An Introduction to Literary Theory and Criticism

An Introduction to Literary Theory and Criticism

Anand B. Kulkarni
Ashok G. Chaskar

Orient BlackSwan

AN INTRODUCTION TO LITERARY THEORY AND CRITICISM

ORIENT BLACKSWAN PRIVATE LIMITED

Registered Office
3-6-752 Himayatnagar, Hyderabad 500 029, Telangana, India
Email: centraloffice@orientblackswan.com

Other Offices
Bengaluru, Chennai, Guwahati, Hyderabad, Kolkata,
Mumbai, New Delhi, Noida, Patna, Visakhapatnam

First published 2015
Reprinted 2016 (twice), 2022, 2023

ISBN 978 81 250 5965 3

037340

Typeset in Adobe Caslon Pro 11/14 *by*
PrePSol Enterprises Pvt. Ltd., Haryana

Printed at
B.B. Press, Noida 201 301

Published by
Orient Blackswan Private Limited
3-6-752 Himayatnagar, Hyderabad 500 029, Telangana, India
Email: info@orientblackswan.com

CONTENTS

Preface *vii*

Part I: Literary Criticism: A Short Introduction 1

Classicism 15

Neoclassicism 32

Romanticism 42

Victorian Literary Criticism 59

Modernism 72

New Criticism 85

Part II: Literary Theory: A Short Introduction 95

Structuralism 106

Marxist Literary Criticism 127

Poststructuralism 150

Psychoanalytic Criticism 178

Reader-Response Criticism 194

Feminist Literary Criticism 206

Postcolonialism 224

Cultural Studies 240

Digital Humanities 260

Glossary *279*

Further reading *296*

PREFACE

It is logical to ask why one more introductory book on literary theory and criticism is needed, when so many are already available. We think it necessary that the answer to this question should start on a deductive note. This is not an ambitious scholarly work that makes tall theoretical claims. It does not deal with all critical approaches and does not fully explore and explicate the plethora of references that every critical approach carries with itself. But it certainly ensures that it does not further complicate matters in the guise of introduction. It is not written for specialists and scholars and so it does not enter into serious theoretical negotiations.

Literary theory and criticism is a prescribed subject at the undergraduate and postgraduate It helps us develop the level in most of the Indian universities. Students are exposed to critical essays with weighty arguments without any groundwork or good introductory books. Quite naturally Indian students find this subject very difficult to understand and very complex to write about. There is an all-pervasive anxiety over this subject in India, and students and even teachers shy away from engaging extensively with it. There are obvious reasons for such anxiety, like the intellectual nature of the subject, extensive theorisation, formidable range of references, and difficult terminology. In addition to this, there are very few books by Indian scholars on this subject that provide a comprehensive and accessible introduction to criticism. The books available are generally not lucid enough, and difficult to comprehend for most students. That is why this book is written. It is a user-friendly book in the sense that it provides all the necessary and vital information about the specific critical approach which will not only give students a grasp over the subject, but also prepare them for various examinations and for qualifying examinations like the NET/SLET/SET.

Literary theory/criticism, since its beginnings, has been a highly intellectual, argumentative and complex field. It has grown into an immensely vast field that covers and encourages many intersecting and contradictory approaches and practices. It is a field that has consistently raised questions about several elements and entities like the author, text, reader and worldview. Literary theory/criticism does not claim to provide answers, and this is due to a strong self-consciousness on its part that there can be as many answers as there are thinking heads, and there can be no final, fixed and permanent answer. Literary theory/criticism is all about plurality and diversity of views. It helps us develop the ability to listen to different and differing views, and to reconsider our postulates about ourselves and the world, that we take to be absolutes. The formidable range of this field, the cross-references and interstices, the terminological complexity and its unique parlance can cause bewilderment both at face value and at a deeper level. Yet, it is an exciting, innovative and challenging field.

We have tried to ensure that the language of the book remains simple, lucid and communicative despite the weightiness of the content. The matter is presented in as precise and compact a form as possible, as it will facilitate the understanding of students. Key points are provided under each section of the critical approach, and supplementary but necessary information is provided in parentheses wherever required. The matter is organised in such a way that students get synoptic yet vital information: a short historical background of critical approaches covering major events, figures and other contexts, salient features, and an introduction to selected critical essays. The unique feature of this book is the addition of a brief introduction to critical essays which are selected in accordance with particular approaches and which truly reflect the spirit and ideas of these approaches. At the end of each critical approach exercises are given with the hope that they will check the understanding of students.

We hope that this book will become a friendly associate to students and teachers alike. It will, we believe, excite the interest of students and will encourage them to study literary theory and criticism at a higher and more contemplative level. This field can seem too complex initially, but draws us in once we actively involve and engage with it.

We express our thanks to our colleagues, friends and well-wishers who were kind enough to express their concern for the progress of the book. It will be an injustice if we do not put on record our deep gratitude to the entire team of Orient Blackswan and especially to Mr Kiran Patro. He has been extremely resourceful in his suggestions, and generous and kind to us through the long while it has taken us to complete the book. The task was difficult and strenuous but we enjoyed every moment of the journey. Vatsala Joshi, the editor of the book, meticulously read through the script and sought explanations and revisions through her comments and queries. We are sure that her efforts towards the book have certainly enriched the quality of the book and have given it a greater appeal.

We welcome suggestions from our readers to improve future editions of this book.

Anand B. Kulkarni
Ashok G. Chaskar

PART I

LITERARY CRITICISM: A SHORT INTRODUCTION

Literary criticism and literary theory are terms used interchangeably and have overlapping issues. However, it is useful to distinguish them for the sake of understanding and also because they have different configurations and they pursue different objectives. Literary criticism has practical application because it often deals directly with individual literary works. Literary theory is usually general or abstract in nature and offers an overarching pattern or set of principles for the study of genres, formal unity or meaning.

Literary criticism is hard to pin down to a single concise definition. This becomes clear when we go through a huge mound of treaties, histories, and introductory books on criticism. However some critics have tried to define criticism and it is useful for us to know them, because they explain different aspects of criticism.

Francis Bacon offers the following advice to critics:

> Read not to contradict, and confute; not to believe and take for granted; nor to find talk and discourse; but to weigh and consider. Some books are to be tasted, others to be swallowed, some few to be chewed and digested.

In his characteristic style Alexander Pope writes about criticism:

> Let such teach others who themselves excel
> And censure freely who have written well.

Matthew Arnold outlines the business of criticism as

> (...) a disinterested endeavour to learn and propagate the best that is known and thought in the world, and thus to establish a current of fresh and true ideas.

Leslie Stephen expects criticism to achieve the scientific spirit

> ... though criticism cannot boast of being a science, it ought to aim at something like a scientific basis, or at least to proceed in a scientific spirit. The critic, therefore, before abandoning himself to the oratorical impulse, should endeavour to classify the phenomena with which he is dealing as calmly as if he were ticketing a fossil in a museum.

T. S. Eliot writes:

> I maintain even that the criticism employed by a trained and skilled writer on his own work is the most vital, the highest kind of criticism; and that some creative writers are superior to others solely because their critical faculty is superior. Criticism is as inevitable as breathing.

F. R. Leavis argues tha:

> the business of critical intelligence will remain what it was: to ensure relevance of response and to determine what is actually there in the work of art.

These and other similar definitions throw light on various aspects of criticism and thereby show that it is a very vast and varied field. Literary criticism is a label that covers a number of different activities. In its limited sense, it refers to the analysis and interpretation of texts. In its wider application, it is concerned with the nature and function of literature including scholarly interpretation, evaluative judgment, prescriptive criticism, literary history and literary theory.

It is difficult to determine when literary criticism began, but it is possible to know its history and the contexts that contributed to the phase-wise development of literary criticism. The history of literary criticism has a large time span of more than two thousand years and includes pioneering critics and their ideas, as well as critical movements. The origin of literary criticism may be traced back to ancient Greek culture and art. The Greek poetry of Homer and Hesiod provided the necessary background and impetus to the growth of Classical criticism. The poetry of this ancient period was self-reflective and the poet was regarded to be both composer and critic. Further, Greek philosopher Plato's views about poetry outlined in his dialogues may be regarded as the earliest instance of literary criticism. His disciple Aristotle based criticism firmly on the ground of logic and reason. In his *Poetics*, Aristotle offered for the first time a well-reasoned and coherently organised description of literary forms, their nature and function. It set the standard for generations of literary critics. Medieval criticism was often religious in its focus and established the religious tradition of hermeneutics (the theory and practice of interpretation that dealt with two types of texts—Classical and Biblical) and textual exegesis (the interpretation of religious texts). The writings of the Italian philosopher St. Thomas Aquinas (1225–74) are perhaps the best example of textual exegesis, in which he reconciled Christian philosophy with Aristotle's philosophy. In succeeding periods literary criticism either renewed the Classical norms and notions like objectivity, unity, coherence, order, grandeur, nobility and diction like Neoclassicism did, or challenged them as Romanticism did in its insistence on subjectivity, freedom from norms, imagination and expression of emotions. In the modern period, especially during the late nineteenth and early twentieth century, criticism developed in many different directions. Critics interested in the traditional historical, moral and biographical approaches were not influenced by the new anti-traditional developments in criticism. They (for example, A. O. Lovejoy, E. M. W. Tillyard and C. S. Lewis) revised the theoretical frameworks of historical and moral approaches and examined literary works within those frameworks. On the other hand, as a move away from these traditional frameworks, New Critics became increasingly objective, practical and textual. New Criticism represents this modern tendency towards objectivity and textual interpretation.

Thus the nature of literary criticism is many-sided and complex. Perhaps the most useful and simplest way to understand it is to comprehend the division that is often made between *intrinsic* and *extrinsic* criticism. *Intrinsic* criticism is an activity in which the critic tries to know the meaning inherent (naturally there) in a literary text; to find out what it is and what its identity is. It includes the study of structural and stylistic features of the text to arrive at a particular meaning. This critical activity includes only interpretation and not evaluation. It keeps away from all kinds of background information and social, political, cultural and economic contexts, and solely concerns itself with the text. This may as well be called the interpretative approach as it concentrates on the meaning in the text. Extrinsic criticism is an activity in which the critic tries to find out the meaning extraneous (not naturally there) of a literary text, to know its relationship to something else, to discover what it signifies. It includes the study of different elements (like social/economic/political) that inform the text. It is also interpretative but it takes into account the background information of a text. We may state that *intrinsic* criticism is *meaning* and *extrinsic* criticism is *significance*. *Meaning* is an investigation into the structural and thematic design of a literary text. *Significance* is the search for the meaning that is not there in the text, or other than the meaning of the text. *Intrinsic* criticism concentrates on the text and its features whereas *extrinsic* criticism deals with the text as well as the contexts. This division covers almost all critical approaches and methods of criticism.

Let us explain the division between *intrinsic* and *extrinsic* criticism with an example. **George Orwell** (1903–1950) was a British novelist, essayist and critic. He wrote a novel, *Animal Farm* (1945). Let us briefly examine this novel in the light of the principles of *intrinsic* criticism. Orwell had subtitled the book 'A Fairy Tale'. We can start with this guideline that it is a witty allegorical fable. Pursued further this guideline reveals that it forms the structure and style of the novel. We can now examine how the consideration of the novel as a witty allegorical fable influences the structure and the style of the novel. First, let us examine the structure of the novel. Look at the words—allegorical fable. Fable is one of the modes of allegory, the other mode being parable. An allegory conveys symbolic meaning; it makes use of personifications and other symbols to communicate more than the literal meaning. The fable, being one kind of allegory, conveys a universal moral truth. It presents its moral at the end of the work. This particular way of writing (allegorical fable) is skilfully used in the novel to give it its structure and style. The novelist organises his material to fit into this frame of writing. However the most significant aspect of this frame is satire. It is, therefore, very important to know that the novel is a satire on totalitarianism and on the corruption of principles. Satire as a genre of literature often subverts traditional story tropes, like a traveller's tale or a moral fable. Orwell follows this tradition, converting the traditional animal story into a political allegory.

Animal Farm can be compared with Jonathan Swift's *Gulliver's Travels.* The substitution of the animal world for the human world is apparent in the fourth part of *Gulliver's Travels*, and in *Animal Farm.* As a fable it presents the story of animals determined to overthrow the tyranny of their master; as a satire it fully exploits the beast fable as a vehicle to criticise the totalitarian state and as an allegory it indicates close parallels with the Russian Revolution and subsequent events. It is therefore important to understand *Animal Farm* as a novel of skilful design fusing together satire, fable and allegory.

The choice and arrangement of words, parts of speech and figures of speech used in the novel exhibit a witty and ironic style. The tone of the novel is also witty and ironic. It amuses us and at the same time makes us aware of the tragic vein in the amusing situation. Words are used to persuade and dominate the animals on the farm. Words promise them a future they had never believed possible, and lead them to dream, and are also responsible for manipulating them into giving up these dreams. Squealer's speech meant to convince the animals of the new decision of not debating any issue is a case in point. His words are: 'Do not imagine, comrades, that leadership is a pleasure! On the contrary, it is a deep and heavy responsibility. No one believes more firmly than Comrade Napoleon that all animals are equal. He would be only too happy to let you make your decisions for yourselves. But sometimes you might make the wrong decisions…' (p. 97, Houghton Mifflin Harcourt, 2009 ed.). The words are rhetorical; there are imperatives and negatives. The imperative 'Do not imagine' is in fact a statement that suggests the feigned superiority and sacrifice that Comrade Napoleon is making for the safety and freedom of the animals. The direct negative, 'No one believes' increases the projected significance of Comrade Napoleon's belief in equality. The words are deceptive; they do not mean what they say. The suggestion that other animals might make wrong decisions, but not Napoleon, reveals the selfish motive behind the leadership. This is because these words contradict the action that follows. Napoleon is portrayed as superior, because his happiness lies in the freedom of other animals but he is afraid of their mistakes and hence, takes on the seemingly cumbersome responsibility of decision-making. Napoleon is responsible, freedom-loving, caring and considerate and not a selfish, merrymaking, irresponsible and cruel leader. These two word pictures simultaneously develop during the speech. The contradiction creates the impression that Napoleon is a cunning and manipulative leader who apparently shows interest in the welfare of the animals but in reality, nurtures strong selfish motives in his mind.

The slogans show the typical style of the novel and convey its theme effectively. In the beginning the slogan is 'Four Legs Good, Two Legs Bad'. By the end of the novel it changes to 'Four Legs Good, Two Legs Better!' and it finally becomes 'All Animals Are Equal But Some Animals Are More Equal Than Others'. The change in the syntax of the slogan shows the change in priority and interest. In the beginning the 'goodness' of four legs sharply contrasts with the 'badness' of two legs, and this shows that the animal government on the farm believes in the equality, unity and interest of all animals. In the next version of the slogan, the contrast between four legs and two legs is removed and two legs are given priority. It is not that four legs are bad, but two legs are better. In the final phase, the idea of equality is newly defined and a special status is given to the ruling animals. The jugglery of words and the change in the tone and expressions together contribute to show that a new corruption has replaced the old one. Thus the structure and the style effectively communicate the tone and theme of the novel.

Let us now briefly examine the novel in the light of the principles of *extrinsic* criticism. Here again we can consider the novel to be an allegory but it is now a political allegory and we are not required to base our criticism on the text alone. We are free to interpret it with the help of extra-textual information as well. We can start with some background information. Orwell disliked all organised political parties. He was a socialist (a believer in the system of thought in which everyone has an equal opportunity to benefit from a country's wealth) and opposed the use of force. He wrote two novels before *Animal Farm*, namely *The Road to Wigan Pier* (1937) and *Coming up for Air* (1939) in which he expressed deep concern for the poor and his dislike of tyranny. This information shows that *Animal Farm* continues the same line of thought as the earlier novels. Orwell's criticism of injustice and intolerance, and sympathies with the weak and the poor is made apparent in these novels. *Animal Farm* makes us aware of the contemporary social and political scene. If we enquire a little further into the near past and relate the novel to the political developments of Orwell's time, we realise that it expresses the frustration caused by contemporary political revolutions. The novel's immediate context is the Russian Revolution. This can be confirmed from at least two sources—the story behind the publication of the novel and the characters modelled on the living leaders of the revolution. We learn that *Animal Farm* was completed during the Second World War in 1943 and published in 1945. Many British publishers refused to publish the novel because it was not a simple fairy tale but a political allegory written against the Soviet Union and Stalin. The character of Old Major, the boar, is based on Lenin, and Major's first speech expresses the ideas of Karl Marx. The characters of Napoleon and Snowball are drawn on Stalin and Trotsky respectively. Both take charge of the farm after Major's death but they quarrel and Napoleon drives Snowball away from the farm by using the terror of dogs. There are many other parallels that show that *Animal Farm* is a satire on dictatorship. Thus the extra-textual details about the novel create space for different interpretations.

This interpretation is only a short attempt at illustrating the two broad categories of literary criticism. Obviously these categories cannot encompass the formidable range of criticism. Critics have endeavoured to define the nature and scope of literary criticism and have proposed frames to classify various approaches. But perhaps the most comprehensive and useful classification is provided by the American critic M. H. Abrams. In his influential study of Romanticism (*The Mirror and the Lamp*, 1953) Abrams tries to cover the vast range of literary criticism from the ancient to the modern time. He describes four major perspectives of critical analysis—the author, the world, the text and the reader. He classifies critical approaches into four major categories—Mimetic Theories, Pragmatic Theories, Expressive Theories and Objective Theories. Mimetic Theories are the most ancient theories about art and they explain art as an imitation of the world. They argue that all art (like painting, poetry, music, dancing and sculpture) imitates the ideas and objects that already exist in the world. Aristotle's *Poetics* is the best example of this kind of critical method.

Pragmatic Theories consider literary works as instruments to achieve desired effects on readers and consequently, desired aims. They examine literary works by their capacity to please and instruct readers. Philip Sidney's defence of poetry may be regarded as a good example of a pragmatic theory. This is chiefly because he considered poetry to be an instrument to achieve pleasure and teach morality.

Expressive Theories consider literary works as a spontaneous expression of the artist's feelings. These theories believe that poetry is the expression or uttering forth of feeling. Wordsworth's theory of poetry is an example of these kinds of theories.

Objective Theories treat literary works as self-sufficient entities. They isolate literary works from all external points of reference and concentrate on their internal merits. New Criticism is an approach that follows the principles of Objective Theories. Rene Wellek and Austin Warren's *The Theory of Literature* (1956, Third Edition) advocates this method that focuses on the internal merits of a literary work. This is a practically useful classification as it imposes some order on the formidable range and mass of literary criticism.

Literary criticism may also be classified into the following two broad categories:

1) aesthetic, autotelic and textual,

2) didactic, moral and prescriptive.

Most critical approaches fall under these two categories and consider the study of literary works to be their prime concern. They study literary works either for their own sake or study them through different contexts. But they commonly assume that literary texts are interpretable. They believe that texts possess meaning or are meaningful. The only difference is that aesthetic and objective criticism discovers the meaning in the text itself whereas didactic and moral criticism discovers meaning somewhere outside the text. It treats the text as the vehicle or medium that carries meaning and can lead its readers to its meaning.

An important variety of literary criticism which can be said to mark a definite shift in the way literary criticism was practised and studied was practical criticism or applied criticism. It emerged in the early decades of the twentieth century and it was mainly a reaction against conventional biographical and subjective criticism. The modern poets and critics who were dissatisfied with conventional criticism turned the focus of criticism from poet/writer to poetry/literary work. It was a shift from subjective and historical criticism to objective and textual criticism. The critics who worked towards this shift were I. A. Richards, T. S. Eliot, William Empson and F. R. Leavis. Each of these critics had developed his own mode of criticism and the only common aspect among them was their dissatisfaction with traditional pursuits of criticism. They focused on literary works rather than on the subjective expressions of writers. There were differences in their approaches. Richards concentrated on the psychological interaction between literary works and readers, Eliot proposed the concept of impersonal art, Empson made prominent the close analysis of literary work that leads to alternate meanings and Leavis insisted on analysing the qualities of the literary work which made it enduring and appealing to all of humanity. None of these critics shared common principles or methods of criticism but they were against the historical and moral interpretation of literature. These critics in diverse ways contributed to the rise and consolidation of practical criticism both in England and in America. Practical criticism has mostly been pedagogical (useful in the course of teaching–learning) and educative and it pays exclusive attention to textual elements.

We may understand practical criticism broadly in two categories. The first is the metrical composition of the text. This includes the study of rhythm, rhyme, stress pattern and meter as well as patterns of sound like alliteration, assonance, consonance and onomatopoeia. This may also include the use of poetic devices like metaphor and personification. The second category is the study of syntax (organisation of words) and lexical arrangement. This may also include the interpretation of the text keeping in view its linguistic features. Let us attempt an analysis of William Blake's famous poem 'London' from this point of view. A full-fledged analysis of both form and content is beyond the scope of this chapter. This is a short analysis and it focuses more on the syntactic arrangement and stylistic features of the poem.

London

William Blake

I wander thro' each charter'd street,
Near where the charter'd Thames does flow,
And mark in every face I meet
Marks of weakness, marks of woe.

In every cry of every Man,
In every Infant's cry of fear,
In every voice, in every ban,
The mind-forg'd manacles I hear.

How the Chimney-sweeper's cry
Every blackning Church appalls;
And the hapless soldier's sigh
Runs in blood down Palace Walls

But most thro' midnight streets I hear
How the youthful Harlot's curse
Blasts the new-born Infant's tear,
And blights with plagues the Marriage hearse.

This poem contains sixteen lines and is arranged into four stanzas of equal length. Each stanza consists of four lines and the rhyming pattern is *abab*. With this initial information about the poem we turn to the title which is simply 'London', and is neither qualified nor modified by any other expression. We may have any inkling of the meaning until we read the entire poem. The title initiates us uninformed into the text. This lack of titular orientation prepares us for a very powerful impact that every line exerts over us. It is like a crescendo that increases its impact with every expression and image. (Interestingly William Wordsworth also wrote a poem with the same title, 'London', with a somewhat similar theme. However there is significant difference between the treatment of the theme by Blake and by Wordsworth).

The entire poem is composed and narrated in the first person. The speaker is closely associated with the scenes he describes and has a deep concern for what he sees and hears. The first person narration suggests involvement and intimacy between the speaker and the scenes of the city. The speaker takes a particular position and that is meticulously maintained throughout the poem. The use of simple present tense reinforces the speaker's position in the sense that it states the existing reality and also suggests its uninterrupted continuity. The existing reality is painful and it will continue to be painful in the future as well because there is nothing and no one that can challenge and/or change it.

Turning to the poem itself, we find that repetition is frequent in the poem. Words like 'chartered', 'cry' and 'every' are repeated with the intention to induce horror about the prevalent conditions in the city of London. The speaker finds each street chartered and this state of being chartered serves as the source/cause of weakness and worry of every resident of the city. Not only are the streets chartered, but also the river Thames. These images of 'chartered street' and 'chartered Thames' very skilfully suggest the complicity of the authorities with the mercantile class which neither cares about the rights of common people nor for their desires. The repetition reinforces this insensitive and cruel contract. As a result of all this, the speaker finds marks of weakness and woe in every face. Significantly there is a singular 'mark' in the third line which becomes plural 'marks' in the fourth line. The singular 'mark' is unqualified but becomes qualified in the plural 'marks' with weakness and woe. This shift from the singular to the plural is meant to suggest the ubiquity of weakness and woe; the plurality of suffering. The repetition continues in the second stanza and there is a highly suggestive play on words. The first line runs 'In every cry of every Man' and the second line runs 'In every Infant's cry of fear'. The syntactic structure of the first line is different from the second line but it is more like the third line. For example the 'every' in the first line is dropped in the second and added in the third line. This deviance suggests the constriction and the reduction of rights and freedom. It also suggests the all-pervasive presence of horror and violence (from infant to man and from man-made street to the natural Thames) and absolute control over the physique and psyche of the people. The image of 'mind-forg'd manacles' suggests this fear and constriction. The next two stanzas reinforce the fear and anxiety with reference to the chimney-sweeper, soldier and harlot. These people have long lost their claims for their rights and are not even entitled to live an ordinary human life. They represent the wretched condition wrought by the absolute exercise of power and absolute loss of freedom.

The contrasting lexical sets intensify the subject matter of the poem. The first set of common people are symbolised by the chimney-sweeper, soldier and harlot. These sensitive, dutiful, acquiescent and dependent people are contrasted with the insensitive, autocratic and commanding Church and Palace Walls which suggest impenetrable insensitivity, cruelty and control. Such insensitivity and inhumanity is the corollary of the 'chartered street' and 'chartered Thames' the bargain between the world of clergymen and the government to unmindfully and forcefully exhaust human and natural resources. This contrast becomes explicit when 'the Chimney-sweeper's cry', 'the hapless Soldier's sigh' and 'the youthful Harlot's curse' are juxtaposed with the 'blackning Church' and the blood running down the palace walls.

The poem may be stylistically interpreted in that the speaker does not passively or neutrally describe the scenes in the city. He has genuine concern for all the suffering people and so he is expository in his narration. Verbs are used in their root form in the poem and all of them are action verbs. The speaker wanders, meets and hears. These action verbs which otherwise stand for mundane and quotidian activities reflect inhumanity, fear and suffering in association with phrases like running of blood, blasting of tears and blighting with plagues. The use of adjectives like 'the *new-born* Infant' and 'the *youthful* Harlot' suggest both innocence and helplessness. The new-born infant and the youthful harlot are forcefully drawn into the chartered world and suffer for no reason. The adjectives 'new-born' and 'youthful' make us conscious of the darkened and horrifying future of infants and harlots. Thus the poem succeeds in exposing the miserable and pitiful conditions of the common people.

CLASSICISM

Historical Background

Greek Classical Literary Criticism

Ancient Greek literary criticism had its origins in Greek poetry. One of Greek poetry's tallest figures was Homer, the celebrated author of the famous epics, the *Iliad* and *Odyssey*. He was a respected poet and skilled composer. His poetry was not only part of Greek education, but shaped the tastes and attitude of the Greek people. It is in his poetry that we find the earliest mention of the nature and function of poetry and the role of the poet. His poetry retold legends of the great heroes of the past, offered pleasure to its readers and deeply moved them. Homer was a profound influence on many great Greek poets. For example **Hesiod**, the peasant poet of seventh century BC, took up Homer's theme of poetic inspiration and developed it. He described how he came to sing about the past and the future. It was due to his meeting with the Muses (nine sister goddesses in Greek mythology that inspired and guided poets, writers, artists, etc.) and divine inspiration from them that he composed poetry. This was of course the extension of Homer's idea of poetic creation. **Pindar** in fifth century BC carried forward the theme of immortality from Homer. He was aware of the mortality of human life and he believed that poetry could make it immortal. His Odes reflected his conviction that poetry survives even after the poet's death. It was one of the earliest attempts to negotiate with the mortality of human life through art. Along with the theme of immortality, truth was another concern of the ancient Greek poets. From Homer onwards, poets claimed that they had special knowledge given by the Muses. Their poetry could tell the truth about human life and the gods. It is notable however that the power of poets was not limited to expression of truth alone. They were also believed to have the opposite power, of misrepresenting or manipulating the truth. Though inspired by the Muses, poets could create their own poetic narratives (storytelling in verse form). They could, therefore, invent their own version of truth and also had the power to excite intense emotions in their listeners. There are many episodes in Homer's poetry where the characters are shown in deeply moving situations.

This deliberate manipulation of the truth showed the poet's ability of re-creation, giving him semi-divine status, but also invited severe criticism from philosophers like Plato. Poets' ability to manipulate the truth had many implications for the future course of both literary and critical development. This very short account of Greek poetry helps us understand the origin and major concerns of Classical literary criticism. We can learn the following points of great importance to Classical literary criticism from the above information:

1) Poetry is inspired by the Muses. This means that it has its origin in divine power. This takes us to one of the important concerns of criticism—the process of poetic creation or how poetry is created. It opened up the debate between inspiration and imitation; between the poet's gift and craft.

2) Poetry expresses truth. Truth, for the Greek poets, lay in inspiration from the Muses. Their poetry offered moral wisdom and guidance to people for practical living and thus led them to the path of truth. However such claims came to be challenged in the Sophist period (fourth century BC) by philosophers. They introduced the theory of mimesis and attempted to prove the falsity of poetry. It initiated the discussion of truth and imitation; reality and representation, in art in general and poetry in particular.

3) Poetry excites emotions. It means that poetry affects human emotions and passions and so it has great affective value. This

refers to two important aspects—the moving power of poetry and its relation to its readers. Poetry was supposed to give pleasure through arousal of emotions and this was as much the function of poetry as it was to give lessons on morality. But some critics were of the view that this affective ability of poetry created tension between reason and emotion.

These themes bring to light some abiding concerns that literary criticism deals with, for example, the relation between ethics and poetry, the relation between the writer and his work, the relation of the work with the world, the theme of imitation/representation, reality and the writer's invention/fiction, etc.

This background information about the status of poetry in the cultural and social life of the Greek people helps us understand the origin and development of Greek literary criticism. It was in and through poetry that criticism developed in Greece in its earliest form. The crucial reason for this was that Greek poetry was self-reflective and contained its own criticism within itself (Greek poetry did not need any formal and independent criticism for its evaluation and it was not until Plato's attack on poetry that sustained and serious literary criticism began). It might therefore be argued that poets were the earliest critics and that the concerns of poets were the concerns of criticism. The concerns of poets were not literary and aesthetic matters but moral authority and ethical value. They regarded poetry and morality as intimately related. So the focus of enquiry was not literary but philosophical. However the rise of prose in the fifth century changed the status and priorities of poetry and by extension, of literary criticism. The Sophist school of thought in Greece was responsible for this change in the nature of poetry and criticism. The Sophists (fifth century BC Greek teachers of rhetoric and philosophy, known for their subtle and clever reasoning power) made prose an important medium of education along with poetry. Now poetry was not taught for its own sake (that is, to understand grammatical and stylistic points in it). It was taught in order to improve the speech of aspiring orators in assemblies and law courts. Poetry came to serve oratory, as speakers began to use verse to enhance their speeches. The art of poetry began to diminish, because of rhetoric taking over poetry, and prose posing a stiff challenge. The term *rhetoric* means the art of speech, an art concerned with the use of public speaking. It is used as a means to convince people. Rhetoric in poetry or rhetorical poetry became more important and literary criticism became less important. It was not only prose and rhetoric that challenged the supremacy of poetry but philosophy also raised doubts about the morality and truthfulness of poetry. For example, the Ionian philosopher-poet **Xenophanes** in sixth century BC criticised epic poetry on moral grounds. He argued that Homer and Hesiod had attached shameful things like theft, adultery and deceit to gods in their poetry. This relating of human faults to gods could have corrupt and adverse effects on readers. Xenophanes' criticism of epic poetry could be seen as the earliest attack on poetry framed by a philosopher and it anticipates the more powerful attack by Plato.

The work of Aristophanes (450–385 BC) could be seen as the next phase of Greek poetry and criticism. He wrote comic plays. They are important because they discuss the role and responsibility of poetry towards socio-political conditions. His famous play *The Frogs* (first performed in 405 BC) presents a literary critical contest between two playwrights—Euripides and Aeschylus. Aeschylus represents old-fashioned values and Euripides, progressive views. The contest shows Aristophanes' dislike of Euripides and respect for Aeschylus. The play is significant because it debates the kind of language (lofty and grand style versus plain and commonplace) a playwright should use, the choice of themes (heroic versus non-heroic) and the duty of poetry to teach virtues and provide guidelines to practical living. Both Aeschylus and Euripides agree that the role of poetry is to teach people morality and offer role models. But they disagree on many other issues and find faults with each other's use of language and poetry. Thus the poets act as critics of each other. These issues recur in subsequent literary-critical discussions.

Gorgias of Leontini (483–376 BC) was a famous rhetorician and speaker from Sicily. His views about the power and use of speech provided many significant issues to literary criticism. He attached equal importance to speech (prose) and poetry, defining poetry as speech in metre. His views on speech were therefore treated as his views on poetry and poetry was accordingly received. He emphasised the ability of speech to arouse emotions and compared the effects of speech on the mind to those of drugs on the body. Like drugs, speech has both good and bad effects. It can give pleasure or pain. Poetry was also thought to have similar effects on readers. His views were mostly antithetical to Plato's views. But it could be observed that they influenced Plato's approach to poetry. Plato's analysis of the bad effects of poetry on the psychology of the audience shows Gorgias' influence as he treated the effect of poetry similar to that of *pharmakon*, a kind of drug. Gorgias' emphasis on emotions like pity and fear anticipated Aristotle's association of emotions with tragedy.

Plato (429–347 BC) offered the first sustained critique of poetry. He formulated very basic and enduring questions about the nature and function of poetry. His questions may be broadly summed up in the following way:

a) He found poetry to be false and imitative.
b) He found poetry to be emotionally exciting and morally corrupting.
c) He found poetry to be inconducive to his ideal state.

He puts his views across in *Ion* and the *Republic*. In *Ion* Socrates is shown cross-examining a rhapsode (singer) on the nature of his art. Socrates tells the rhaspode that the poet composes in a fit of divine inspiration by the Muses, in a state of possession, and not through his own talent and ability. In other words he calls poets and their poetry inspired and irrational. The rhaspode's art is equally irrational in the sense that it lacks art and knowledge. Socrates challenges the rhaspode's art by referring to his understanding of Homer's poetry.

In the *Republic,* Plato deals more intensely and elaborately with poetry. He treats it philosophically and to some extent ideologically, as his aim is to replace poetry with philosophy. He proposes his theory of *mimesis* (imitation) for the first time in Book III of the *Republic*. In this book Plato divides literature into two kinds of narration: *diegesis* (narrative) and *mimesis* (imitative). He does not criticise poetry, and expects deep involvement of the actor while reciting poetry. But in Book X of the *Republic* the tone and theme changes completely and he declares poetry to be a false activity. In order to support his critique of poetry, he examines it in the light of his theory of Forms. He shows that poetry falls short of the required standard of reality. For Plato the physical world is not independent and self-sustained. It depends upon another world of ideas. This ideal world is accessible only to reason and not to physical sense perceptions. Thus, in other words, the objects in the physical world get their essence and qualities from the ideal world. Plato gives the example of a bed to substantiate his central point of reality. A bed in the physical world is not perfect because it is only a copy of the ideal bed in the world of Forms. Poetry, like the bed in the physical world, depends upon the ideal world of Forms and deals only with appearance and not reality. Poets imitate the objects that are already twice imitations of reality. He then criticises the emotive power of poetry. It pleases its audience by appealing to their emotions and does not improve them morally. It evokes their emotions and passions and weakens their reasoning power. It is harmful because it corrupts. So poets should be banished from the ideal state.

With his master, Plato, **Aristotle** (384–322 BC) is another great pioneer of Western philosophy and literary theory. He logically formulated his views about art in general and poetry in particular and provided a rational base to literature and criticism. His two surviving treatises *Poetics* and *Rhetoric* show his rational thinking and scientific method of analysis.

It is helpful to know the difference in mode of thinking and method of analysis between Plato and Aristotle:

1) Plato is idealistic in his thinking whereas Aristotle is pragmatic. Plato examines everything against his concept of Form which is abstract. Aristotle evaluates everything in a concrete and scientific way. Plato thinks deductively, that is, he draws particular conclusions from general objects whereas Aristotle thinks inductively, that is, he draws general conclusions from particular objects.

2) Plato analyses poetry from a philosophical point of view whereas Aristotle analyses it as an independent art form with its own logic. Plato treats poetry as the result of an inspiration and therefore, an irrational activity, whereas Aristotle considers it as a craft with a determinate structure.

3) For Plato poetry offers false imitation and for Aristotle poetry can teach human beings more than particular facts. Poetry, according to Plato, is morally harmful and according to Aristotle, it refines our emotions and passions.

4) Plato uses dialogue form to illustrate his views whereas Aristotle uses a straightforward propositional form. Plato provides a dramatic account of poetry with value judgments whereas Aristotle examines poetry as an object and studies its elements through differentiation and classification.

Aristotle answers Plato's questions about art and poetry in his *Poetics*. He takes the idea of poetry as an imitation from Plato but he defines it very differently. He disagrees with Plato's view that imitation is a lower activity and art is an inferior imitation. He argues that imitation is a basic human instinct. We all imitate to learn and to get pleasure. This takes Aristotle to another important argument about reality and its imitation or representation in art or poetry. A poet imitates things not in a crude and mechanical form, but in a lively and refashioned way. He presents things as they are (factual), as they appear (appearance) or as they ought to be (ideal). He does not produce the exact copy of an object but its verisimilitude (likeness to reality) or its ideal version. Thus Aristotle interprets the poet's imitation as a refining lens with which to view the world, and poetic mimesis as a natural and common activity which helps the audience to improve upon their mental and moral faculties.

Callimachus (305–240 BC) was one of the finest Hellenistic poets and a scholar who worked in the library of Alexandria. He is important in the development of literary criticism because he brought new approaches to the art of composition and criticism of poetry. He introduced completely new standards of verse composition and of judgment. He rejected traditional types and subjects of poetry. He advocated small and short poems based on new themes. For him allusiveness, wit and subtlety were the important factors in poetry, and not length, continuity and past themes. He argued that poetry should be judged as an art and judged by a cultured scholar. We notice two important points in Callimachus' views. The first is that he calls for experiments with types and themes of poetry and secondly, that he insists on critical activity as a specialised activity.

Roman Classical Literary Criticism

In this phase of historical development, the centre of literary and critical activities moved from Athens to Rome. This age, known as the Augustan age, was different from the Greek Classical age. Poets and not philosophers dominated the literary and critical world and the Roman emperors gave patronage to poets. The age was represented by distinguished poets like Virgil, Horace, Ovid and Livy.

Horace (65–8 BC) is particularly important to the development of literary criticism. He wrote his famous *Ars Poetica* (an epistle addressed to a father and two sons) and expressed his views about poetry and drama. Horace followed the views of the Greek classicists on art, especially the views of Aristotle, but he introduced his own views as well. In his advice to poets, he explains his views about poetry and in turn demonstrates how criticism of a literary work can be written. According to him, the function of great poetry is to delight and instruct the audience. He argues that poets should strictly adhere to brevity and plausibility in their writing. He attaches importance to technical perfection in verse composition. He states that a sensible critic should expose flaws like harsh verse, ugly lines, obscure passages and defective phrases.

Longinus was the author of the famous critical work *On the Sublime.* Nothing is known for sure about the author and the date of the composition of the work. However the work was believed to be written in the first century AD. Longinus says, in his work, that sublimity is what marks out truly great literature from the rest. True sublimity fills the audience with joy and lifts their souls to noble experience. A work of literature is sublime only if it pleases all men at all times. If a work is appreciated and enjoyed by men with different interests and ages, then it may be said to possess sublimity.

Sublimity is described as arising from five sources. These are—grandeur of thought, capacity to feel strong emotions, proper use of figures of thoughts and speech, noble diction and dignified word arrangement. The first two sources arise from inborn genius, but the poet's latent talent should be disciplined and brought into order by technique. Thus Longinus describes sublimity as a harmonious balance between inborn genius and honed technique.

Longinus also discusses the faults which prevent a work from achieving sublimity. *Turgidity*, which arises when an author aims at grandeur but instead writes in a bombastic and insincere style, is the first fault. The second fault is *puerility*, which literally means childish behaviour. It arises when an author's writing and ideas are shallow and lacking in any real substance. The third fault is *parenthysus* or false sentiment. This is the overuse of emotion where it is not required. Another fault is *frigidity*, which literally means being extremely cold or insensitive. It is occasioned by triviality of mind and insensitivity to others. It is the tendency to find faults in the works of other writers.

Longinus' views draw from his background of the rhetorical tradition, but are sufficiently different in that he describes good writing as a mix of talent and technique. His theory was a great influence on a new aesthetic approach called Romanticism that flourished in the nineteenth century.

Salient Features of Classicism

1) Classicism in general is characterised by emphasis on reason because it was considered to be both the creative and shaping faculty of human life. Plato's insistence on ideas and rejection of materiality is indicative of the decisive role of reason in the Classical mode of thinking. It became the hallmark of excellent literary work.

2) Classical criticism gave importance to structural organisation, to elements like order, sequence, coherence and unity in both composition and critical appreciation of literary works.

3) It was believed that all poetry was inspired by the Muses, or in other words, had a divine source. It was thus held to express the ultimate truth about life and human nature; however it was also believed to excite emotions, and was deemed harmful for the general populace. These assumptions influenced the composition and criticism of Greek poetry. Literary criticism thus focused extensively on poetry's ethical value, and not as much on its literary or aesthetic aspects.

4) Literature was expected to present model examples for people to emulate and to reinforce ideals so that tastes could be enriched and behaviour could be improved. Authors were supposed to be objective in their portrayal of human life and create high standards of morality.

5) The three unities of time, place and action were to be compulsorily observed by poets.

6) Early Greek poets dealt extensively with the themes of immortality, truth and wisdom. A few examples include Homer, whose poetry was self-reflective and contained its own criticism within itself, followed by Hesiod and Pindar.

7) The rise of prose brought about changes in poetry and also literary criticism. Poetry began to be viewed as subordinate to oratory, while rhetoric and philosophy further challenged poetry as an intellectual discipline.

8) The chief critical positions of the Classical era were Plato's and Aristotle's. Plato criticised poetry as being false and imitative, morally corrupt due to its capability to emotionally excite the audience, and thus harmful to the social fabric. Aristotle defended poetry against Plato's charges by saying poetry, by imitating living action, served to refine human faculties and provide an outlet for negative emotions. He further stated that grand style and themes, decorum, and moderation were what characterised good literary works.

9) Other important critics included Horace and Longinus. Horace was a Roman critic who authored *Ars Poetica.* The function of poetry, according to him, was to delight and instruct; and of criticism, to show the faults of the poet. Longinus, whose famous work *On the Sublime* identified the 'sublime' element which distinguished great works of literature, influenced the eighteenth-century literary movement, Romanticism.

Introduction to Aristotle's *Poetics* (Chapters 1–10)

Poetics is often thought to be Aristotle's response to Plato's criticism of poetry. He does not directly refer to Plato but it is very revealing to study the work in the light of Plato's charges against poetry. *Poetics* is the first theoretical work of literary criticism devoted entirely to the discussion of types, nature and function of literature. It contains twenty-six short chapters. It deals mainly with tragedy as an art form. It is believed that it had a second part that dealt with comedy but it was lost. Here is a synopsis of certain chapters.

Chapter 1 to 5

Aristotle begins his discussion with the varieties of art forms. These are poetry, music, dancing, painting and sculpture. They are all forms of imitation and they differ from each other in three important respects. These are:

1) *Medium of imitation* – Art forms (poetry, music, dancing, painting and sculpture) present human action through rhythm, language and melody. However they employ the three mediums separately or in combination. For example, music uses rhythm and melody only, dance uses rhythm alone and poetry uses language alone whereas dithyrambic poetry uses all these mediums.

2) *Object of imitation* – All art forms present men in action but with different objects. For example, poetry presents men as better, true to life or worse. Homer presents better men, Cleophon (an Athenian tragic poet of the fourth century BC) presents men as they are and Nichocares (the author of *Deiliad*) worse than they are.

3) *Mode of imitation* – All art forms differ in their modes of imitation. In the case of poetry, for example, imitation may be performed through— a) narration where the poet becomes another personality (an omniscient narrator), b) narration in one's own person (first person narrator), c) narration where the poet presents all characters in action (third person narrator).

While providing a brief account of the origin and history of poetry, Aristotle states two reasons for the rise of poetry— i) man's natural tendency to imitate things ii) man's tendency to enjoy works of imitation.

Poets, and their poetry, were of two different kinds, depending on the nature of individual poets. The first group of poets was serious minded and they represented noble actions of noble persons. The second group was trivial and they represented mean actions of mean persons.

Tragedy originated from dithyrambic songs and over time settled into its natural form of dramatic plot, dialogue and iambic verse.

Comedy originated from phallic songs and imitated base characters. It presents faults and disgrace in characters but it does not show them in a destructive or painful manner.

Epic, like tragedy, imitates serious action in grand and lofty words. However there are certain differences between epic and tragedy. These are:

Epic	Tragedy
makes use of a single metre	free to use any kind of metre
narrative in form	not narrative in form
no limits of time	usually takes place in a single day
does not include all the elements of tragedy	includes all the elements of epic

Chapter 6 to 10

Aristotle defines what constitutes tragedy in these chapters and the following points can be highlighted in the definition— i) tragedy imitates serious and complete action of a certain length, ii) it imitates such action in rhythmic words, iii) it does not use narrative form for its presentation but only presents action, iv) it provides an outlet for negative emotions like pity and fear.

Aristotle then moves on to discuss the six elements of tragedy. I order of importance they are: plot, character, thought, diction, melody and spectacle.

Plot is the most important element of all because: a) it imitates action and not a person, and actions decide the success or failure of a person, b) tragedy is not possible without plot or action but possible without well-defined characters, c) plot cannot be replaced by any other element, d) plot gives unity and accuracy to the arrangement of other elements.

Characteristic features of plot:

i) *Completeness* – It means that a tragedy should have a beginning, middle and end. This means that plot is based on a definite and well-knit order of cause and effect determined by the tragedian. The order of Sophocles' tragedy, *Oedipus Rex,* serves as a good example of Aristotle's view of completeness. The play begins with the plague in Thebes and Oedipus tries to find out its cause. In the middle of the play Oedipus tries to find out the events that led to the death of Laius. The play ends with Oedipus' discovery that he is himself responsible for the plague.

ii) *Magnitude* – It refers to length of the plot. The plot should neither be extremely long nor extremely short. It should be in proportion with the memory of the audience. But Aristotle also argues that a long plot makes tragedy beautiful because it shows the change in the fortunes of the characters from good to bad or bad to good through the sequence of beginning, middle and end.

iii) *Unity* – It refers to the organisation of subject matter. Aristotle recommends that all the action in a tragedy should be organised around a common theme or idea.

iv) *Determinate Structure* – A plot should have a structure that unites all parts of the action. This structure should be so compact that removal of any part disturbs the unity of the whole.

v) *Universality* – Poetry according to Aristotle, expresses universals. The universal is the tendency of a character to speak or act like most people in a given situation. This works as per the law of probability.

Aristotle outlines the elements that make a plot work. These are:

i) *Astonishment* – It occurs when events turn out contrary to the expectations of the audience.

ii) *Recognition* – It shows the change from ignorance to knowledge. The persons involved in the action understand each other well and their identities become clear. For example, in *Oedipus Rex*, a messenger comes to give good news to Oedipus and free him from his worry about his mother. But he produces the opposite result on Oedipus with his news.

iii) *Reversal* – It is a change in the fortune of the main character from good to bad.

iv) *Suffering* – It is a painful or destructive action as a result of recognition or reversal.

Aristotle classifies plot into two types—*simple* and *complex* plot. A simple plot does not emerge out of reversal or recognition whereas a complex plot develops out of reversal or recognition or both.

Aristotle then discusses the difference between poetry and history. He introduces the law of probability in his discussion and proves the universality and superiority of poetry. He does not consider the point of prose and verse as the point of difference between poetry and history. The difference is that history tells us what has happened whereas poetry tells us what might happen. The other difference is that poetry expresses universals and history expresses particulars. Poetry is therefore more philosophical and worthy of attention than history.

Key Points

- Aristotle begins by establishing that all forms of art are imitations of real life.
- He identifies three different forms of poetry—comedy, tragedy and epic, and describes each form briefly.
- In chapters 6 to 10, he extensively discusses tragedy as an art form.
- He identifies six elements of tragedy. In order of importance they are—plot, character, thought, diction, melody and spectacle.
- Plots are of two kinds—simple and complex.
- The plot of a tragedy must have a definite and well-knit order, be organised around a common theme, demonstrate unity of action, be neither too short nor too long, and imitate real-life situations and people as closely as possible.
- The elements which make a plot engaging are—astonishment, recognition, reversal of fortune and suffering of the main characters.
- Aristotle believes that poetry expresses universal emotions and dilemmas, and is therefore superior to all other forms of knowledge.

Exercises

Answer the following questions in about 100–150 words.

1) What are the three mediums of imitation?
2) What are the objects of imitation of poetry?

3) Briefly describe the differences between tragedy and epic.

4) Enumerate the elements of tragedy.

5) What, according to Aristotle, is the distinction between poetry and history?

Answer the following questions in about 250–300 words.

1) Explain Aristotle's definition of tragedy.

2) Why does Aristotle call plot the soul of tragedy? Justify your answer.

3) Discuss the characteristic features of plot.

4) What are the elements that make a plot functional?

5) How does Aristotle defend poetry against Plato's charges?

NEOCLASSICISM

Historical Background

Neoclassicism was an intellectual movement in literature and other art forms that began in the early seventeenth century and lasted till the late eighteenth century in Europe. This was a time when works by the ancient Greek and Roman writers were being rediscovered and translated into modern languages. Neoclassical writers, thus, looked to the Classical period for inspiration from the model works of ancient writers. This included imitation of styles, techniques and values of the ancient Greek and Roman authors. The recourse to Classical models began as early as the fourteenth century when Petrarch (1304–74) in Italy regenerated interest in the study of Greek and Latin literature. With the recovery of Aristotle's *Poetics*, interest in Greek and Roman literature grew in Italy. Many editions of *Poetics* with commentaries were brought out. The most popular among them were J. C. Scaliger (1561) and Castlevetro's (1570) commentaries which took *Poetics* from Italy to different parts of Europe and sparked off interest in the study of the ancient works.

Neoclassical literary criticism first took root in France. Jean Chapelain introduced Classical ideas to France through Scaliger and Castlevetro's commentaries. These commentaries greatly influenced French intellectuals. The establishment of the French Academy in 1635 and the insistence on Classical ideas like probability and decorum further strengthened interest in Classical ideas and works. This led to the rise of French Neoclassical literary theory. The major theorists and practitioners of French Neoclassicism were the writers Corneille and Boileau.

A short account of these theorists will provide the necessary background to the understanding of French Neoclassical literary criticism.

Pierre Corneille (1606–1684) was chiefly a playwright. His literary criticism emerged out of the need to defend his position as a dramatist and his dramatic practice. He wrote *Three Discourses on Dramatic Poetry* (1660) as a defence of his play *Le Cid* (1637). The play became immensely popular but also caused controversies. It was criticised for violating the Classical rules and for the absence of any moral message. Such criticism was striking because Corneille himself was a Neoclassicist writer. He wanted to provide a wide base to Classical ideas by adapting them to the modern stage, and his experiments necessitated a more fluid understanding and interpretation of Classical norms. He succeeded in producing these adapted plays and wrote well-reasoned essays to defend them. These essays/discourses can be treated as an excellent example of Neoclassical criticism. In his third *Discourse*, titled 'Of the Three Unities of Action, Time, and Place', he explains the impact of Classical ideas on his writing and the rationale behind his plays.

Nicolas Boileau (1636–1711) was a poet and critic of great reputation. He influenced French, as well as English and German poets and critics. His critical work, *The Art of Poetry*, first published in 1674, was translated into English by John Dryden. This critical text was written in verse form and aimed to advise poets about the craft and labour of verse composition. It systematically formulated and expressed the principles of French Neoclassicism. It drew on Aristotle and Horace, and influenced English Neoclassical poets like Pope. It set the standards of French Neoclassicism and relieved French literature from non-Classical Italian and Spanish influences. It cultivated the literary taste of the French people and enabled them to appreciate the works of contemporary writers like the famous tragedian **Jean Racine** (1639–99) and the comedian and actor **Molière** (1622–73, pseudonym of Jean-Baptise Poqueline). Boileau insisted on three qualities in the composition of literature—reason, nature and decorum. These included qualities like the unities of time and place, poetic control, moderation and the imitation of Classical works.

The other branch of Neoclassicism flourished in England. It was mainly under the influence of French Neoclassicism. **Ben Jonson** (1572–1637, the English dramatist and poet) was the precursor of Neoclassicism in England. He frequently referred to ancient Roman and Renaissance-era Italian literary ideas and works. But the real motivation was provided by John Dryden's translation of Boileau's *The Art of Poetry*. It is, however, noteworthy that the English men of letters did not passively accept the French version of Neoclassicism. They were choosy and discrete in their approach to French Neoclassicism. Dryden himself objected to the servility of the French critics to the royal court. He argued for a free and independent exercise of the Classical rules in England. Along with Dryden, Alexander Pope and Samuel Johnson were the most important practitioners of Neoclassicism in England. These writers formulated a moderate and flexible type of Neoclassicism, which struck a balance between the qualities of ancient and modern writers. As a result, they ensured that Neoclassicism on English soil became native, accessible and useful.

John Dryden (1631–1700) was one of the pioneers of Neoclassicism in England. He wrote the *Essay of Dramatic Poesy* (1668), his most famous work, and many other prefaces, reviews and prologues. His critical work consisted of commentaries on genres like epic, tragedy, comedy and satire, and the qualities of the ancient and modern writers. Unlike Boileau, his French contemporary, who wrote in the form of dogmatic statements, Dryden used the dialogue form in the *Essay*. By doing so Dryden was able to present many critical views of his time. He debated issues like the nature and composition of drama, the merits of the ancient and modern writers, and the relative excellence of the French and English writers in this work. It is obvious from the *Essay* that Dryden did not accept Classical ideas unchanged, in their ancient form. He discussed almost all the Classical ideas in the light of the changes in modern literary works and favoured English writers who interpreted them to suit modern audiences.

He reaffirmed the importance of the Classical unities of time, place and action but showed how even the Greek masters failed at times to observe them. Dryden acknowledged the usefulness of Classical ideas but did not approve of their rigorous and unmindful application. He tried to broaden the applicability of these ideas.

Alexander Pope (1688–1744) was another important practitioner of Neoclassicism in England. His *An Essay on Criticism* (1771), written in verse form, clearly and categorically expressed the principles of Neoclassicism. Pope's *Essay* can be summed up in these three points: he brought his vision of humanism to a Classical set of principles, he rigorously followed the Classical principles of art and beauty, and he adopted the style of the ancient rhetoricians in his *Essay*. Along with other Classical virtues, Pope gave more importance to nature and wit in the composition and judgment of literary work. Nature for him is the force that represents order, harmony and the beauty of creation. Wit was variously interpreted as being an accessory to Nature, and as important as Nature because it is the objective and honest expression of the universal truth. Pope interpreted Wit as the ability of the writer/critic to express truth and morality. When the point of comparison between literature and criticism came up Pope argued that poets and critics need the same qualities to create and judge literary works. In his words:

> Both must alike from Heav'n derive their Light,
>
> Those born to Judge, as well as those to Write. (Essay, ll. 13–14)

His precept was that excellent poets make excellent critics. He gave a long list of qualities which a good critic must have, but the most important of them are the critic's ability to recognise the overall unity of a work, unbiased assessment and moral sensibility.

Samuel Johnson (1709–84) was the crowning figure of English Neoclassicism. His prodigious personality and critical ability greatly influenced his contemporaries and successors. His *Preface* to Shakespeare's plays firmly established Shakespeare as a genius dramatist. His account of the lives of many English poets defined various qualities of good literature in general and laid the foundation of the English literary canon. He was a Classicist in his insistence on reason, probability, truth and moral function of literature. Like Pope, he also gave importance to Nature and believed that the greatest excellence of art lay in the imitation of Nature. However he made it emphatically clear that the imitation of Nature should be proper and should express truth in general and universal terms. Johnson firmly believed in Classical ideals but he did not follow them blindly. He broke away from Classical rules whenever he found them rigid and restrictive. He recognised and defended the merits and qualities of great writers and their innovations that did not fit the Classical standard. For example, he famously celebrated the mixing of the genre of tragedy and comedy in Shakespeare's plays. He did not approve of the Classical rules which dictated the number of characters on the stage, the limitation of a play to five acts and the unity of time whereby a play's action must play out in a day.

It may be stated that the key figures of English Neoclassical criticism are Dryden, Pope and Johnson. Dryden introduced Neoclassicism to England by adapting Classical ideas and rules to the English taste. Though he appreciated Shakespeare's plays, he found much to criticise as well, because they did not suit Neoclassical ideas.

Pope's version was English Neoclassicism in the strict and perfect sense of the term. He insisted on following Classical norms both on a creative and critical level. Johnson preferred to tread the middle path. He was against any unnecessary violation of Classical rules by writers/critics, but also cautioned against an extreme and rigid use of the Classical rules. As a Neoclassicist he favoured the use of heroic couplets and admired Pope for doing so. But at the same time he dismissed the unity of time and place as unnecessary to a play and insisted on the unity of action alone.

Salient Features of Neoclassicism

1) Neoclassicism is a return to Classical literary works and a revival of Classical rules and modes of writing.

2) Imitating the ancient writers and their works is encouraged. This is because a good writer should aim for the correct depiction of nature—both physical and human. The ancient writers depicted nature perfectly and thus a close imitation of their style and form is desirable.

3) Decorum and moderation were valued in Neoclassicism. A good writer was expected to use the appropriate language and writing style for different characters and genres, and avoid excess and extremes, in depictions as well as writing style.

4) Unity is one of the important features of Neoclassicism. It implies that the writer should perfectly and rationally organise his material. Writers must follow the three unities of action, time and place. The unity of action mandates that the chain of actions in the plot must proceed logically, and must be connected with one another. The unity of time limits the action of a play to twenty-four hours and the unity of place restricts the show of action to a particular place.

5) Neoclassicism can be said to have originated as a critical movement in France. The most prominent French Neoclassical critics were Pierre Corneille and Nicolas Boileau. Corneille was a playwright who adapted Classical ideas to best cater to contemporary audiences, and also authored essays outlining his critical stance on Neoclassicism. Boileau wrote prescriptive criticism for

writers and stressed on three principles being essential to good writing—reason, nature and decorum. His ideas influenced various French, German and English intellectuals.

6) English Neoclassicist critics included Ben Jonson, John Dryden, Alexander Pope and Samuel Johnson. Dryden translated Boileau's *Art of Poetry* and insisted on a strict adherence to Classical ideas. Pope had a humanist vision towards Classical ideas, and exemplified the Classical vision in his own writing. Johnson laid emphasis on the principles behind Classicism, and stressed that reason, probability, truth and a moral function were the hallmarks of good literature.

Introduction to Dr Samuel Johnson's *The Rambler, No. 4 [On Fiction]*

The Rambler was a twice-weekly periodical by issued by Dr Johnson during 20 March 1750 to 14 March 1752. There were 208 issues of the periodical, and it featured essays on a wide range of subjects.

The Rambler No. 4 deals with the emerging genre of the novel in Johnson's time. It shows how a sagacious critic grounded in a particular mode of thinking receives a new kind of literature. As a true Neoclassicist he emphasises the elements of morality and responsibility in the writing of the novel. He makes the novelists aware of their duty towards their readers and exhorts them to create examples of good behaviour for young readers to follow. He briefly outlines the nature and faults of fiction writing of the last age and explains his expectations as a critic from the fiction writers of his age.

The essay begins with an epigraph from Horace's *Ars Poetica* and its English translation. In the opening paragraph Johnson comments on the works of fiction of his age and sums up their qualities. These works of fiction, according to him, show human life in its true state and the passions and qualities that can actually be found in human beings. Johnson takes care to distinguish this new kind of writing from the fictional writing of the last age, which he terms as the comedy of romance. The comedy of romance consisted of entertaining stories of love and adventure often based on elements of fantasy and myth. The fiction of Johnson's time, on the contrary, brings out natural events by easy means without resorting to improbable plot devices. He distinguishes it from the improbable and incredible action of the comedy of romance. The writers of this sort of fiction did not study hard, did not have the knowledge of nature, and did not know human life well. So they continued to deceive readers with the help of their imagination.

Next, Johnson describes the duty of the writers of his generation. According to him writers should glean knowledge not just from books, but through the observation of real life. They should ensure that they present only credible and faithful pictures of human life. Another duty of the writers is towards young and inexperienced readers. Young readers are ignorant, idle and impressionable. They neither have any knowledge of human life nor determination of mind. While reading works of fancy and wonder they fall victim to false presentation and a partial account of life. Therefore writers should be on guard against any false and misguiding account of human life in their works, no matter how entertaining. Johnson points out that the romances of the earlier age were not closely related to life and therefore not easily imitable. But the novels of his generation offer examples from real life and therefore, there is the risk of imitation by young readers. It is their moral duty to present only the best examples. They must select only those objects and individuals that are worthy of imitation. The object or individual they have chosen to depict should be like a diamond, whose lustre can be polished by art. As a Neoclassicist, Johnson emphasises that art should imitate nature. But he knows the dangers involved in indiscriminate imitation. The novelists should identify the most proper parts of human nature that are free from bad qualities like passion and wickedness. They should not show only that which appears to them, but that which is found suitable and presentable through observation and experience. The purpose of novels is not limited to showing human beings as they are but to provide them with examples by which they can learn to live by virtue and fight against treachery and fraud. However, Johnson observes that many writers mix good and bad qualities in the creation of major characters in their works. Such characters merely give pleasure to readers and have no didactic value. Influenced by such portrayals, readers neglect their own faults.

Johnson clears the misconception that virtue and fault emerge from the same passion and so any description of virtue in isolation is improbable, and a believable character must also partake of vice. He quotes Jonathan Swift, who observed that men are equally grateful and resentful. Swift's observation assumes that man's behaviour is based on uncontrollable and violent impulses. But Johnson argues that such violent impulses can be controlled and sublimated with the help of reason. Novelists should distinguish good from evil with the help of reason, and through the presentation of rational and judicious characters, encourage readers to separate right from wrong.

Johnson urges novelists to show the most perfect idea of virtue. He explains that characters should not be angel-like and improbable. Novelists need not show that which human beings can never attain, but should show the highest and the purest level of virtue that human beings can achieve. They should also depict vice, but in such a way that it excites disgust in readers.

Key Points

- Johnson's *Rambler no. 4* deals with the emerging genre of the novel in Johnson's time.
- Johnson, as a Neoclassicist critic, insists on morality and responsibility.
- His advice to fiction writers is keep young readers in mind and to create model examples for them to emulate.

- He argues for strict adherence to reason, nature and factual presentation of human life in novels.
- Johnson wants novelists to create characters that are life like and that are personifications of the highest purity and virtue.
- He argues against Jonathan Swift's argument about the violent nature of human beings.
- According to him, reason can control violence and so novelists should portray restrained characters that exhibit ideal behaviour.

Exercises

Answer the following questions in about 100–150 words.

1) What are the faults of the writers of the comedy of romance?
2) Where should writers get their knowledge from?
3) What type of readers are young people?
4) What kind of selection from nature should novelists make?
5) What, according to Johnson, is the purpose of novels?

Answer the following questions in about 250–300 words.

1) How does Johnson distinguish the comedy of romance from the novels of his age?
2) What, according to Johnson, are the tasks of novelists?
3) What kind of imitation of nature does Johnson prefer?
4) How does Johnson prove the importance of reason in separating virtue from vice?
5) What qualities of Johnson as a Neoclassical critic emerge from the essay?

ROMANTICISM

Historical Background

Romanticism was an intellectual movement which began in the late eighteenth century, and lasted well into the nineteenth century. Romantic writers and critics valued what they deemed was 'natural'—the beauties of the countryside, individual untaught genius, spontaneity and emotion. It was characterised by a rejection of Neoclassical norms of reason, balance, order and artifice. Romanticism was a powerful influence on the cultural world of Europe, and several works produced during this period form part of the English literary canon.

There are certain socio-political contexts and artistic reasons responsible for the rise of Romanticism as a cultural movement in Europe. The Enlightenment, the American and French Revolutions, industrial development and the urbanisation which followed, and the emphasis on rationalism provided the socio-political and intellectual background to Romanticism. These developments in Europe influenced and were reflected in the literature of the time. Romanticism proposed a new and revolutionary aesthetic that stressed subjectivity, imagination, artistic genius, and themes and language borrowed from common people. Its historical development as a literary movement can be better understood by studying it as three versions—German, French, and English Romanticism. Of course, these movements did not develop in isolation, and influenced each other. Romanticism later spread to different parts of Europe and America. Given below is a short outline of how Romanticism as an artistic movement began and played out in the above mentioned nations.

German Romanticism

It is remarkable that German Romanticism found its true and comprehensive expression in literary criticism and not in creative literature. It was literary critics and theorists and not poets or playwrights who laid the foundations of Romanticism and developed it into a recognisable movement in Germany. Because it flourished within and through criticism it was organised, self-conscious and argumentative. The driving intellectual force behind this kind of thinking was the philosopher **Immanuel Kant** (1724–1804). Kant expressed his views on beauty, art, imagination and poetry in his critical philosophy. His views provided a theoretical base to German critics and influenced other European Romantic critics as well. It is therefore helpful to know his views related to art and poetry in a nutshell.

1) Kant proposed that the mind can construct its world. Such a construction would obviously be subjective. Applied to poetry and other forms of literature, this was a philosophical sanction to the subjectivity of poet's mind which the Romantics fully utilised.

2) He made a distinction between art and craft. He privileged art over craft because he argued that art is free of artificial constraints and that fine art (poetry) arouses a feeling of spiritual pleasure. Craft, on the other hand, is mercenary and mechanical. It gives concrete shape to the object in mind but cannot give a feeling of true spiritual pleasure.

3) He thought 'genius' to be a natural disposition and not something to be earned through hard work and reason. It cannot be taught or learnt; it is natural. It means that there can be no rules for the creation of art; art follows its own rules. A work of art shows the rules of its creation.

4) According to Kant, imagination is an 'animating principle' of mind. It gives concrete form to an aesthetic idea. It creates

another nature/world out of the material that Nature provides to it.

5) He rates poetry to be the finest form of art because it offers full scope to the imagination and expresses the inexpressible.

It is clear from this sketch that Kant disagreed with many Classical ideas and proposed to free art from the strictures of rules and reason. He influenced two generations of notable critics and theorists in Germany. The first generation consisted mainly of theorists who were directly influenced by Kant's ideas about art, beauty and sublimity. A prominent member of the first generation of German Romantic critics, **Friedrich von Schiller** (1759–1805) was a poet, dramatist and critic. He further elaborated upon Kant's ideas about art and aesthetics. He looked upon art as a solution to many world problems. He appealed to writers to turn away from reality and to turn towards the ideal world. The writer's role, according to him, was to recreate this ideal world made available to him by his imagination.

August Schlegel (1767–1854) was another influential first generation Romantic critic and philologist. His association and devotion to Romanticism started with his translation of William Shakespeare's plays into the German language. He gave lectures on Shakespeare's dramatic art and literature and became a famous figure in England. The noted English Romantic critic William Hazlitt, and William Wordsworth praised Schlegel's views. Coleridge was influenced by his lectures when he was forming his own views on Shakespeare's plays. He successfully defined the ideal of Romantic art which consisted of notions like beauty for beauty's sake, the union of poetry and life and the absolute freedom of the artist to express his experiences.

Another prominent figure was **Friedrich Schelling** (1775–1854). In his book *System of Transcendental Idealism* (1800) he reinterpreted the idea of consciousness and proposed that knowledge of the external world comes to consciousness through self-consciousness. This amounted to the removal of contradiction and effective interaction between the realms of subject and object; mind and nature. He believed that the human mind achieves its highest self-consciousness in art and thereby suggested that art can be the best possible source of resolving contradictions. Schelling's theory greatly influenced many intellectuals across Europe, one notable example being English critic S. T. Coleridge, who borrowed Schelling's ideas to explain his theory of poetic creation. The principle of interaction between mind and nature helped Coleridge to form his theory of poetic imagination as the reconciler of opposite qualities.

The second generation consisted of writers like Clemense Brentano, Achim Arnim, Ludwig Ulhand, and Joseph Goerres. This generation did not formulate views on Romanticism independently and largely followed the lead of the first generation theorists.

French Romanticism

Like German Romanticism, French Romanticism was also a movement based on commonly shared principles. But it had its distinctive nature and mode of expression. If German Romanticism was philosophical, its French counterpart was artistic and social. The French Romantic writers and artists largely restricted their ideas to the domain of art and did not apply them to politics and religion as thoroughly as the Germans did. French Romanticism was assertive, aggressive and violent because it had to react to the stronghold of eighteenth-century Neoclassicism. **Jean-Jacques Rousseau** (1712–1778), the renowned social thinker of the period, provided the necessary intellectual inspiration and theoretical orientation to French Romantics. Rousseau outlined the roadmap of French Romanticism in his work by challenging Enlightenment principles.

Following are some of the highlights of his thoughts:

1) Rousseau historically belonged to the Enlightenment movement but rejected the principles of the movement, especially the principle of reason. He argued that reason deprives man of sympathy for fellow beings, making him self-centred and selfish.

2) Man's worth does not depend on his intelligence but on his moral nature. Moral nature consists of feeling. Feeling is the only common thing that all men possess and therefore it can create equality and justice in human beings.

3) Rousseau gave the call—'return to nature'. This idea of nature is based on freedom from all methods of learning and education. It is free communion with nature and it cultivates the feeling necessary to deal fairly and humanely with others. Thus, man in a 'natural environment' becomes truly liberal and moral.

These ideas greatly influenced the French and other Romantics. We find the echoes of Rousseau's ideas in the theoretical formulations of critics and the themes of creative writers. Rousseau provided artists and critics of this period with a range of ideas that stood squarely against the traditional, and especially the Enlightenment worldview. These ideas included distrust in reason, search for innocence and an uncorrupt world, urge for true liberation and nature as the source of knowledge and delight.

Madame de Stael (1722–1817) was the precursor of French Romanticism. She wrote the first piece of criticism which treated literature as a product of social history and environment. Her bold personality and extraordinary talent made her the source of inspiration for many French Romanticists. She firmly believed in a progressive view of life and boldly spoke for justice. Her rebellious lifestyle and work featured most of the principles of Romanticism. Her novels and critical writing openly supported the freedom of writers and women.

Francois-René de Chateaubriand (1768–1848) could rightly be termed as the Father of French Romanticism. He wrote a defence of the Christian faith, titled *Le Genie du Christianisme* (1802) and contributed to the revival of the church in France. The work was significant from the point of Romanticism because through his impassioned love of Christianity, Chateaubriand championed the imaginative freedom of the individual. He eloquently expressed the emotional and imaginative appeal of religion to the deepest instincts of man's nature. His two successive fragmentary works based on tragic romance and solitude further illustrated his Romantic attitude. Autobiographical features which reflected in his work, like his own hypersensitive poetic nature, his love for the beauty of nature, the power of imagination in his work and its emotional intensity made him the pioneer of French Romanticism.

Victor Hugo (1802–85) was the central figure of the Romantic movement in France. He was a poet, novelist and dramatist of great eminence and was instrumental in giving French poetry a Romantic orientation. He introduced new subjects, changed diction and versification and thus brought freedom to French poetry. The poet, according to Hugo, is the true master of his age and the most sensitive indicator of the spirit of his age. Apart from poetry, he made a great impact with his plays and novels. In plays he violated the unities and other Neoclassical norms and his two novels, *Notre-Dame de Paris* (1831) and *Les Misérables* (1862), immensely influenced the French people.

English Romanticism

English Romanticism started around the mid-eighteenth century and reached its culmination during the beginning of the nineteenth century. Like their European counterparts the English Romantics supported the cause of the French Revolution and believed their literary works were revolutionary. They strongly opposed Neoclassical rules and restrictions like poetic diction, faithful imitation of characters and objects and reason. The opposition could be seen both in their creative and critical writings. Wordsworth rejected Neoclassical rules for poetry in his composition and emphatically argued against it in his canonical Preface. His 'Preface' to *Lyrical Ballads* (1800) was primarily an introduction to and justification of the kind of poetry he and Coleridge had attempted. It stated the Romantic concept of poetry in clear and effective terms. Apart from Wordsworth's 'Preface', Keats's letters could be studied as excellent pieces of criticism. Keats did not write an independent treatise to state his theory of poetry but his letters very effectively and convincingly elaborated his views on poetry. But the critical statement of this period that was theoretically most developed and comprehensive came from Coleridge. He was a critic of great range and perception. His brilliant views on concepts like reason and understanding, symbolism and allegory, organic and mechanical form, and culture and civilisation were pathbreaking. His most towering contribution was his concept of poetic imagination. In his *Biographia Literaria* he made a distinction between fancy and imagination. But he could not develop this concept into a full-fledged theory.

Apart from Coleridge, Shelley showed a critical bent of mind. He offered a powerful defence of poetry against the charges made by critics like Thomas Love Peacock, who said poetry was immoral and of no use (1785–1866, English satirist, essayist and poet). These poets conceived Romanticism in their characteristic individual ways and practiced it accordingly in their compositions.

The pre-Romantic poets like Thomas Gray (1716–71), Robert Burns (1759–96) and Oliver Goldsmith (1730–74) prepared the way to High Romanticism. For the sake of convenience we may divide the English Romantics into two groups—the early group of poets like William Blake, William Wordsworth and S. T. Coleridge, and the later group consisting of P. B. Shelley, John Keats and Lord Byron. It is important to know that these poets shared certain common goals like freeing poetry from the burden of rules and artificiality, depicting nature as an endearing world that contrasts with the man-made world and championing freedom from all kinds of bondage. They pursued these goals differently in their poetry and thus contributed to or extended the principles of Romanticism.

In the early group of the English Romantics **William Blake** (1757–1827) was the first important figure. Blake's Romanticism was different from the writers who were his contemporaries, as well as those who succeeded him. Blake regarded the poet as a visionary, and believed the poet's gift of imagination gave him prophetic powers. As a citizen of England he was alert to the political developments and social ills of his time. As a sensitive artist he believed that his task was to harmonise opposites and contradictions. His interest in arts like engraving and painting further deepened his artistic vision. His poetry was prophetic, mythological and visionary and therefore difficult to understand. His poems are characterised by a blend of political fervour and visionary ecstasy. His poetry often portrays the suffering and painful realities of his time. He speaks out against evil and injustice and has compassion for the weak and the exploited. He offers both a positive vision of the world as in *Songs of Innocence* (1789) and a negative vision as in *Songs of Experience* (1794).

The novelist **Walter Scott** (1771–1832) also ought to be given credit for introducing Romantic elements into English literature, especially in fiction. He was the pioneer of the historical novel in England. But his Romanticism was very different from the High Romanticism of the poets. His Romanticism was rooted in the local landscape and heavily influenced by Scottish legends about heroes and aristocrats of the past. His metrical romances often expressed a nostalgic urge for past glory and love for the nation.

William Wordsworth (1770–1850) along with his friend Coleridge was responsible for the beginning and growth of Romanticism as a movement in England. He was a passionate supporter of the French Revolution. He thought that it would turn republican ideals like liberty, equality and fraternity into reality. He celebrated the promise of the revolution in the following words:

> Bliss was it in that dawn to be alive
>
> But to be young was very Heaven! O times,
>
> In which the meagre, stale, forbidding ways
>
> Of custom, law, and statute, took at once
>
> The attraction of a country in romance! (Prelude, XI, 108–113).

But the revolution disappointed him and his generation and he distanced himself from radical politics and idealism. In collaboration with Coleridge he published an anthology of poems titled *Lyrical Ballads* (1798). He proposed a new theory of poetry in the preface of this anthology, which became the manifesto of English Romantic poetry. In the preface, Wordsworth argued against Neoclassical artifice in poetry. He emphasised the freedom of art and the artist, his individuality and autonomy. He championed the use of real language and real-life themes in poetry. His view of the poet was of 'a man speaking to men', albeit one gifted with visionary faculty. He regarded poetry as springing 'from emotion recollected in tranquility'. He stressed the qualities of emotional intensity, simplicity, spontaneity, love for nature and bliss of solitude.

Samuel Taylor Coleridge (1772–1834) was a poet, critic and one of the most influential figures of English Romanticism, along with Wordsworth. Like his friend Wordsworth, he was also influenced by the promise of the French Revolution but the later political developments disillusioned him. He turned to German intellectuals like Kant, Schlegel and Schelling for inspiration. His views on the dramatic art of Shakespeare were influenced by Schlegel, and his formulation of poetic imagination, by Schelling. A poem, in Coleridge's view, is a metrical composition that opposes the works of science because its object is to give pleasure and not truth. The poet, according to him, is born and not made.

He has the magical power of imagination, which helps him create visions in his poetry. Coleridge's own poetry possesses a dream-like quality where borders are blurred between dreams and reality (his difficult poem, 'Kubla Khan', for example.) He made a seminal contribution in at least two respects—he gave a new direction to the critical study of Shakespeare's work in England, and he proposed his celebrated concept of fancy and imagination. He convincingly argued that fancy is different from imagination because it is more common. Imagination is a rare gift that reconciles opposite qualities and gives delight to the reader. While explaining the creative role of imagination he distinguished between primary and secondary imagination and termed secondary imagination to be poetic imagination. Apart from a handful of enduring poems, *Biographia Literaria* (1817) was his most notable work.

In the later group of the English Romantics, **Lord Byron** (1788–1824) was a stylish and exciting figure. He was notorious for his lifestyle and yet exerted great influence on English Romantic poetry. Byron, in the early stage of his writing career, imitated the favourite themes of earlier Romantic poets, like descriptions of landscapes and attributing human feelings to nature. But later, he developed his own distinctive version of Romanticism, best exemplified in his famous creation, the 'Byronic hero', in his long poem *Childe Harold's Pilgrimage* (1812–18). The 'Byronic hero' is a lonely person, proud but unhappy. He stays away from family, friends and society but enjoys the company of women. He loves freedom and opposes regimentation and systemic oppression. He uses artificial and affected language. It is obvious that the hero was a prototype of Byron himself.

P. B. Shelley (1792–1822) alongside his fellow Romantic, Byron, presented a very radical version of Romanticism in both theory and practice. He was widely read and was knowledgeable about the classics, contemporary science and philosophy. Like all other Romantics he strongly believed in liberty, individuality and compassion for the oppressed. He hoped for a better world where there was no repression or social evil. He defined the poet as 'a nightingale who sits in the darkness and sings to cheer its own solitude with sweet sounds'. He thought poetry to be 'the record of the best and happiest moments of the happiest and best minds', and assigned a redeeming role to the poet. Poetry for him was both a source of pleasure and beauty and an instrument to bring about social change. It is noteworthy that the early and later generation of Romantic poets tried to escape from the irreconcilable contradictions and opposites of modern life, but Shelley bravely depicted it in the form of a mixed picture of idealism, hope and faith on one hand, and scepticism, doubt and despair on the other (for example his 'Ode to the West Wind').

John Keats (1795–1821) was the last significant English Romantic. Like Byron he was also influenced by the major themes employed by earlier Romantic poets, like the urge for freedom from all bondage, love for nature, and the significance of emotions and imagination. His poetry is famed for his passionate descriptions of beauty and its sensuousness. His 'Odes' are the best examples of Keats' sensual writing. In his letters he expressed the view that the poet should possess what he called 'negative capability', give up his personal identity and share the identity of the objects he is attempting to describe, in order to create a faithful description.. The task of the poet, according to him, is to transmute the passing beauty of the world into a permanent work of art. He defined poetry as a natural event, like leaves blooming on a tree.

Salient Features of Romanticism

1) Romanticism is a reaction to Neoclassicism. The Romantics strongly criticised the Neoclassicist vision of human life. The Neoclassicist vision was based on the rational (and not emotional) understanding of human life and universally applicable (and not limited to individual application) characteristics of human behaviour. The

Romantics on the other hand favoured sentimental and individual descriptions of human life.

2) Apart from this philosophical difference, the Romantics broke away from the Neoclassical rules of literary style and subject matter. Their writing was marked for its passionate appeal, deep longing and intense feeling. Their style was characterised by a preference for boldness over restraint, suggestiveness over clarity, and freedom from the rules of composition, genre and decorum.

3) Love for nature is the defining feature of Romanticism. The Romantics regarded it as a living and liberating force, as opposed to the utilitarian rationalist view of nature. It was through nature that they tried to establish communion with the entire world. It appealed to them in different forms and offered the whole range of human experience—pleasure and pain, temporariness and permanence, mortality and immortality, beauty and truth.

4) Imagination is the key term of Romanticism. This was a change from the mimetic theory (art as an imitation of the Classical models) of art to the expressive theory (art as a creative expression). The Romantics thought of imagination as a dynamic, active and unifying faculty. It helped them recreate reality and unite both reason and feeling.

5) Individualism is another important feature of Romanticism. The Romantics did not follow already established views and conventions but believed strongly in the authority of experience. They were democratic in their approach and regarded individual freedom and thought highly.

6) The Romantics disliked the unpleasant, mechanical and competitive nature of city life and preferred the simple, primitive and uncorrupted lifestyle of the country. They

hated the moral mediocrity of the middle-class world.

7) As a literary critical movement, Romanticism can be studied as three versions—German, French and English.

8) The German version of Romanticism was largely philosophical and religious in nature, and influenced by the philosopher Immanuel Kant's ideas on the principles of art, beauty and sublimity. Important German Romantic critics included Friedrich von Schiller, August Schlegel and Friedrich Schelling.

9) French Romanticism had an aesthetic and artistic tilt, and was greatly influenced by Jean Jacques Rousseau's philosophy. Noted French Romantic writers and critics included Madame de Stael, Francois-René de Chateaubriand and Victor Hugo.

10) English Romanticism included writers and poets who also produced literary criticism outlining the ideals of their movement. William Blake and Sir Walter Scott are now classed as being the earliest Romantic writers, but writers and critics began to self-identify as Romantic from the eighteenth century onwards. The first generation of Romantic writers and critics included William Wordsworth and S.T. Coleridge, while Lord Byron, P. B. Shelley and John Keats were among the second generation.

Introduction to Wordsworth's 'Preface' to *Lyrical Ballads* (1802)

Wordsworth added his 'Preface' to the second edition of *Lyrical Ballads*, published in the year 1800 and revised it for the subsequent edition in 1802. He was writing after the painful disappointment caused by the failure of the French Revolution in achieving its stated objectives. He was writing for and in favour of common people living in the company of nature and not for sophisticated people living in the mechanised cities. This background provides a good context to understand Wordsworth's position and views in the 'Preface'. The 'Preface' primarily deals with the use of real and natural language in poetry but it also addresses other important issues like a) the view of the poet and b) the purpose of poetry. It justifies the style, subject matter and language of the poems included in *Lyrical Ballads* and also makes general statements about poetic language and the nature and scope of poetry.

In the very beginning of the 'Preface' Wordsworth makes it clear that he is against the grand, stylised and artificial use of language. He points out that the long use of such polished language by poets turned it into a rigid poetic diction and replaced ordinary speech. He states certain reasons for his choice of language of the common people in the poems of the present anthology:

1) The chief object behind the poems in *Lyrical Ballads* is to choose incidents and situations from common life. Such incidents are to be related or described in the language really used by men.
2) Such a choice gives full scope to the imagination, and in turn, imagination makes ordinary things look unusual and interesting.
3) Wordsworth explains in detail the reasons for his choice of low and rustic life as the themes of his poems. In a nutshell they are— a) it can better express essential passions, b) it is not constrained by structural and thematic restraints, c) it makes use of simple and emphatic language. According to Wordsworth, the language of rustic people is more permanent and philosophical than the capricious and arbitrary language used by poets. It is clear that Wordsworth rejects the language used in the city and the court and prefers the language used in the fields and farms. He prefers the language of rustic people because the passions of rustic

people are influenced by their daily communion with nature, and their language contains the best part derived from such beautiful and permanent passions.

Wordsworth dismisses the important features of Neoclassical poetry—poetic diction and the personification of abstract ideas. It is because they are artificial. On the contrary, he says, 'good poetry is the spontaneous overflow of powerful feelings' where he emphasises spontaneity of feelings.

Wordsworth then takes up the issue of the poet, his nature and role. He examines the institution of 'poet' in relation to its definition, nature, its association to readers and its use of language. For Wordsworth a poet is not a singer of great glories or a teacher of good morals. He is 'a man speaking to men'. He has certain qualities which set him apart, though, like sensibility, enthusiasm, tenderness, and a greater knowledge of human nature. It is notable that Neoclassical poetics demands the observation of rules by the poet but Wordsworth expects many more qualities. He frees the poet from Neoclassical rules but puts greater demands on him. He requires the poet to be individual in his approach and to possess qualities different from others, and this leads to the idea of poetic genius. Wordsworth distinguishes the poet from the man of science. The man of science seeks truth as a remote and unknown benefactor and celebrates it in solitude. He works in isolation and celebrates alone. The poet on the other hand sings a song with other humans and rejoices in the presence of the truth. He contributes to build the vast empire of human society with the help of passion and knowledge.

The Classical purpose of poetry is to teach people to think reasonably and behave acceptably. Wordsworth rejects this didactic purpose. According to him the purpose of poetry is to give immediate pleasure to human beings. Poetry is not the result of reason or rules; it is the result of imagination. He famously defines it as 'the spontaneous overflow of powerful feelings: it takes its origin from emotion recollected in tranquility: the emotion is contemplated till, by a species of reaction, the tranquility gradually disappears, and an emotion, kindred to that which was before the subject of contemplation, is gradually produced, and does itself actually exist in the mind.' This may be simply stated as–the poet seeks inspiration and develops his emotions in nature. His emotions are excited and are made into a poem with the help of images of in nature. The images of nature in the poem are the expression of the emotions in the mind of the poet. The poem, when read, excites in the reader emotions similar to that of the poet.

Wordsworth also discusses the point of the use of metre in poetry. He does not approve of the use of metre because he thinks that it imposes restrictions on the power of poetry to excite powerful emotions.

Key Points

- Wordsworth strongly opposes the Neoclassical principles of grand, stylised and artificial language, and abstract and sophisticated subjects.
- His preference is for ordinary language and incidents from the life of ordinary people as themes.
- Such ordinary language and incidents are eternal and exciting.
- The poet is not an educator or singer of great glories but 'a man speaking to men'.
- Wordsworth distinguishes between a poet and man of science thus—a poet enjoys truth in the company of others and a man of science celebrates truth in isolation.
- Poetry is not the result of reason, art and objectivity but the result of imagination, spontaneity and individuality of the poet.

Exercises

Answer the following questions in about 100–150 words.

1) What is the chief objective behind the poems in *Lyrical Ballads*?
2) Why does Wordsworth prefer the language of rustic people?
3) What features of Neoclassical poetry does Wordsworth dismiss?
4) What is Wordsworth's definition of a poet?
5) What are the qualities of a poet?

Answer the following questions in about 250–300 words.

1) Write a short account of Romanticism as a cultural movement in Europe.
2) Comment on the features of Romanticism, as explained by Wordsworth.
3) What, according to Wordsworth, are the reasons for his choice of using the language of rustic people in his poetry?
4) Discuss Wordsworth's views on the poet.
5) What, according to Wordsworth, is the purpose of poetry?

VICTORIAN LITERARY CRITICISM

Historical Background

With rapid changes in the socio-political structure of English society and the increasing influence of scientific attitude and rational thinking, English Romanticism lost its sway around 1830 and gave way to Victorianism. The Victorian period, technically, is the period of Queen Victoria's reign, and begins in 1837 and ends in 1901. Her accession to the throne marked the beginning of the Victorian period in literature and art, and her death, the end of the period. It was a period of wealth and stability in England. The English had extended their colonial empire to nearly a quarter of the globe by the end of the nineteenth century. The wealth brought in by the colonies, as well as the Industrial Revolution, had substantially altered the English economy, as well as its sociopolitical structure. England moved towards an industrial, urban-centric society, from an agrarian one, in which ownership of land determined social class. The economic shift created a more democratic society in some ways, and the Victorian era heralded the rise of the English middle class. The Victorians emphasised a rigid adherence to convention, and viewed appropriate behaviour, practicality, utility and reason as noble and socially enriching. However, there was another side to Victorian society. Widespread poverty, squalid urban slums, child labour and prostitution characterised the Victorian era, as much as its affluence and rigid morality. These contradictions immensely influenced literary output and critical practice.

Unlike Romanticism, Victorian literary criticism was not a reaction or a revolution against any dogmas or rules of creative writing and critical practice. We can say that the Victorian period was more of a transition period between Romanticism and Modernism. It had its own features and problems but the creative writers and critics of this period did not propose new and revolutionary theories that could orient the literary world to a new aesthetic.

In a world of excessive materialism, utilitarianism and scientific advancements questioning faith, the Victorians found the earlier thought and practice of Romanticism increasingly inadequate to meet new challenges. They needed art, and more particularly, criticism, to become a social and moral teacher and address contemporary issues *judiciously* (this term meant the promotion of intellectual culture and balanced view of life to the Victorians). Such lessons into social behaviour and morality could help them formulate their worldview and enjoy the beauties of human life. These attributes and needs influenced the artistic and critical minds of the period. They were tied to the service of their society, and the revival and protection of morality was the most important medium through which such service could be effectively rendered.

Victorian critics could not, however, formulate a unified theory or one dominant school of thought. Victorian criticism therefore represents different critical tendencies in different phases. It is strongly idealistic in its first phase; moralistic, objective and truth seeking in the second phase; and aesthetic in the last phase. These critical tendencies drew on European philosophical and critical approaches prevalent at the time. Idealism was the dominant mode of thinking in Germany, Realism and Naturalism were the important movements in France and aestheticism had its sway in Italy. These movements across Europe influenced Victorian critics and helped them formulate their respective views about literature and criticism. The following description is a very short account of these three critical tendencies of the Victorian period and the critics referred to are representative of the three tendencies.

There are not too many influential critics/theorists in the Victorian period. But the account of this period should start with **Thomas Carlyle** (1795–1881). He was a social critic, historian and biographer. He was not a critic per se in the sense that he did not propose a critical theory or write a sustained and substantial critical work. He was more of a cultural custodian who ensured that the morality of the Victorians should not be corrupted by the materialist and utilitarian views and tendencies very much in vogue in his time. He expected literature to play the role of a teacher of morality and idealism. He criticised Romanticism but himself was a Romantic mystic in his way of thinking, as he often tried to reconcile his Romantic ideas with the sociopolitical facts of his time. He was deeply influenced by German philosophy and literature and he brought much of the German idealism into English literature and criticism.

The philosopher **John Stuart Mill** (1806–73) presented his views on poetry and proposed the subjectivist theory of poetry, similar in theme to Wordsworth's theory. **John Keble** (1792–1866), Professor of Poetry at Oxford argued that the art of poetry is a kind of medicine divinely bestowed upon man. Other reviewers and critics of the time expressed similar kinds of views about poetry and art in general. They served more as links between the Romantics and the aestheticians of the Modern Era.

The most notable and commanding voice of literary criticism of the mid-Victorian period was **Matthew Arnold** (1822–1888). He was held in high respect and severely criticised by the critics that followed him. Much like Carlyle, he was a cultural custodian and an 'institution' in his own right who criticised the Victorians for their moral corruptness and greed for material possessions. He was acutely concerned with the falling moral standards and fading reasoning power of the people of his time, and he expected criticism to have the functions of correction and resurrection. As a literary critic he was judgmental in style, prescriptive in argument and didactic in purpose. In his preface to his *Poems* published in 1853, Arnold says that a poetical work should be an accurate and interesting representation. He takes up a subject which was hotly debated in his time—that of the merits of poetry from the distant past. Several intellectuals of the time had biased arguments, but Arnold shows a more mature view and argues that great poetry is timeless and cannot be dismissed as ancient or modern. It shows human actions that are eternal. He elaborated upon this view in his later critical essays. For example in his essay 'The Function of Criticism at the Present Time' Arnold asserts the value and function of criticism in relation to literature and society in general. The duty of the critic according to him is to create a favourable atmosphere for writers to write and enrich the knowledge of common people through their work. He prescribes qualities like disinterestedness, truth and objectivity for the critic to cultivate, and requires him to create a current of true and fresh ideas. He regards poetry as the highest art form because it expresses ideal things in universal terms. On the whole, it may be stated that as a critic, Arnold respected Classical literature, and ignored much literature which came later. He strongly desired and recommended objective standards and believed that literature and criticism helped to improve the taste and temperament of common people.

Walter Pater (1839–94) was another prominent critic who rose to prominence towards the end of the Victorian period. His *Studies in the History of the Renaissance* (1873) outlined his aesthetic ideas and subjective model of analysis. He was an ardent lover of beauty and a devoted supporter of aestheticism in England. His views and vocabulary were very different from those of Arnold and other critics of his time. He dismissed morality, idealism and objective disinterestedness as hallmarks of good criticism, and stated that the only method of critical analysis was to examine the impressions that a work of art creates on the audience or reader. The job of the aesthetic critic, therefore, is to explain subjective impressions without venturing upon moral and metaphysical questions. He rejected all absolutes like truth, morality and objectivity and focused on the individual experience as the only guiding principle. Beauty, he argued, must be defined not in its abstract form but through concrete manifestations. He made direct sensation of the beauty of an object the only standard of critical judgment and thus undermined the traditional objective standards of criticism. Pater believed that literature should be studied not for the revelation of the truth, but for the sensations it induces.

Salient Features of Victorian Literary Criticism

1) Victorian literary criticism is not a uniform literary/critical movement or school and it does not make a substantial body of critical work. It is not spontaneous but derivative in nature. The Victorian critics did not have a revolutionary agenda like the Romantics but believed that art and literature should cease to be just a source of beauty, happiness and freedom, and should turn to social and moral issues to correct and elevate people from meanness and materiality.

2) Victorian criticism may be conveniently divided into three phases— i) the first phase of idealism proposed by Thomas Carlyle, ii) the second phase of moral and objective criticism proposed by Matthew Arnold and iii) the third phase of aestheticism proposed by Walter Pater. Carlyle was more of a social philosopher but Arnold and Pater were critics in the true sense of the term. Arnold emphasised the social orientation and moral function of literary criticism. Pater on the other hand insisted on the examination of impressions that a work of art creates on the audience/readers.

3) Victorian criticism (especially that of Arnold) tries to follow the Classical tradition—realising the beauty of life and literature through intellect/reason. It tries to remove all signs of excess in both ancient and modern writing and strike a balance between them. The desire for truth and moral discipline characterise Victorian criticism

which contrasts with the passion and individualism of the Romantic period. The rise of the puritanical middle class and England's shift to an industrial urban society from a rural agrarian one revived moral strictness and rational thinking in Victorian society and by extension, in the critics of the age, causing the influence of Romanticism to dwindle.

4) One of the important features of Victorian criticism is its didactic and prescriptive nature. The Victorians looked upon literature as a vehicle for the advancement of society and criticism as a mediator of knowledge and truth. They thus stressed that both literature and criticism are moral in nature.

5) Victorian criticism provided certain standards and set in motion the process of canon formation in English literature. Moral strictness (codes of conduct), search for truth, objectivity, universality and intellectual pursuit informed the process of canon formation. There was another important aspect to this process—the idealised notion of what was typically 'English'. The notion of 'Englishness' was interpreted as a model that could provide a set of standards and codes of conduct not only to the English people but also to the native people of colonised countries. The critics drew on this idealised notion of 'Englishness' and tried to consolidate it in their writing.

Introduction to Matthew Arnold's 'The Study of Poetry' (1880)

This essay was written as an introduction to the book *The English Poets*, edited by T. H. Ward in 1880. In this introduction, Arnold does not simply introduce the English poets featured, but offers his judgments about them and their poetry. He defines the nature of poetry, comments on the qualities of the best poetry, compares English poetry with European poetry and claims that poetry has a supreme place in civilised society. He argues that poetry has to play a vital role in modern life because another source of truth, knowledge and morality—religion—is on the decline. Only the best poetry can assume the role of a substitute for religion and the best poetry is not necessarily English poetry. He substantiates his value judgments about the nature, qualities and future of poetry by referring to poets like Homer, Dante, Shakespeare, and Milton and quoting extracts from their poems.

The essay begins with Arnold's quotation taken from his introduction to the book *The Hundred Greatest Men.* Arnold, in this quotation, considers poetry a supreme art with a bright future because it deals with ideas and never links ideas with physical objects or presents them as facts. Therefore it will never lose appeal, interest and relevance as religion has done. He explains that his purpose in the present introduction is to examine the stream of English poetry which is a part of the river of world poetry. Poetry is meant for higher uses and higher destinies. It has the power to interpret life, and can console and sustain us. It is superior to philosophy and religion and so it will replace both, and complete science.

But for the achievement of these lofty aims, poetry should be of a high order and excellence; a fine blend of thought and art. It should be free from 'charlatanism', which, Arnold says, causes the divisions between truth and falsehood, excellent and inferior, and sound and unsound to be blurred. The best poetry, according to Arnold, will have the 'power of forming, sustaining and delighting us'. He warns against getting distracted from the best poetry and the strength and joy that it can give to us. There are two such distractions that can deprive readers of real enjoyment—the historic estimate and the personal estimate of poetry. Readers may give more importance to the historical development of poetry in general and the piece of verse on hand as a stage in that development. This is all very interesting and attractive but it distracts readers from the actual poem and forces them to overrate it. Secondly readers' personal likings, affinities and circumstances may affect the interpretation of poetry. Readers may interpret a poem using their personal biases and thus may be carried away from the actual poem. Arnold argues that these are natural faults but it is important that readers refrain from them. He compares English readers of poetry with the French, and finds the French to be more diligent students of their poetry. He cites the French critic, M. Charles d'Hericault, who argues that the Classical writers deified by critics (who praise and worship ancient writers without attempting to know historical facts about them) prevent young students from a historical and human understanding of their poetry. Arnold calls this a piece of negative criticism but seeks its enabling side as well. He agrees with d'Hericault to the extent that a Classical poet should not be blindly studied, and his faults should not be ignored. But he disagrees with him because of his emphasis on the historical method and appeals for a deeper enjoyment and appreciation of the Classical poets' work, rather than focussing on mere historical and philological details about them. To illustrate his point he takes the example of schoolboys who learn philological details to appreciate Greek and Latin authors. But they hardly know and enjoy the works of these authors due to excessive attention to philology and a shortage of time. This is the case also with a reader/critic who pays too much attention to the historical origins of poetry, rather than appreciating the poem itself. It is obvious from this discussion that Arnold is decidedly against historical and personal methods of criticism.

He points out that historical criticism can affect the reader/critic's judgment when he deals with ancient poets, and personal criticism, when he deals with modern poets. He refers to another eminent French critic M. Vivet who is all praise for the poem *Chanson de Ronald* (a heroic poem based on the Battle of Roncevaux in 778 and the oldest surviving major work of French literature) and sees it as a genuine epic. Arnold, however, compares the French epic with Homer's *Iliad* and finds it lacking in many respects. He argues that Vivet's praise is extreme and undeserved. With his comparison of the French epic to Homer's famous Greek epic, Arnold proposes his famous *touchstone method*. He appeals for the comparison of any poetry, contemporary or otherwise, with the poetry (he calls them the 'classics') of the great masters. Such a comparison works as a touchstone that enables the critic to find out the presence or absence of high poetic quality in the poetry that is placed by the side of great poetry. The comparison of short passages or even of single lines will serve the purpose. In order to substantiate his argument Arnold quotes lines from the great master poets—Homer's *Iliad*, Dante's *Paradiso* and *Inferno*, Shakespeare's *Hamlet* and Milton's poetry. The highest poetic quality is the common factor between all these great poets. The comparison of lines from the poems of other poets with lines from the poems of these great poets reveals the worth and merit of other poems. Arnold wants critics to give up abstract evaluations about the highest poetic quality and instead turn to concrete examples from established great poetry and compare them with other poetry.

Arnold then specifies certain characteristics of the best poetry. The characteristics are related to and emerge out of the matter and substance of poetry and the manner and style of poetry. Truth and seriousness must characterise the matter and substance of great poetry, while good diction and movement are essential characteristics of manner and style. These characteristics are interrelated and interdependent and together they form the best and highest quality of poetry. Arnold appeals to English readers/critics to look for these characteristics in poetry. He once more refers to French poetry both to distinguish it from English poetry and to show its great quality. He refers to the romance poetry of twelfth and thirteenth century France. During this period, French literature, especially poetry, dominated all of Europe. It provided role models in substance and style to all European poets. But by the fourteenth century this scene changed and gave way to poets in different parts of Europe. In England, Geoffrey Chaucer (1343–1400), who was influenced by French romance poetry, emerged on the poetic scene. The language he uses poses some difficulty, but his poetry is a source of joy and strength. His poetry is superior to French romance poetry in his subject matter and style, due to his clear-eyed yet sympathetic view of human life. Arnold refers to the views of Dryden and Johnson about Chaucer and calls Chaucer the 'the father of our splendid English poetry'. His diction and style have a lovely charm. Chaucer's legacy can be seen in later poets like Spenser, Shakespeare, Milton and Keats. In order to prove this claim about Chaucer's poetry having an impact on English poets who came after him, Arnold quotes some lines from Chaucer's *The Prioress's Tale* and from Wordsworth's poetry.

Arnold points out some of the qualities of Chaucer's poetry and yet he does not consider his poetry as one of the great classics. His poetry is superior to French romance poetry, to his contemporary English poetry and to poetry till the rise of Elizabethan poetry. But Arnold finds him lacking when compared to Dante. Chaucer's poetry possesses a large scope, freedom, shrewdness and benignity but lacks the high seriousness of the great classics. Arnold contends that Shakespeare and Milton are indisputably the greatest classics of English poetry.

Arnold then moves on to the Augustan poets John Dryden (1631–1700) and Alexander Pope (1688–1744). He points out that based on historical judgment English critics have long regarded Dryden and Pope the classics. But this is only historical judgment and not real criticism. He praises both poets for their poetic talent and mastery of words but argues that as inaugurators of prose and reason for a new age Dryden and Pope can be called the classics of English prose but certainly not the classics of poetry. Arnold calls a succeeding poet Thomas Gray (1716–71, famous for his *Elegy*, and was instrumental in changing the Neoclassical trend of lucid and clear writing towards obscure and sublime writing) as the poetical classic. He did not write prolifically and did not naturally possess the gifts of poetic genius and style. But he studied the Greek masters and acquired these qualities through hard work. Arnold gives him the double-edged compliment of being the 'scantiest and the frailest classic'.

Arnold then discusses Robert Burns (1759–96). He notes that this was the period when historical criticism gave way to personal criticism. Critics began to judge poetry based on personal, regional and national biases. Burns, according to Arnold, is more at ease and appealing in his Scotch poems than his English poems. But his Scotch poems create an exclusive world which cannot hold the interest of non-Scotch readers, and therefore can give them no enjoyment. Arnold says that Burns is a great poet when he writes about the independence, equality and the dignity of man. But he lacks sincerity and the high seriousness characteristic of the great classics.

Arnold ends his analysis by reasserting the importance of real criticism based on the touchstone method. He makes a passing reference to the Romantic poets—Byron, Shelley and Wordsworth, and argues that their poetry is also appreciated on a personal level and no real criticism has been attempted of their work.

Key Points

- Poetry plays a vital role in modern life as source of truth, knowledge and morality.
- Poetry will replace religion as the site of morality in the age of science and industrialisation.
- Examples of the best and highest poetry include the poetry of Homer, Dante, Shakespeare and Milton.
- Poetry has a bright future and will assume a supreme position in society because of its truthfulness and high cultural value.
- Arnold opposed historical and personal criticism.

- Historical criticism is based on high praise and historical details of the poets and can affect our understanding of ancient poets. Personal criticism is based on personal bias and can affect our understanding of modern poets. Arnold advocates the touchstone method, which is the comparison of poetry of the time, or of other ages, with the poetry of the great Classic poets.
- Qualities of the best poetry
  - truth and seriousness in poetic matter and substance
  - good diction and movement in poetic manner and style
- Chaucer's poetry is superior to French romance poetry and the English poetry of his time, but lacks in accent and high seriousness.
- Dryden and Pope's writing cannot be included among the classics of English poetry but they find a place among the classics of English prose.
- Thomas Gray's poetry can be regarded as a poetical classic.
- Robert Burns' poetry lacks sincerity and high seriousness.

Exercises

Answer the following questions in 100–150 words.

1) Why does Arnold think poetry can replace religion?
2) Who does Arnold identify as the classics of poetry?
3) Why does Arnold reject historical and personal criticism?
4) Briefly define the 'touchstone method'.
5) Why is Chaucer not a classic of English poetry?

Answer the following questions in 250–300 words.

1) Describe in detail the salient features of Victorian criticism.

2) Why, according to Arnold, are Homer, Dante, Shakespeare and Milton classics of poetry?

3) What are the qualities of the best poetry, according to Arnold?

4) Write in detail about Arnold's 'touchstone method'.

5) Why does Arnold reject historical and personal criticism?

MODERNISM

Historical Background

Broadly speaking, Modernism may be defined as a tendency to challenge tradition and to explore alternatives to conventional assumptions. It is a shift away from tradition and aims to create a new and contemporary world order. Modern artists, thinkers and critics found Victorian ethics and values increasingly illusory and irrelevant in the face of rapid social change and important developments in science. As a result they started questioning the existence of an omniscient Creator (God), the value systems of religions, and the prevalent aesthetic and philosophical ideas of the Enlightenment, a term generally used to describe an eighteenth-century intellectual movement in Europe. It was mainly based on the economic theory of the English thinker Adam Smith and the philosophical ideas of the German thinker Immanuel Kant. The major characteristics of the movement are: a) belief in the emancipatory power of reason, b) the precedence of science, c) freedom from superstition, d) scepticism, and e) empiricism. This movement prepared the high road for Modernism by supplying it with many anti-traditional ideas).

The Modernist movement drew on three epoch-making thinkers—**Friedrich Nietzsche** (1844–1900), **Karl Marx** (1818–83) and **Sigmund Freud** (1856–1939). Their ideas caused paradigm shifts in the thinking, methodology and objectives of all disciplines of knowledge in the modern and even postmodern period.

Nietzsche was perhaps the most assertive and vociferous among the three in his defiance of all kinds of traditions. He introduced nihilistic ideas in the fields of religion, philosophy, psychology and literary criticism. He announced the death of God and offered a sustained critique of Christianity. He criticised objective analysis and praised the self-assertive and rhetorical aspects of philosophy. He was also a trenchant critic of European modernity, declaring values like growth, progress, reason and maturation decadent. Nietzsche is regarded by some as the first postmodernist, who tried to reverse the entire Western system of thought.

Karl Marx's groundbreaking theory of economic relations and how they shape society gave a new direction to how economics, government and a society's sociocultural life were perceived. He rejected a utopian, idealistic and essentialist conception of history and society and instead attempted to construct a worldview from a materialist framework. He proposed that human beings are creatures of need and therefore the material side of human life is primary and basic. He argued that every society is composed of productive forces (tools, machinery and labour) and their association with particular social 'relations of production' (property, economic relations, division of labour). He encapsulated this statement in the metaphor of 'base' and 'superstructure'. His thought gave rise to a discipline called Marxism which has influenced every conception of modern intellectual life—culture, art, science, politics, economy and globalisation. Marx revolutionised the conception of society which enabled intellectuals across the globe to understand how material conditions affect the mode of thinking and existence.

Sigmund Freud was the founder of psychoanalysis whose work on the nature and working of human mind had far-reaching consequences on the perception of the mind and individual. He challenged the traditional assumption of the mind as an undivided, autonomous and abstract entity. He proposed that the mind works on unconscious drives and desires, thereby demolishing Cartesian notions of individual autonomy. While having a profound impact on medicine and pathology, psychoanalysis also influenced new movements in art and literature.

These thinkers, through their diverse theories and interpretations, brought to light several previously unconsidered aspects of thought and behaviour, creating what can be called a Modernist consciousness.

It would be incorrect to think of Modernism as a monolithic movement, however. Modernism in art and literature was so varied, differently conceived and practised that it would be sensible to think of 'Modernisms' (even a cursory look at the versions of Modernism like Symbolism, Expressionism, Dadaism, Imagism, Vorticism, Futurism and Surrealism will give us the idea of its immense range and complexity) instead of a singular nomenclature. Significantly, all these were chiefly literary movements (except Dadaism) and they contributed to various experiments in style, structure and themes in literary works produced during this period.

It is difficult to state an exact time period for when Modernism began and developed, owing to its multifariousness, but the two decades from 1910 to 1930 may be regarded as the prime period of literary Modernism. This was the period in which Ezra Pound's *Hugh Selwyn Mauberley* (1920), D. H. Lawrence's *Women in Love* (1920), T. S. Eliot's *The Waste Land* (1922), James Joyce's *Ulysses* (1922), Virginia Woolf's *To the Lighthouse* (1927) and W. B. Yeats' *The Tower* (1928) were published. (This is the list of the most prominent English writers. There were other great European/ American writers like Marcel Proust, Franz Kafka, Albert Camus, Bertolt Brecht, Joseph Conrad, Robert Musil, William Faulkner, Wallace Stevens and Rainer Rilke). These works set the tone, texture and perspectives of literary Modernism.

T. S. Eliot (1888–1965), an American emigrant to England, was probably the most influential figure of this period and his experiments both in poetry and in criticism continue to be widely read even today, as seminal works of literary Modernism. His poetry expressed anxiety, loss of faith and the disintegration of the self characteristic of modern life in a very ironic, allusive and obscure style. He wrote an impressive bulk of criticism on diverse topics from the early *The Sacred Wood: Essays on Poetry and Criticism* (1920) to later essays in which he critically examined the act of literary criticism itself, like *To Criticize the Critic* (1965). His criticism was more of an elaboration and justification for the fragmented content and experimental style of his poetry. He was a self-declared Classicist and this was most clearly evident in his criticism. He was against the Romantic conception of art in general, and poetry in particular. He prioritised art, skill and impersonality over the Romantic emphasis on imagination and the poet's personality asserting itself through his compositions. He also disapproved of focussing on the moral, religious or social background of a literary work and the biographical details of the writer. He redefined the concept of tradition, arguing that a literary canon ought to be a dynamic and comprehensive category that carries forward the ideas of the past and at the same time, has room to promote new experiments and individual talents. He coined new critical concepts, which are now widely used, like 'objective correlative' and 'dissociation of sensibility'. His criticism was a strong dismissal of Romantic and Victorian critical assumptions, and a reassertion of formalist principles.

F. R. Leavis (1895–1978), a critic and professor of English at Cambridge University, was culturally conscious and critically sophisticated in his practice of literary criticism. He was much like his predecessor, the Victorian critic Matthew Arnold. He insisted that literature had a key role to play in an age of crisis. His books *Revaluation* (1936) and *The Great Tradition* (1948) did much to establish the canon of English literature and to institutionalise literary criticism. In *Revaluation*, he attacked the Victorian and Georgian poets and praised the poetry of Eliot, Pound and Hopkins (Gerald Manley Hopkins [1844–89], the famous English poet known for his love of beauty in nature and man, his technical interest in prosody and his originality). In *The Great Tradition*, he turned the focus from poetry to prose and analysed the literary qualities of certain novelists, including Jane Austen, George Eliot, Joseph Conrad and Henry James. His selection of novelists and his judgments about authors were more informed by his personal bias than objective and substantial interpretation, and his criticism tended to be abstract and unspecific. Leavis was a strong advocate of elite culture and he thought that literature could play a vital and redeeming role in building a culture of responsive and sophisticated people.

I. A. Richards (1893–1979) was a critic, poet and professor who proposed practical criticism as an alternative to traditional abstract criticism. He was very rational and methodical in his theory and provided a quasi-scientific framework to literary criticism. He dismissed the Victorian obsession for 'beauty', the emphasis on rhythm, stress and character, and the random generalisations which characterised the criticism of F. R. Leavis and his followers. He championed the method of close analysis of the association between the reader and the text. His books *Principles of Literary Criticism* (1924) and *Practical Criticism: A Study of Literary Judgment* (1929) laid the foundations of practical criticism in England and provided the theoretical impetus to 'New Criticism' in America. An experiment he conducted with undergraduate students in Cambridge, in which he asked students to critically evaluate a set of poems, without knowing the names of the poets, resulted in the students rating poems by lesser known poets higher than poems by established poets. This objective method of analysis revolutionised the teaching and study of English literature. He criticised vagueness, sentimentality and laziness on the part of both writers and critics and advocated the evaluation of a literary work solely on its intrinsic merits, without taking into account biographical details, sociopolitical influences, and so on. His theory of practical criticism examined the effects of the text over the reader in psychological terms without losing sight of the form and the structure of the text. His approach is different from earlier critics in that he developed a scientific approach to mental events that regulate the process of reading.

William Empson (1906–84) was a student of I. A. Richards and a poet, critic and professor of English. His landmark book was *Seven Types of Ambiguity* (1930), in which he discussed at length the seven categories of ambiguity, and their differing complexity and depth. His method involved a close analysis of poetry. His criticism was largely responsible for the rise of New Criticism in America.

Salient Features of Modernism

1) Modernism as a movement in literature was experimental, formally complex and elliptical (characterised by extreme economy in the usage of words and difficult to understand, like Ezra Pound's Imagist poetry). There were experiments with styles, forms and themes and everything traditional was challenged, replaced or recreated. The First World War and the impending Second World War, scientific advancement and the impact of industrialisation shook the foundations of conventional morality, religion and the existing system of values. This disintegration, loss of faith and scepticism was reflected in literature and criticism as well.

2) Artists and writers of this period conceived freedom in separation from realism, materialism, traditional genres and forms. They were radical in their aesthetic views, language, technical innovations and expression.

3) There was a widespread disappointment with the traditional methods of literary analysis. Traditional methods were largely biographical, historical and social in approach and critics did not devote as much attention to individual literary works as they did to the collective work of a particular era. As a result criticism had become prescriptive, subjective, didactic and sentimental. Modern criticism went against the grain to make the objective study of literary texts the standard of critical judgment.

4) Critics and professors of English literature were anxious to discover new ways of critical analysis. Eliot and Richards, by introducing new critical frameworks and techniques, caused a shift from historical criticism to textual criticism.

5) The critics of this period vigorously asserted the autonomy and integrity of art. They conceived of art as a complete and unified whole in itself that did not need to conform to external standards of morality and ethics.

6) The important feature of Modern English criticism was its insistence on the redeeming role of literature. The critics thought that literature could work as a cultural purifier and create standards of excellence both in speech and action. This was more strikingly evident in Eliot and Leavis' criticism. They became increasingly culture-conscious and went beyond literary criticism to write cultural criticism.

Introduction to T. S. Eliot's 'Tradition and the Individual Talent'

This essay first appeared in *The Egoist* in 1919. It is divided into three parts: the first part explains Eliot's concept of tradition, the second part elaborates his theory of impersonality and the last part concludes the discussion on the note that the personality of the poet should be kept aside for a sound judgment of his poetry. The essay may be seen as an announcement of Eliot's critical stance and concerns, his rejection of the Romantic theory of poetry and a defence of his style of writing poetry. He opens the essay with a reference to the prevalent view about tradition. Tradition, as a term, has come to acquire negative connotations. He compares French people to the English, and states that the English deride tradition, preferring the original and individual aspects of poetry instead. Eliot believes that there is an unnecessary emphasis on individuality. Critics should not be prejudiced in their approach, and upon close scrutiny, will find that the poets of the past exert an influence on the best and the most individual parts of a poet's work. Eliot then redefines the term 'tradition'. It is a yardstick against which he judges the goodness and worth of poetry. Tradition for him does not mean blindly following conventional practices. He is against the mere imitation of the past and supports innovation. He thus frees the term from its narrow connotations and gives it a wider significance. He defines tradition not as something one can inherit from the past but something one should acquire through hard work. It is not a stasis carried forward from one generation to the other but an awareness of the continuity obtained through painstaking efforts. These efforts include possessing deep knowledge about the writers of the past and being able to discern what is worth carrying forward from the poetry of the past. Tradition involves the 'historical sense'. Eliot defines historical sense as the perception of the pastness of the past and of its presence; that is, the poet should be aware of the past and the present status of poetry and be able to trace a continuity. For Eliot, tradition is literary tradition, from the ancient Greek poet, Homer, down to the present time. It is the duty of a poet to be aware of this tradition. A poet who has the historical sense is aware of his contemporary literary world and aware of the past poets as well. Tradition thus means three things for Eliot: knowledge of the continuity of literature, critical ability to discover past writers who continue to be significant in the present, and devoted scholarship leading to a deep knowledge of past writers.

Eliot does not conceive of tradition as stationary, or a changeless state. It is a dynamic, ever-changing and multiplying process. It changes the understanding of the poets of the past and the present status of poetry, and is itself changed in the process. To explain this point, Eliot relates the individual writer to the literary tradition. The significance of a poet and appreciation of his poetry is possible only in relation to tradition and not in isolation. A poet can be properly evaluated only through comparison with the past poets. Only this method can satisfactorily explain the worth and significance of the poet and what he has added to the literary tradition. It can also suggest changes and modifications in the individual poet's work. Thus, tradition informs us what is new and original in the work of a poet and is itself transformed by fresh literary innovations. The great poets of the past form an ideal order among themselves and new poets modify this order. However, Eliot also warns us that a comparison between the works of past poets and present poets should not be made arbitrarily; neither should the work of a new poet be judged by the standards of the past.

Eliot wants poets to know of the literary tradition because it develops a sense of tradition in them. However they should not be indiscriminate in their understanding of past works, and should evaluate their significance and worth. They should also be careful not examine only a few poets or a particular literary period, but should know the whole range of poets. This is because it is not only great poets who constitute tradition, but also the minor poets. Eliot also addresses the objections that his propositions may raise. It could be said that Eliot demands too much scholarship, and that too much knowledge kills sensibility. It may also be argued that every great poet in the past was not a learned person. Eliot thus recommends that poets make judicious use of their critical judgment in acquiring knowledge of past poets. They should learn as much as their capacity allows and continue to learn more as their poetic career progresses.

In the second part of the essay Eliot elaborates on the theory of impersonality. He argues that poets must submit themselves to the literary tradition because that is more valuable and enduring than their individual status as artists. He illustrates his theory by drawing an analogy between the poet's mind and the catalyst (a chemical substance that causes a reaction to happen more quickly). Just like a catalyst causes a chemical reaction to take place, the poet's mind works as a catalytic agent and combines different emotions into a unified whole. Eliot describes the procedure of the chemical process to further explain the resemblance. In the chemical process there is a jar that contains oxygen and sulphur dioxide. When a fine filament of platinum is introduced in the jar the two gases combine to produce sulphurous acid. The gases come together only in the presence of the filament of platinum. The filament causes the reaction but is not affected by it. It remains neutral and unaffected. The poet's mind must be like this catalyst. It is necessary for the combination of emotions and experiences but must remain unaffected by the process of combination. The mature poet manages to withhold his personal emotions from his composition. The ideal poetic mind does not find expression in composition but only makes the composition possible. Eliot regards poetry not as an expression of personality but as an extinction of personality. Thus he makes impersonality a criterion for the evaluation of poetry.

Eliot regards poetry to be skilful organisation rather than inspiration. For this he compares the poet's mind to a jar or a receptacle that contains many feelings and emotions. These remain in the receptacle of the mind in disordered form until all the particles necessary for the unity of emotions and feelings enter the mind. The greatness of the poem does not, therefore, depend upon the intensity of emotions but upon the intensity of the process of poetic creation. The more intense the process of poetic creation, the better the poem. Eliot differentiates between artistic emotion (which is the emotion expressed in poetry) and personal emotion (which is the poet's emotion that does not find place in his poetry). He cites John Keats' 'Ode to Nightingale' as an illustration of this where there are many emotions which have nothing to do with the nightingale. He argues that the poet need not express new emotions or only refined and complex emotions. The poet may express ordinary emotions but he should do it after imbuing them with a new significance. Eliot applies this theory of impersonality to Romantic poetry. He dismisses Wordsworth's concept of poetry as merely sentimental and subjective. Poetry, as

Wordsworth states, is not the overflow of emotions but an escape from emotions. He calls Wordsworth's theory an inexact formula and rejects the view that the process of poetic creation concentrates on emotion recollected in tranquility.

In the last part Eliot sums up his views about poets, poetry and their relation to literary tradition. He reasserts the aim of literary criticism: to attend upon poetry and not the poet. It is not the poet's emotions but the emotions in poetry, or artistic emotions, that count the most. The critic should examine the poet's technical excellence in expressing significant emotions in poetry. Attention should also be paid to whether the poet surrenders himself completely to the work and thus becomes a part of the literary tradition.

Key Points

- The essay is divided into three parts: a) Eliot's concept of tradition, b) theory of impersonality and c) conclusion.
- Eliot redefines literary tradition as a dynamic, ever-growing process which determines truly great writing, and ranges from the ancient Greek poet Homer, to present-day writers.
- The tradition does not mean an unconditional acceptance of ancient writers. But Eliot deems a thorough knowledge of the literature of the past as very essential.
- Historical sense is essential for a literary critic, and Eliot defines this as the awareness of the 'the pastness of the past', as well as its enduring presence and influence in the present.
- Eliot's definition of tradition thus can be summed up as follows— a) knowledge of the continuity of literature,

b) critical ability to discover the past writers who continue to be significant in the present, and c) thorough knowledge of the significant writers in the past, leading up to the present.

- Eliot proposes his landmark theory of impersonality, in which he states that it is essential that a poet must have an impersonal attitude to his composition. He draws an analogy between the poet's mind and catalyst (a chemical agent that expedites the chemical process). Just as the catalyst in a chemistry experiment produces reactions, the poet's mind brings various emotions and images together and produces a unified literary work.
- The poet's mind does not participate in the process of poetic creation but only makes it happen. It does not become a part of the poem and remains unaffected. Great poets never express their individual personalities and personal emotions in their poetry.
- Eliot rejected the Romantic theory of poetry (as defined by Wordsworth) as an inexact formula. He argued that poetry was not an expression of the poet's emotions and personality but an escape from it.

Exercises

Answer the following questions in 100–150 words.

1) What is Eliot's essay about?
2) What, according to Eliot, is the problem with English critics?
3) How does Eliot define tradition?
4) Why does Eliot compare the poet's mind with a catalyst?
5) What is poetry, according to Eliot?

Answer the following questions in 250–300 words.

1) Explain the process of poetic creation, as described by Eliot.
2) What is Eliot's concept of tradition?
3) Explain Eliot's theory of impersonality.
4) What arguments does Eliot propose with regard to the Romantic theory of poetry?
5) Do you think Eliot's description of a literary tradition contributed to the formation of a English literary canon? How?

NEW CRITICISM

Historical Background

New Criticism, which emerged in the 1940s in the United States of America, advocated a method of based on close reading of the text alone, and ignored all extraneous factors dominated American literary criticism in the mid-twentieth century, and was responsible for the growth of literary criticism as a formal academic discipline. The publication of John Crowe Ransom's book, *The New Criticism*,in 1941 is considered to be the starting point of New Criticism as a critical approach in America. New Criticism was a culmination of a series of experiments in the interpretation of literary texts and traditional critical methods. It owes much to the following theorists and their theories—Aristotle's description of formal unity and his discussion of the various kinds of style and structure in literature, the critical ideas and practices of modern Anglo-American critics like T. S. Eliot, I. A. Richards, William Empson, F. R. Leavis and Yvor Winters, and the influence of Formalist Russian critics like Roman Jakobson, Boris Eichenbaum and Viktor Shklovsky. It sought to move away from traditional critical approaches based on biography, intentions of the author and social impact, and shifted the focus away from the author and contexts, to the formal aspects of the text alone.

John Crowe Ransom (1888–1974) is generally considered to be the founder of American New Criticism. He was instrumental in establishing New Criticism as a useful and effective method of literary interpretation. His editing of the literary journal *Kenyon Review* gave him the institutional visibility and support necessary to explicate his ideas, and thereby establish New Criticism as a valid critical method. As a critic, he was careful to distinguish between science and poetry. According to him, science only skims the surface with regard to the nature of things, whereas poetry probes deep into the inner essence of things. He criticised the Romantic and Victorian ideas about poetry and the traditional critics who insisted on studying literary history, without paying attention to the structural organisation and aesthetic effects of individual literary works. He urged critics to be more scientific, precise and systematic, and to examine the technique and form of poetry. He emphasised the structural properties of poetry—meter, inversion of syntax, tropes and figures of speech. He distinguished poetry from prose, and like Formalist critics, believed that poetry is different in its special use of language. He called this the 'texture'—the form that organises content into a unique structure. For him 'texture' was both the form and content of poetry and the critic's job would be to discover and interpret it accordingly.

Allen Tate (born John Orley Allen Tate, 1899–1979) was a famous American poet, essayist and critic. He was against the moral, historical and didactic criticism prevalent in his time. He wrote extensively about the nature and quality of poetry and strongly advocated the close reading method of literary analysis.In his influential essay, 'Tension in Poetry', Tate proposed his formula of poetry, which stated that poetry was the expression of tension. According to him, the job of the critic was to find out the tension in a poem, because that is its single most important quality. He supported his theory with an analysis of several poems. His theory is that poetry consists of *extension*, which is denotative, or literal meaning, and *intension*, which is connotative, or the meanings associated with an object. Great poetry achieves an equilibrium between these two parts. He proposed that 'tension' connects both extension and intension, making the poem a coherent whole that balances extremes and gives poetic pleasure to readers.

R. P. Blackmur (1904–1965) was a literary critic, poet and professor known for his insistence on close reading of the linguistic details of texts. Blackmur was alert to the linguistic nuances of literary work and stressed the significance of paying individual attention to words in the composition and criticism of literary work. In his famous works of criticism, *The Double Agent* (1935) and *Language as Gesture* (1952) he investigates how language shapes our understanding of the form and meaning of poetic text. He conceptualised 'technique' as the principal object of analysis and classified it into four categories: a) the first category of metre and plot, b) the second category of linguistic techniques, c) the third category of visual and dramatic techniques, and d) the fourth category of idiomatic language and symbolic imagination.

Cleanth Brooks (1906–1994) was an influential literary critic and professor. His most important contribution was that he revolutionised the teaching of poetry in American universities. His critical works *Modern Poetry and the Tradition* (1939) and *The Well Wrought Urn: Studies in the Structure of Poetry* (1947) elaborately explained his critical method of analysis. In collaboration with R. P. Warren he authored many bestselling course books which explained how poetry could be studied through close reading. Like all other New Critics, Brooks was also against moralistic and didactic criticism and condemned any attempt at reducing poetry to a single message. He was also against impressionistic criticism and cautioned critics not to be guided by their emotional responses to literary works and evaluate them on the basis of their effects on readers. He concentrated on the technical elements and patterns of poetic texts. His concern was to discover the unity in a text; how the parts related with each other and formed a unified autonomous whole. For him form and content were not separate. His formula of close reading was asearch for irony, ambiguity and paradox in poetic texts.

W. K. Wimsatt (a professor of English at Yale University) and **Monroe C. Beardsley** (a philosopher of aesthetics) are two other prominent New Critics. They co-authored the stimulating *The Verbal Icon: Studies in the Meaning of Poetry* (1954). They argued for an objective criticism which avoids both the intention of the author (they famously called it the *intentional fallacy*) and the individual impressions of readers (the *affective fallacy*) in the analysis of poetry.

Salient Features of New Criticism

1) New Criticism is an Anglo-American version of Formalism. Formalism originated in Russia and Formalist critics like Roman Jakobson, Boris Eichenbaum and Viktor Shklovsky emphasised the autonomy of the literary work and made the study of language central to the analysis of poetry. But this early Russian Formalism underwent several changes as various critics offered several different perspectives (for example Mikhail Bakhtin, who proposed materialist Formalism). The influence of Formalism spanned from the early decades of the twentieth century to the late 1960s. New Criticism therefore can be treated as a version of Formalism that derived certain basic ideas from it, like the emphasis on the language used in a text and the autonomy of art, but developed these ideas in unique directions.

2) New Criticism does not propose any coherent literary theory as such, but sought a change in critical methods. It changed the emphasis from the biographical or historical contexts to the formal features of the work. It is, therefore, pedagogical in its emphasis and practice and is not ambitiously theoretical like structuralism or Marxism.

3) It concentrated on the text alone as an autonomous, self-sustained whole. In this sense it was intrinsic and excluded extrinsic considerations like morality, religion, society, history, politics and culture. It focused on texts and dismissed contexts.

4) It prefers poetic texts over narrative or dialogic texts for interpretation because it mostly examines aspects like ambiguity, irony and paradox.

5) A text is an organic whole for New Critics. They study words, their arrangements, their symbolic significance and emotive association in texts. Famous New Critics often discovered one element among others of a text as the single most significant element that not only organises the structure of the text but gives meaning to it. This focal point varies with each critic's perspective. Ransom studied the poem as texture, R. P. Warren as symbol, Allen Tate as tension, Blackmur as gesture and Brooks as paradox.

6) Wimsatt and Beardsley made the following observation in their book *The Verbal Icon* (1954). It explains very clearly the assumptions and methods of New Criticism: 'A poem should not mean but be. A poem can only be through its meaning—since its medium is words—yet it is, simply is, in the sense that we have no excuse for inquiring what part is intended or meant. Poetry is a feat of style by which a complex of meaning is handled all at once'.

Introduction to John Crowe Ransom's 'Criticism Inc.'

This essay appeared as a part of the book, *The World's Body*, which Ransom wrote in 1938. In this polemical essay, Ransom describes the pros and cons of literary criticism with reference to his contemporary critical scenario.

Ransom opens the essay with a discussion of the business of criticism. He points out that there are no competent and qualified critics to speak about the role of criticism, even though there are many amateur critics with readymade commentaries about criticism. (Ransom disapproves of the amateur critics because they are unskilled.) According to him there are three types of individuals who are qualified to work as critics. These are: the artist himself, the philosopher and the university teacher of literature. Out of these Ransom's choice is obviously the university teacher of English literature. There are certain reasons for this choice. Ransom points out that professors of literature are learned but not critical (that is, they do not commit themselves entirely to literary judgment). The professor, thus, is professional in his critical activity.

He refers to the modes of criticism prevalent in his time, like New Humanism and Marxism, and says that these critical perspectives mislead readers into focusing on extra-textual perceptions and positions. Ransom then refers to the literary criticism practised in the universities. The university intellectuals pay attention to backgrounds, sources and intentions instead of the literary work on hand. This method of study prevents students from acquiring the skills necessary to understand the structural organisation and technical aspects of literary works. After pointing out the current problems in the interpretation of literary works, Ransom turns his attention to the role of the professors of English literature. He appeals to teachers and students to practise criticism rigorously, and apply themselves to finding out the special textual qualities that separate poetry from prose. He opines that stylistic devices like imagery, metaphor and metre can give precision and objectivity to the understanding of poetry. Ransom wants criticism to be scientific, precise and systematic and pleads for professionalism and students to be trained in criticism proper.

In the second part of his discussion Ransom refers to the views of the Chicago critic, R. S. Crane. Crane, in his paper titled, 'History Versus Criticism in the Study of Literature', argued against the historical study of literature and appealed for a shift towards a critical analysis of literature. Ransom credits Crane as the first great professor who advocated objective criticism. He appreciates Crane's perspective and turns towards the school of New Humanism in America (It was a critical movement in the USA between 1910 and 1930. It was based on the literary and social ideas of the Victorian critic Matthew Arnold. He appealed for recreating a civilisation based on the values of morality, ethics and reason, and was opposed to materialism and industrialisation. Irving Babbitt (1865–1933) and Paul Elmer More (1864–1937) were the prominent practitioners of this approach, and were against Romanticism, Naturalism and Realism. Their ideas were viewed by many as cultural elitism and the critics as supporters of social and literary orthodoxy.). Ransom argues that while New Humanism was a diversion from orthodox criticism, it is not the kind of criticism that he endorses. The New Humanist critics were moralists and did not study the aesthetic aspects of literature. They evaluated Romantic literature from an ethical point of view but not from an aesthetic perspective. Ransom offers a brief comparison between the views of Irving Babbitt and T. S. Eliot towards Romantic literature. Babbitt criticised Romantic literature on moral grounds (such as on the ground that it dealt with emotions rather than with principles). Eliot on the other hand judged Romantic literature on aesthetic grounds. Ransom also criticises Marxist critics as guilty of judging literature on ethical grounds. He scrupulously distinguishes between historical scholarship and criticism, saying that pestablishedlack the critical judgment necessary to evaluate He argues that criticism should be taken seriously by professors of English and should be painstakingly practised in their departments.

In the third section Ransom continues his attack on the historical method and urges professors of English to engage in serious criticism. He dismisses literary appreciation, prevalent in many American universities at the time as a valid method of criticism, as a faulty method of literary interpretation, because what is essentially a private act becomes public. The whims and personal biases of the professor teaching in the classroom tends to influence students; as a result they may unable to form objective judgements of literature. He does not deny the contribution historical scholarship has made to English literature and rule out its importance, but argues that an overemphasis on historical facts complicates a text's aesthetic interpretation, and prevents the critic from unraveling the structural design of the text.

In the fourth section Ransom discusses the nature of criticism. His definition of criticism is based on exclusion, that is, he states what it should not do or deal with. He borrows from Crane's exclusion of New Humanism and Marxist analysis based on historical scholarship, but also adds his own criteria to determine what truly objective and aesthetic criticism is. First, the critic should avoid bringing into play the impression the text creates on him as an individual reader. Second, the critic should avoid writing a mere synopsis or paraphrase of text, in place of an evaluation. The third criterion is that the critic should not refer to the general literary background, the author's biography, and other historical details. The fourth is that the critic should stay away from a linguistic study into the meaning of words. The fifth exclusionary criterion is that the critic should refrain from any kind of moral view. The last point of exclusion is any other special studies which may distract the critic's attention away from the text.

In the last section of the essay Ransom elucidates his idea of criticism. Criticism, for him, is an act dissociated from historical and other scholarly studies and devoted entirely to the interpretation of literary texts. He distinguishes criticism from the review of books and argues that the study of the techniques used in a text is real criticism. These techniques include the study of metre inversions, solecism (wrong use of words), tropes and figures of speech. Ransom argues that the critic should regard the poem as a desperate ontological or metaphysical exercise. The poet, through his composition, tries hard to save his order of existence, which is at risk of crumbling in real life. The poet wishes to defend the existence of his poem from enemies like practicality and utility, and the critic should know what and how the poet is implementing his defence. Thus Ransom brings the critic face to face with the text and wishes him to be serious and objective in his interpretation.

Key Points

- Ransom criticises New Humanism and Marxism as methods of literary criticism, arguing that they mislead readers/critics into focusing on extra-textual perspectives and positions at the risk of ignoring the text itself. He believes that New Humanism as a critical method is a diversion from objective criticism towards moral criticism, while Marxist criticism emphasises the ethical, rather than aesthetic aspects of a literary work.
- Ransom also decries historical criticism, saying that historical scholars lack critical judgment.
- For Ransom, criticism must be dissociated from contexts and devoted to interpretation of the text alone.
- Real criticism, according to Ransom, is objective criticism and it is in the discovery of special textual qualities that critics can separate poetry from prose. It involves examining the imagery, metaphors and metre in the text, and ignoring extraneous factors. This alone can bring precision and objectivity into literary critical interpretation.
- Ransom believed that the following elements should be avoided in the interpretation of a literary work—impressionism, synopsis and paraphrase, historical studies, linguistic studies, and moral studies.
- Ransom drew a distinction between literary appreciation and literary criticism, saying the former was an easy and private act and the latter, a public and specialised act.
- He appealed for criticism to be viewed as a profession and for critics to be trained as a specialist in any other field would be.

- Three kinds of individuals were qualified to be critics, according to Ransom—the artist himself, the philosopher and the professor of English literature.
- Ransom's first choice for his ideal literary critic is the professor of English literature.

Exercises

Answer the following questions in 100–150 words.

1) What are the two critical methods that Ransom rejects?
2) Why does Ransom appeal for professional criticism?
3) Who are the three kinds of individuals qualified to be critics, according to Ransom?
4) Why does Ransom refer to R. S. Crane's views?
5) What is the difference between appreciation and criticism?

Answer the following questions in 250–300 words.

1) What are the features which mark Ransom's views as belonging to New Criticism?
2) What must the critic avoid when evaluating a text, according to Ransom?
3) What are Ransom's expectations from the professor of English literature?
4) Why does Ransom reject New Humanism and Marxism as critical methods?
5) Explain Ransom's concept of literary criticism.

PART II

LITERARY THEORY: A SHORT INTRODUCTION

Literary theory, like literary criticism, evades definition. Some critics argue that since literary criticism emerged out of theory and is its application, they are not separate from each other. Other critics have emphasised the difference between them, arguing that they have independent pursuits and that theory is more general, abstract and overarching in nature whereas criticism is more particular, empirical and practically applicable. Both arguments are valid in their own way but for the sake of our understanding it is helpful to know the differences and similarities between them.

The relationship between literary theory and literary criticism is complementary and yet mutually exclusive. It is therefore tenable to some extent to regard that literary theory and literary criticism have formed and re-formed each other in different historical phases.

Literary criticism, especially in the first half of the twentieth century, has undergone a sea change in its nature, aims, objectives, methods, approaches and functions. It is no longer what it was before theory appeared on the scene. Literary criticism has undergone several renewals, revisions and recreations, with various sociological, psychological and biographical approaches being brought into critical discussions. As a general trend, American New Humanist critics like T. S. Eliot, I. A. Richards and Ezra Pound insisted on objective, practical criticism and British critics like C. S. Lewis and E. M. W. Tillyard devoted their energies to moral and historical criticism. With English practical criticism and American New Criticism, the pendulum of criticism was thrown back to the Classical principles of unity, coherence and objectivity. They narrowed the focus of critical analysis from plural contexts to a singular study of text as a complete unit with its own independent verbal system of organisation. This was a significant shift in the sense that the author, the world and the reader were entirely eliminated from the critical scene and the literary text was studied as a unique construction of language. It was influential for roughly fifty years. But its reductionist and monolithic practice was bound to be challenged. With the advent of literary theory both the traditional and modern methods of literary criticism were questioned and sidelined. Literary theory does not have an exact historical point of beginning. This is because while Anglo-American critics explored the change in focus and emphasis within the field of literary criticism itself, European critics were experimenting with the very nature and configurations of language and literature. F. R. Leavis and many other critics who believed in the humanist tradition complained that disciplines other than literature and language, like psychology, sociology, anthropology, philosophy, history and culture were encroaching upon the space reserved for literary criticism proper.

The new theories of language emerging from linguistics and philosophy radically altered linguistic assumptions and compelled scholars and critics across all disciplines to reconsider their disciplinary premises. They came to literature and language with their characteristic preoccupations and methods of analysis and displaced the analytical methods of literary criticism. Thus literary criticism as a discipline lost its previously specific, coherent and unique identity and gave way to several extra-disciplinary explorations into language and literature. These explorations came to be known as literary theory. For a precise understanding of the features and differences (there are striking differences and only occasional similarities) between criticism and theory let us attempt a comparison.

Literary Criticism	Literary Theory
It is interpretative in nature. Its basic search is for the meaning of the work that it deals with.	It is not interpretative in nature. It does not look for meaning but for textual aspects that make 'the' (definite) meaning impossible.
It is disciplinary and institutionalised. It has its stated aims and objectives (like enrichment of tastes and morality, delight and instruction), methodology and evaluative approaches.	It is anti- or interdisciplinary. It is against any institutionalisation (and yet some of its versions became established practices) so it does not have definite aims and objectives like the discovery of meaning.
It is not entirely linguistic in its orientation. This does not mean that it does not take into account the language aspect of literary work. It is historical in its approach to language and it seeks to discover how the specific and creative use of language makes literature different from other types of writing.	It is entirely linguistic in its orientation. It, however, does not continue the traditional study of language but reconsiders the nature and function of language in radical terms.
Traditional criticism is biographical, historical and psychological. Modern criticism broke away from these approaches and introduced textual and practical criticism.	Theory is not strictly limited to biographical, historical and psychological approaches. It cross-references many of these approaches and consists of many terms and methods they represent. But it radicalises or subverts them in an attempt to show their singularity of approach and inadequacy of methods.

Modern criticism is objective, rational, scientific, textual and pedagogical.	Theory does not follow the ideas of modern criticism because it rejects the very project of modernism as the extension of the essentialist worldview.
It does not intend to propose any comprehensive theory about the nature, elements, role and relevance of literature and language. It applies certain frames of analysis to literary texts. It is more concerned with individual texts than with analysing texts belonging to particular genres or forms collectively.	It raises basic questions about the nature, role and relevance of literature and language. It provides certain overarching theories, or broad frameworks and offers a set of principles that are or can be applicable to texts in general. Northrop Frye's theory of archetypal patterns and Gerard Genette's theory of narrative may be cited as examples of this kind.
Traditional criticism is author-centred, and modern criticism is text-centred. But in all, criticism has discovered certain central organising principles, source or foundation to base its practice upon. It believes and relies on some kind of universal or absolute.	Theory denies any kind of centre or source. It is decidedly anti-foundational so it dismisses all universals and absolutes. It does not believe in the authority of the author or accept the coherent and unified notion of text.
Traditional criticism does not bother about text; it pays more attention to biographical and historical contexts. Modern criticism fully concentrates on text as the unified whole.	Theory addresses certain social and cultural issues but it is not tied to a particular critical approach or context. It redefines text as 'a tissue of cultural quotations drawn from different sources' (This is Barthes's interpretation). Text is not seen as a unified whole based on coherence, unity and order but on discontinuities and breaks.

Traditional and modern criticism both disregard the role of the reader in the interpretative process.	Theory emphasises the role of the reader in the reading process. Of course, the reader is not an individual or a specified subject but a consciousness; a reservoir of several responses.
Modern criticism is practical and textual. It studies text to reveal the structural and verbal organisation and also to discover the inherent meaning.	Theory also advocates close reading of the text but not with the intention of revealing meaning. It discovers how a text subverts any attempt to understand it in a logical, uni-dimensional way.
Traditional criticism does not pay much attention to language aspects but modern criticism looks into the language aspects like of a text, metre, rhythm, tropes and stylistic variations. However literary criticism does not consider theoretical aspects of language and does not problematise it.	Theory brings radical issues to language like its relation to reality, its communicability, its ability to express truth, and so on. It changes the focus from communication to signification. It redefines language as a signifying practice that does not relate words directly to meaning but words to other words. Such relation complicates the meaning that we think words communicate.

It is interesting and insightful to know how any theory can be applied to a literary work. Such application not only demonstrates the utility of theory but also helps better understand its basics. Owing to such a need a modest attempt to examine John Keats' famous poem 'Ode on a Grecian Urn' from a deconstructive point of view is made below. It is not a definitive analysis so it is always incomplete and you can try your hand at your own reading of the text.

Ode on a Grecian Urn

John Keats

Thou still *unravish'd* bride of quietness,
Thou foster-child of *silence* and *slow time*,
Sylvan historian, who canst thus express
A flowery tale more sweetly than our rhyme:
What leaf-fring'd *legend* haunts about thy shape
Of deities or mortals, or of both,
In Tempe or the dales of Arcady?
What men or gods are these? What *maidens* loth?
What mad pursuit? What struggle to escape?
What pipes and timbrels? What *wild ecstasy*?

Heard melodies are sweet, but those unheard
Are sweeter; therefore, ye soft pipes, play on;
Not to the sensual ear, but, more endear'd,
Pipe *to the spirit ditties of no tone*:
Fair youth, beneath the trees, thou canst not leave
Thy song, nor ever can those trees be bare;
Bold Lover, never, never canst thou kiss,
Though *winning* near the goal yet, do not grieve;
She cannot fade, though thou hast not thy bliss,
For ever wilt thou love, and she be fair!

Ah, happy, happy boughs! that cannot shed
Your leaves, nor ever bid the Spring adieu;
And, happy melodist, unwearied,
For ever piping songs for ever new;
More happy love! more happy, happy love!
For ever warm and still to be enjoy'd,
For ever panting, and *for ever* young;
All *breathing* human passion far above,
That leaves a heart high-sorrowful and cloy'd,
A *burning* forehead, and a *parching* tongue.
Who are these coming to the sacrifice?

To what green altar, O mysterious priest,
Lead'st thou that heifer lowing at the skies,
And all her silken flanks with garlands drest?
What little town by river or sea shore,
Or mountain-built with peaceful citadel,
Is emptied of this folk, this pious morn?
And, little town, thy streets for evermore
Will silent be; and not a soul to tell
Why thou art desolate, can e'er return.

O Attic shape! Fair attitude! with brede
Of marble men and maidens overwrought,
With forest branches and the trodden weed;
Thou, silent form, dost tease us out of thought
As doth *eternity*: Cold Pastoral!
When old age shall this generation waste,
Thou shalt remain, in midst of other woe
Than ours, a friend to man, to whom thou say'st,
"*Beauty is truth, truth beauty*,—that is all
Ye know on earth, and all ye need to know."
(Italics ours)

A critical reading of this poem primarily involves a search for meaning. It may be interpretation, analysis or both but it amounts to meaning-making. The poem is a constellation of many sense units which frustrates all attempts to gather one single meaning.

On the surface, the speaker of the poem finds a Grecian urn with many scenes inscribed on it and narrates to us the beauty and elegance of the urn. But this is not the whole of it. The speaker speaks to the urn and describes it to readers. The speaker's address to the urn and his description to readers constitute two separate perspectives. His address to the urn celebrates the artistic beauty and eternity of the urn and the mood and tone are joyful and flamboyant. His description to readers, on the other hand, brings out the transience and misery of human life. It does not remain a mere description but an act of narration where the speaker has to assume a position either as an objective narrator or as a narrator irrecoverably overwhelmed by the beauty of art and intensely involved in its inner workings.

But this 'commonsense' interpretation of the speaker is ripped apart by the narration of the urn itself. The urn has continued to narrate its story to several generations and this act subverts the speaker's perception and expression about the urn. The narration of the urn is not verbal but visual. The visual narration of the urn subverts the speaker's verbal narration, thereby showcasing the limits of the verbal medium and by extension, of the speaker's understanding of art. These two narrations that simultaneously work in the poem to undermine each other undermine any stable view or understanding that an audience/reader can supposedly discern.

The title of the ode further disrupts the relation between the speaker and the urn. It is not an ode addressed to but *on* a Grecian urn. It is unlike 'Ode *to* a Nightingale' where the speaker uninhibitedly addresses the nightingale, establishes intimacy with the bird and desires to identify himself with it. Such intimacy is absent in the present ode and this is suggested by the shift from *to* to *on*. The use of *on* is therefore suggestive of the speaker's distancing from the urn. The perfection of the urn is set against his own imperfection and incompleteness. The speaker knows that the urn possesses the qualities of enduring beauty and perfection, and that he does not and can never attain such a state of thorough perfection. All this amounts to the contradiction between imperfect life and perfect art. However, despite this binary opposition of art and the human world, with art being seen as superior to the latter, the urn only proves the limitations of art, especially in relation to truth and beauty. The truth and beauty of the urn as an object of art are assumed and relative. They are not absolute—they require the contradistinctive human world which is full of falsehood and misery. The point here is that not only human world/life, but even art fails to achieve a state of absolute truth and beauty. The urn cannot represent pure and enduring art as it is a human construct. It is not free from its inevitable association with human world and it has its existence only because it represents fleeting and imperfect human life. It may represent the speaker's dream world of art that is perfect, beautiful, permanent and true but the reference to it as 'foster-child' reverses this privileged order as against mutable and temporary human life. Such reversal and destabilisation of the apparent order and stability is resurgent in the very text of the poem.

In the opening line the speaker calls the urn 'unravished bride of quietness'. This expression has sexual overtones and the unravished state of the bride may be taken as an appreciation and valorisation and also as a disparagement. The relational word *bride* evokes the whole range of assumptions associated with the institution of marriage. Physical possession is a mandatory ritual in the institution of marriage and it has many other contours. Patterson (1968:7) while dealing with this point argues 'It is natural for brides to be possessed physically...it is unnatural for them not to be' ('Passion and Permanence in Keats's *Ode on a Grecian Urn*' in *Twentieth Century Interpretations of Keats's Odes*. ed. Jack Stillinger). It is evident then that the speaker is effecting a contradiction to a culturally naturalised act either by valorising its state of being unravished or disparaging it for being unravished. But such valorisation gets suspended when we realise that it is not a bride wedded and still unravished but an urn that is thus addressed and perceived. The urn as an embodiment of art has remained unravished or unconsumed until the poet speaks about it. But with the speaker relishing its beauty, interiorising its scenes and addressing them, the urn gets ravished and consumed. The speaker not only speaks to the urn but also on behalf of the urn. He consumes the beauty of the urn and the pleasure it offers by entering into its inner artistic world. He thus ravishes the unravished urn and subverts the established meaning.

This element of consumption upsets the apparent hierarchical meaning of the opening lines of the second stanza. The lines imply that the music that we do not hear is sweeter than any music really heard because it is imaginative and ideal. An ideal song exists beyond all real songs because it does not actually exist and exists only as essence of the song and so it is eternally fresh. But this very ideal non-existent state of the song makes it the subject of real consumption and part of the material world. Heard melodies are real and material and yet they contain traces of the ideal and perfect. Unheard melodies are ideal and perfect and yet they contain traces of the real and material. The ideality of art cannot be conceived without considering its materiality. Something can appear as an art form only when it is structured into some kind of consumable object. Art is art not because it is ideal and non-existent but because it has all the possibilities of existing in a real and tangible form.

The remaining lines of the second stanza and the entire third stanza describe the scene of trees, lovers and musicians. The speaker points out that tune of musicians will not be heard and lovers will not be able to meet. But he confidently states that trees can never be bare, tunes can never be stale, the beloved can never lose her youth and the lover can never lose his love. This assurance is further positively reinforced by the repeated use of the word 'forever' in association with warmth and youth. This is possible because the urn is an art form and art is eternal and immortal. Adverbial expressions like 'never' and 'forever' emphasise the timelessness and immortality of art. But this leads to a new interpretation that the urn is static. The absence of life which can activate change and development has eternally perpetuated beauty, youth and pleasure in the art form of the urn. However this interpretation is undermined by the urn itself. In the first place the scenes wrought on the urn are not in stasis but in the state of motion. The use of present participles like *winning, piping, breathing* and *burning* suggest both time and action which inevitably associate the urn as an art form with mutable human life. Secondly the scenes of art forms on the urn spring to life in every onlooker's mind and he/she imparts eternity and immortality to them. The urn as an art form exhibits only a limited world and its maker must have had a feeling of incompleteness and imperfection, similar to the one that the speaker experiences when narrating/describing the beauty of the urn. This is supported by the description of another scene in the fourth stanza. This scene inscribed on the urn contains only a procession of individuals; the rest of the scene (the altar, the town) is imagined by the speaker. This extension signifies that art does not and cannot cover the entire and varied range of the human world and also cannot express a large part of eternity and perfection. The speaker supplements the details from the fleeting and mortal world to 'complete' the artistic appeal of the urn.

In the final stanza the speaker explicitly associates the urn with eternity and permanence and introduces a mutually inclusive equation of truth and beauty. The proposition is that permanence is achievable when an art form is both true and beautiful, and the urn as an art form has qualified this test. The proposed superiority of art is undermined by the art itself because it needs certification of its permanence from the human world. Art can claim to be eternally true and beautiful only when it is contrasted with mortal human life.

STRUCTURALISM

About *Structure* in Structuralism

Structuralism as a critical approach originated with the revolutionary ideas of the Swiss linguist **Ferdinand de Saussure** (1857–1913). Saussure used the word 'structure' in a very peculiar and innovative way. Structuralist critics do not use the word *structure* to mean a building or a construction. It refers to a set of interrelations between invisible principles and the visible form of those principles within a system. The invisible or underlying principles organise the structure into its concrete form and control its functioning. For example, consider a colony that contains buildings of the same size and design. An architect can study the structure of one of the buildings and can try to find out the underlying principles that made the structure of all buildings possible. *Structure* thus becomes a set of underlying principles that controls the organisation and working of any system. This awareness about the word *structure* takes us to the basic idea of Structuralism. Structuralism proposes that every system has two levels—surface structure and deep structure. Surface structure is physical and observable, and can be observed in a number of human activities, behaviours and objects. Deep structure is a set of principles that lies below the surface structure. It is abstract and invisible. To understand better, let us take the example of a computer. The surface structure of a computer is its monitor, keyboard and mouse. This is the structure that meets our eyes. We may come across many computers of different sizes and makes. But these various sets are based on some underlying principles and that is its deep structure. It is this structure (the underlying set of principles) that organises computers of all kinds into their physical forms.

Language is another example of a system where we can observe such levels of structural organisation. Language consists of millions of words and that is its surface structure. But the use of these words use by speakers in different situations and in specific patterns constitutes its deep structure. Sounds are uttered in many different ways when used by different speakers for different purposes. This creates a particular set of underlying principles for the sake of utterance and the study of such principles is called phonetics. Along with pronunciation, organisation of words (which we call grammar in more general terms) into patterns is also based on certain underlying principles. This underlying structure makes the exchange of words meaningful. For our convenience let us consider the following utterances. They show the working of surface and deep structure:

a) Raju plays tennis.

b) Surendra is clever.

These utterances are surface structures. They are based on the deep structure:

Subject + Predicate

We can form several hundreds of utterances by using this deep structure. The word *structure* thus refers to the conceptual frame that underlies any physical or visible structure.

Let us discuss another aspect of *structure*—its function. A structure works as a unit. Its parts are not independent. They are related with one another and with the structure as a whole. The interesting point here is that the whole of a structural system is independent of its parts even though it is made of those parts. Due to the interrelationship of the parts and the whole, the structure remains active and keeps on changing. It accepts changes, enters into new relations, organises and is organised. It produces new elements (in the case of a language, new utterances) in its process of change. These new elements are the part of that structural system and they follow the rules of that system.

Structuralism believes that structure (now we can call it deep structure) originates from the human mind. In other words, the human mind creates structures (conceptual frameworks) and according to these structures organises and classifies activities or objects in nature. Thus we know the world as our mind brings it to us, in its structural form. This basic understanding of the word *structure* helps us to know its elaborate application in the fields of linguistics, anthropology, psychology and literature.

Historical Background

Structuralism was an intellectual movement in Europe in the early half of the twentieth century. It originated from the revolutionary ideas of the Swiss linguist, Ferdinand de Saussure. Saussure studied *philology* (the traditional term for the study of language) at Leipzig and published his major work on the Proto-Indo European vowel system in 1879. He was a professor of Sanskrit and Comparative Grammar at the University of Geneva. He is known for his pioneering work *Course in General Linguistics* (1916, translated in English in 1959). This work was in fact a collection of his lecture notes and other materials taken down by his students. Saussure analysed language as a structural system. This analysis was against the traditional view of language. Before we turn to Saussure's analysis, let us think for a while about our view of language. We, as common users of language, consider language as a meaningful medium of communication. We believe that language can express our feelings, ideas, thoughts and opinions. We believe so because we are taught to think so by social conditioning. This means that our beliefs about language are shaped by society. Traditionally, language is supposed to have a definite origin at some point in the past. It evolved over several centuries and acquired the present form. It can be studied historically—how it developed through several phases and how individual words in it changed. Traditional scholars compare old and new forms of words in a language and try to discover rules that make such changes possible. Saussure called this traditional approach *diachronic* and dismissed it. Another idea he discussed was about language and its relation to reality. Traditional scholars believed that words directly refer to the objects they describe. For example, the word 'fan' refers directly to a thing that has three blades which move in a circle. The word in this case is assumed to contain the meaning it refers to. Saussure rejected this assumption as well. He adopted a very different approach. He considered the study of how language changes over a period of time less important than studying how language works. He called this approach *synchronic*. He followed an ahistorical (free from historical views) approach to language. He concentrated on language itself and proposed to study it as it is. Saussure's revolutionary ideas changed the traditional approach. These changes in approach may be outlined as below:

a) Language is separated from its history of development.

b) Language comes to be regarded as a structural system rather than a collection of words with individual histories.

c) Language does not remain an individual's possession but the possession of a society.

Saussure's *synchronic* approach paid more attention to discovering the deep structure (underlying principles) that makes a language work instead of the individual history of words. He coined two terms—*langue* and *parole*—to describe the deep and surface structure respectively. *Langue* is a set of underlying principles/rules that govern the working of language (or any system for that matter) and *parole* is specific use or utterances in language. He defined language as a system of signs. *Sign* is the key term Saussure used in his analysis. It is the basic linguistic unit. It consists of two aspects: *signifier* and *signified*. Saussure defined *signifier* as sound image and *signified* as concept. We may call signifier 'word' and signified 'meaning' for our convenience. Word (*signifier*) and meaning (*signified)* depend on each other and work in association. This association between them is called *signification*. Saussure says this association is purely psychological or conceptual. The same word (*signifier*) may stand for a different meaning (*signified*). Take the word, *play*. It is a sign consisting of:

→ *signifier* : the word *play*

→ *signified* : activity engaged in for recreation and enjoyment

a theatrical production

a sporting match

perform on a musical instrument

The signified meaning of the word *play* depends on the context in which it is used. The same signifier signifies different meanings, in different contexts.

Saussure here makes a very important point. It is that words *(signifiers)* do not get their meaning from the things they refer to; that is, there is no direct relation between words and their meaning. This point can be more logically understood in two ways. The first is that a particular object or thing does not give meaning to a word and the second, that word does not refer to any real thing in the world. Words only refer to images of things in our mind and not the things directly. Saussure gave the example of the word *tree* to explain this point. The word *tree* does not refer to any fixed single object but a class of many objects. This means that the word *tree* does not have a fixed meaning or object and that it is not by nature meaningful. We associate the word with the meaning in our mind and then the meaning becomes clear. Applied to language as a system, this point leads to a series of difficult questions. What is the relationship between language and reality? Does language exist before reality or vice versa? What gives meaning to words—the real things in the world or the place of words in a linguistic system? Does the fruit apple, for example, give meaning to the word *apple* or does the word *apple* help us to see the apple as a separate variety of fruit? Saussure's answer to all this is that language exists before reality and that it constructs reality for us.

Language as a sign system works as a mediator between us (users of language) and the world around us. It serves to signify, and our mind identifies the proper and necessary messages from it. Words as units of language are not meaningful by themselves and do not become meaningful simply because they refer to certain things. Words can have meaning only because they are part of a system called language. By this bold move, Saussure rejected the traditional referential view of language and proposed a relational view of language.

Here we come to two important principles of *signs* proposed by Saussure. These are **arbitrariness** and **difference**. He argued that *signs* are arbitrary. The relation between words and their meaning is arbitrary because one word may refer to many objects and an object may be referred to by many words. We shall take two examples of the *signifier* (word) and *signified* (meaning) separately to know Saussure's point. The first example is *board* as a word or *signifier*. Now think of the objects that this word may refer to. It is a piece of wood, a group of people, an organisation, meals at a rented place of accommodation, a kind of examination, etc. The word *board* is not fixed with any one of these objects and no object can make it meaningful unless it is placed in relation with other words (*signs*). The second example is *home* as an object or *signified.* Think of the synonyms that we can use to refer to this object: house, flat, apartment, etc. This linguistic relation of one word (*signifier)* with many objects and of one object (*signified)* with many words is purely arbitrary. What does all this mean? Does this mean that we can use any word to refer to any object? That will create confusion. Saussure was aware of all this and therefore he called language as 'a given, an inheritance of the past'. We as users of language do not create language for ourselves and cannot change any *sign.* When we use language for some purpose of communication, we use the reservoir of words already available to us. We follow the established conventions of language. Words are linked with particular objects/meanings because we have collectively agreed that words mean particular objects/meanings. Social convention gives words their meaning in a linguistic community. A sign is not meaningful in itself. It has to relate itself with other sign/s to become meaningful. This relation between signs is based on the idea of *difference*. The idea is that each sign in a linguistic system is meaningful because it is different from other signs. Saussure stressed on the negative difference of signs. Signs are meaningful not because they represent something but because they represent differently. Take the word *man*. *Man* does not have any meaning in itself as it is not informed by any 'man-ness'. But it has meaning because it is different from *can*, *van* or *fan*. It is this differential relation between signs that gives them meaning. Here Saussure introduces another term for meaning—*value*. A sign has no absolute value if it is not in its system. Its relation with other signs gives it its value. Saussure uses another term, *signification*, with *value*. *Signification* is the relation between the signifier and the signified. We can briefly put these technical terms as below:

Value: the relation between one sign and the other sign

Signification: the relation between two parts of a sign—the signifier and the signified

To explain the term *value* Saussure gives the example of the game of chess. Chess is a rule-bound game with its own system. There are pawns, bishops, knights and queens in the game. However they are not pawns, bishops, knights and queens on their own, independent of the game. They are made so by the rules of chess. The rules give them their respective value and so pawns become pawns, knights become knights and so on.

We have thus far to understand the basics of structuralism. It was originally a theory of language as a sign system proposed by Saussure. However it can be applied to literary texts. Critics like Jonathan Culler, Robert Scholes, Tzvetan Todorov and Gerard Genette have already applied structuralism to literary texts and have shown the usefulness of this approach. Literary structuralism adopts the structuralist method to study literature. This means that a structuralist critic tries to know the rules and conventions that underlie the practice of literature. A literary text may be understood as *parole* and the entire system of literature as *langue*. The critic places a particular text in the literary system where it actually belongs and where it can become meaningful. This kind of study involves both *abstraction* and *comparison*. Literature is considered to be an objective system and an individual literary text as the essential element of that system. *Abstraction* means studying a literary text without taking into account its external factors, its contexts. The critic draws comparisons between a literary text and other literary text/s in order to know their common elements. He tries to discover the rules/conventions underlying the system of literature. This kind of criticism was earlier practised by the **Russian Formalist critics**. As the word 'Formalist' suggests, the critics focused their attention on formal or structural aspects of literature. For them form was the most vital and organic part of every literary work. It organised a literary work into a coherent structure and gave meaning to it. They ignored the content (subject matter) of literary works as less important, as they believed that form dictated the content. However they could not explain the unity and oneness of content and form in literary texts and the relation between one literary text and the other. Structuralism came up as an advance over Formalism and convincingly answered both the questions. It studies a literary work as a whole, that is, the relation between the whole and its parts. Such study reveals the nature and working of the relations between parts and the whole and thus shows unity of the text. Secondly it examines a literary text as a structure and compares it with other structures. Thus it finds out the relation of the literary text with other texts. The Russian structural linguist **Roman Jakobson** (1896–1982) was instrumental in developing structuralist theory beyond Saussure's theory. He was influenced by Saussure's views but he did not approve of Saussure's division of the *synchronic* and *diachronic* study of language. He argued that language could be studied structurally across time. In his landmark study of poetry, Jakobson attempted to discover the grammar of poetry. He believed poetry to be a structured system and examined the linguistic structures that contribute to the overall effect of poetry. He influenced many contemporary theorists like Claude Levi-Strauss and Jacques Lacan.

Saussure's structuralism generated seminal studies across different disciplines like philosophy, anthropology, psychoanalysis, sociology and literary theory. His ideas were taken up by French structuralist critics and applied to different fields. These include **A. J. Greimas**' model of narrative analysis, **Claude Levi-Strauss**' anthropological structuralism, **Roland Barthes'** semiotic study of cultural institutions, **Tzvetan Todorov**'s project of grammar of narrative, **Jacques Lacan**'s search for the unconscious mind, **Michel Foucault**'s ideas about power and historiography, **Loius Althusser**'s redefining of Marxism and **Gerard Genette**'s application of structuralist ideas to narrative and discourse. However not all of these applications are directly related to literature and literary criticism. Those directly related to literature are A. J. Greimas' model of narrative analysis, Gerard Genette's model of narrative and discourse analysis and Tzvetan Todorov's project of grammar of narrative. (Roland Barthes' analysis is not limited to literary texts as he analysed non-literary cultural texts as well.) These models deal with literary texts and they form an independent kind of literary structuralism called *narratology*. It is useful for us to know these two important terms—*narrative* and *narratology*. A narrative is a story in prose or verse. It includes events, characters, action and dialogue. More technically speaking, a narrative is a form of communication which presents a sequence of events caused and experienced by characters. Novels, short stories, epics and romances are examples of narrative. Narratology adopts a very different approach to narratives. It rejects the traditional approach to narrative as a fictional representation of life. It deals with narrative as a systematic formal construction. It does not focus on the content of the narrative but on the structure of narration. The study of the content is the study of the subject matter and the study of the structure of narration is the study of the mode of narration. The difference is between what is told and how it is told. Narratology studies how a story is told. It tries to find out a comprehensive model of narration that can cover all the possible ways of story-telling. **A. J. Greimas**' (1917–1992) model of narrative analysis is a case in point. Greimas in his book, *Structural Semantics* (1966), proposed his model of *actants* to deal with narratives. With the help of this model, Greimas tried to describe all elements and their combinations in narrative. He presented two aspects of his model: *actants* and *actors.* Interestingly these two aspects are very much like Saussure's aspects of *langue parole.* Actants are like langue, the deep structure, and actors are like parole, the surface structure. Actants are formal elements in a narrative. They are abstract and they organise the narrative in its concrete form. Actors on the other hand are visible and concrete elements of a narrative. Greimas conceives of six basic elements of actants in three pairs: subject-object, sender- receiver and helper-opposer.

1) In the first pair of subject-object, subject is the central element in the action of a story and object is the objective/end that the subject hopes to achieve. The subject tries to achieve his/her objective through his/her actions and the subject's action takes the story ahead. The relation between this pair (subject-object) is based on desire or quest.

2) In the second pair of sender-receiver, a person, god or an institution appears as the sender. The sender sends the subject in search of the object which the receiver finds. The relation between this pair (sender-receiver) is based on communication.

3) In the third pair of helper-opposer, the helper helps the subject achieve his/her goal and the opposer opposes the subject by creating obstacles in his way. This pair often forms sub-plots of narratives.

We may take these three pairs as the three patterns of plot. These pairs make different combinations with one another. They act in opposition or in support with one another as per the nature of narrative. As far as the aspect of *actors* is concerned, subjects and objects bear names and possess physical appearances. In other words, actors are the visible forms of actants. Actants and actors are interrelated. But an actant and an actor do not always share a one-to-one relation. One actantial role may be played by many actors and one actorial role may be played by many actants. Greimas' model can be explained with the help of the Mahabharat (the great Sanskrit epic). In Sanskrit, it means 'the big story'. Indeed it is a mega narrative that contains many episodes. We may consider Lord Krishna as the sender, Arjuna as the subject, the kingdom of Hastinapur as the object and the entire Pandav family and their followers as the receivers. Duryodhan works as the opposer and Vidura as the helper to the Pandav family. We can read the pairs in many different ways and we find the actants and actors changing their roles. In the narrative of the Mahabharat, we find actors playing different actants when the subplot changes. For example, in the episode of Draupadi's *vastraharana* (a scene in which Duryodhana attempted to forcibly take away Draupadi's clothes in the presence of her husbands, the king and other distinguished courtiers), the king of Hastinapur becomes the sender, Duryodhana the subject, Draupadi the object, Arjuna the opposer and Lord Krishna, the helper.

Gerard Genette's (b. 1930) model offers a typology of narrative discourse. Genette identified different levels of narrative discourse: the story (*histoire*) that is told, the account itself (*récit*), and the way the account is narrated (*narration*). These levels interact with one another for the development of the narrative. Their interaction is based on three categories: *tense, mood* and *voice*. The first category of tense is the arrangement of events in the narrative in relation to time. It consists of the frameworks of order, duration and time.

Order involves the relationship between the chronological order of events (the order in which the events happened) and the narrative order of events (the order in which they are narrated). We may better understand this relationship in the following way:

a) The narration may temporarily lag behind the chronological order of events as we may find in a flashback.

b) The narration may go with the chronological order of events.

c) The narration may go ahead of the chronological order of events as the narrator thinks about the future.

Duration is the relationship between the time an event has taken up in reality and the time it takes to narrate that event. To maintain an equal duration of time for both events, the narrator needs to compress time. For example, a character studying a degree course will take three years to complete it but the narrator may describe it in just three lines. The narrator may also choose to increase the duration of an incident; for example, a visit to a friend's house, though lasting for only an hour, may be described with great detail in many pages.

Frequency/time involves the relationship between the recurrence of an event in a story and its recurrence when it is narrated. Usually an event that occurs many times is described only once, to avoid unnecessary repetition. The opposite kind of narration is also possible. An event that occurs only once may be repeatedly described, by different characters with different viewpoints.

The category of *mood* helps to create the atmosphere of the narrative. It is created by *distance* and *perspective*. *Distance* is created when the narrator is one of the characters in the narrative. The notion of distance depends on two factors: the nature of the narrator and the proportion of the descriptive detail. The more involved the narrator in the narrative, the greater the distance between narration and story. It means that minimum presence of the narrator and maximum description of details reduces the distance between narration and story.

Perspective is concerned with point of view. (Gennete used the word *focalisation* for perspective). Perspective differs with the role of narrator. For example, if the narrator in a novel speaks, we need not consider that it is his point of view. It may be the point of view of other characters in the narrative.

The category of *voice* refers to the voice of the narrator. It helps the reader to decide the narrator's attitude towards the story. The narrator's voice may be different from the point of view in the narrative. *Voice* helps to understand the narrator's relationship to the story being told and the way it is being told. Gennete's model thus shows that free combinations of levels and categories reveal the underlying principles on which a narrative works.

Tzvetan Todorov (b. 1939) is a Bulgarian critic who lives in France. He has sought to develop *poetics* as the framework which can work as the 'science of literature'. This involves a broad framework of analysis based on sets of principles that govern the nature and function of literature as a structured system. In pursuit of this project Todorov has attempted to find out stable underlying principles that can explain the phenomena behind a literary text. In his early works like *Introduction to Poetics* (1968), *The Poetics of Prose* (1971) and *Genres in Discourse* (1978) he tried to study literature in two broad categories—poetics and interpretation. In the category of poetics he worked to find out abstract structures that control and regulate literary genres. The category of interpretation was more concerned more with the meaning of individual texts where no abstract structures could regulate the meaning of texts. In his *Genres in Discourse* Todorov identified three aspects of literary texts—semantic, syntactic and verbal. With the help of these aspects he tried to work out a structural frame of literature. He did not approve of the traditional concept of seeing the literary text as composed of several semantic units; instead seeing the text as a dialogic and intertextual work drawing from both literary and non-literary matters. For him the 'syntactic' structure (the organisation of words in a certain order) of a literary text is not grammatical but narrative. This implies that he did not consider the syntactic organisation as based on the rules of grammar but on the structure of narrative. The verbal aspect of a literary text works on the categories of time, voice and perspective and helps the reader build a fictional world. Todorov found that these aspects are present not just in literary texts but in all types of writing. Throughout his work Todorov is aware that poetics as a science of literature cannot define the aspects specifically meant for literature and so the need to explore other aspects. His study revealed that structuralist analysis can identify the characteristic features of an individual text and cannot develop a broad frame applicable to a whole range of texts.

Among other applications of structuralism **Roland Barthes'** study is highly insightful and significant even though it is not limited to literature. He was perhaps the most innovative critic of the twentieth century in the sense that he developed ingenious models of literary and cultural analysis. He never stuck to a particular position or critical approach but constantly tried new approaches and methodologies. In his early period his ideas about language were strongly influenced by Marxism and existentialism. But then he moved towards semiology and structural linguistics which is evident in his work *Writing Degree Zero* (1953). In this work he introduced his theory of writing called 'ecriture'. This was a double-edged theory. He insisted that the writer should free himself from the conventional ahistorical notion of writing and should understand that some kind of ideology works in every piece of writing. At the same time he argued that the writer cannot influence society and cannot bring any social change. He argued that writing is neither entirely historical nor entirely personal. It emerges out of the writer's encounter with society. In a later stage of his career as a critic, he wrote *Elements of Semiology* (1964) and *S/Z* (1970) and produced a structuralist analysis of various literary texts. Barthes' method of analysis became increasingly complex and comprehensive as his critical career progressed. For example, in *Mythologies* (1958), he adopted Saussure's notion of signs and applied it not only to literary but to non-literary cultural texts like food, clothing, toys, film, fashion and advertising.

We briefly discuss below his semiological and structuralist analysis of two very ordinary and simple things, in order to reveal Barthes' innovative application of semiology and structuralism. The first instance is his semiological analysis of French toys. He showed how toys in the hands of children present the world of adults to them and prepare them to accept their roles in the future. Toys are based on imitation and they make children owners and users but never creators. They deprive them of creativity and pleasure and mould them into readymade roles. Thus toys represent bourgeois ideology on the level of form and on the level of substance as well. An example Barthes gives to illustrate this is plastic toys, which, according to him, are the products of chemistry and are cold and inhuman. They have replaced wooden toys, which are products of nature, and thereby capable of a firmness, softness and natural warmth of touch which plastic can never provide. The second example is his analysis of a photograph. He showed how a simple thing like a photograph of a black soldier saluting the French flag on the cover of a magazine called *Paris-March* can suggest bourgeois ideology. It signifies that since the colonised subject demonstrates his respect and allegiance towards the French nation, everything is all right with the imperial rule of the French bourgeoisie. In his seminal essay, 'Introduction to the Structural Analysis of Narrative', he made use of a sophisticated structuralist methodology to analyse the working of narrative texts. Even in his structuralist analysis, Barthes often crossed the limits of structuralism and semiology. His breakaway from structuralism was evident in his celebrated essay, 'The Death of the Author' (1968). The essay made the powerful argument that the reader, the 'modern scriptor', had turned down the conventional supremacy of the author. The same poststructural mode of analysis is carried forward in his next work *S/Z* (1970). In this work Barthes analysed Balzac's story of *Sarrasine* with the help of codes. He divided the text of *Sarrasine* into 'units of reading', that is, into units of a few lines each and classified these units into codes. The relationship between 'units of reading' and codes is not one to one. This is because one unit may refer to many codes. Barthes showed that a text believed to be unified and having a fixed meaning is in fact full of cross references and different meanings. His *The Pleasure of the Text* (1975) offered a typically poststructuralist analysis both in its style and method. He adopted the framework of psychoanalysis and analysed reading as a form of pleasure (*jouissance*) that a reader derives through a free play of meaning with the text. Reading thus became a sexual act with erotic body of language which is neither fixed nor permanent.

Salient Features of Structuralism

1) Ferdinand de Saussure, a Swiss linguist, laid the foundation for Structuralism, a theory of language which rose to prominence in the early half of the twentieth century. His *Course in General Linguistics* revolutionised the study of language.

2) Saussure invested the word 'structure' with a different meaning from its former conception as a building. He spoke of all language being one structure, and functioning as a unit, with each of its parts related to the whole.

3) Language, essentially, is a system of signs that are interrelated on the basis of difference. This system is in possession of a society and not of any single individual.

4) A sign is split into two—the signifier and the signified. The relation between these two parts of a sign is called signification.

5) Signs also function as signifiers and signified to one another, in a system. The relation between one sign and the other is known as its value.

6) Saussure said every language system had two components—a surface structure, which is physical and observable, and a deep structure, which is abstract and invisible. The two terms he used to describe these components are langue and parole. Langue is a set of underlying principles/rules

that govern the working of language, while parole is the specific use of a signifier in language.

7) Saussure rejected the diachronic model (origin, historical development and varieties of language) of language study. He instead supported the synchronic model (the present status and working of language) of language study.

8) There have been several applications of structuralism in literary criticism. Some notable examples include A. J. Greimas' model of narrative analysis, Gerard Genette's model of narrative and discourse analysis and Tzvetan Todorov's project of grammar of narrative.

Introduction to Tzvetan Todorov's 'Structural Analysis of Narrative'

Todorov explains the basic assumptions of the structuralist approach in this essay and demonstrates its application to literary works. He regards the structuralist approach to be objective and general in its application, like science, and therefore he discards the individual specificity and meaning of literary works. He clears up the difference between structuralist approach and other prevalent critical approaches like New Criticism, Marxism and psychoanalytic criticism. The New Critical approach is internal in its focus because it concentrates on the literary work itself and ignores external aspects/contexts. It examines the internal organisation of the work and concludes with paraphrase in its attempt to search for the meaning of the text. Marxist or psychoanalytic criticism are both external in their focus because they do not concentrate on the literary work itself but attempt to explain the abstract social or psychic structure that the work expresses. The structuralist approach differs from both these approaches. It neither attempts to understand the work and its meaning nor does it relate to any external context. It tries to discover the abstract structure (literary properties) that informs and organises literary works. It is a search for the common properties that literary works share with one another. It does not explain the characteristic commonalities of individual works. Todorov proceeds to reveal the scientific inclination of the structuralist approach. He says it is a preliminary step to creating a future science of literature.

In order to substantiate his claim of the structuralist approach being a scientific study of literature, Todorov refers to the objections raised by writers and critics. One such reference is to Henry James' objection to using scientific terminology and methods of analysis to describe concepts in literature. James contends that unlike science, which studies physical objects, a 'pure dialogue' or a 'pure description' will never be found in a real text and that breaking apart a text to study individual components is unnecessary and harmful because 'the novel is a living thing all one and continuous' (from Henry James' *The Art of Fiction*).

Todorov's answer is that in a structuralist analysis there is no need to find any concept in its pure state. The pure state of any abstract concept cannot be observed at a physical level. In physics, for example, temperature is a property which we cannot observe by itself. It is observable only in a particular body that possesses other properties like resistance and volume. Thus, it is studied only as a theoretical concept and not in its pure state. The concept of description is also theoretical and does not exist in a pure state. As for James' second objection Todorov replies by saying that studying individual components of a literary text is like studying any part of the body. The fact that we find them together does not mean that we cannot distinguish them from each other. Thus the oneness that James talks about can, in fact, be understood separately and it does not affect the oneness of the novel. Todorov then refers to another important objection to the introduction of scientific method and principles into literary analysis. The objection is that science is objective whereas the interpretation of literature is subjective. Todorov argues that the critic's choice of perspective decides the degree of subjectivity in his interpretation. If he chooses to examine the properties of the literary work instead of its historical significance there will be a minimum degree of subjectivity. Todorov points out that no social science (like economics or anthropology) or even natural science is completely free from subjectivity. The only difference is that the economist or the linguist is aware of such subjectivity and he tries to minimise it in his work. This can be made possible in the interpretation of literature as well. In order to explain how the interpretation of literature can take place with scientific principles, Todorov takes the plot to be the principal abstract structure. He analyses the narrative organisation of four different stories from the famous Italian writer, Giovanni Boccaccio's *Decameron*, on the basis of the commonality of plot as the abstract literary structure. In these stories he finds the common elements that organise them. He uses a schematic formulation to express the common elements of the four plots. These elements are in fact categories that he discovers in his analysis of the narrative structure of *Decameron* and they are based on the model of the sentence as consisting of subject, predicate and adjective. As per Todorov's formulation X and Y in the stories are proper nouns that serve as the subject or object of the clause. Verbs like 'violate', 'punish' and 'avoid' work as predicates. They denote an action that modifies an earlier situation. The analysis of other stories would show the third part of the narrative speech—adjective. It corresponds to a quality, which does not change a situation. Todorov refers to other categories of the abstract structure of the stories like modality (how the action would take place), point of view (how an action is perceived), causal relation between clauses and sequence (it is the impression that the story is complete and it is caused by repetition of the initial clause—punishment). He points to three other categories that can help reveal the commonalities of the selected narrative. These are the a) study of narrative syntax, b) study of theme and c) the study of rhetoric. Todorov dismisses the question of the purpose of this kind of structuralist analysis of a literary work. This is because structuralist analysis does not aim to understand the work or its meaning but only its abstract structure.

By the end of his essay Todorov presents the result of his analysis. It is that the plot of the stories moves from an equilibrium (a term that Todorov derives from genetic psychology, which means the equal balance of mind between two conflicting motives. Here, it means a balanced, calm and stable situation) to disequilibrium and concludes with a new equilibrium. The story begins with a state of equilibrium which is broken by a violation of the established law. The disturbed equilibrium can be restored by punishment but it is avoided. This avoidance creates a new equilibrium in the story. Todorov ends his analysis with the reassertion that an abstract literary structure can help us better understand the universe that literary works create.

Key Points

- Todorov says that the structuralist approach is objective and scientific in its approach and method. It is different from other prevalent critical approaches like New Criticism, Marxism and psychoanalytic criticism.
- Structuralist criticism is the search for an abstract structure that can explain the structural design of literary works.
- Todorov believes that structural analysis is the first step to a future science of literature. He defends it from allegations which questioned the degree of objectivity this method allowed for, saying the critic's choice of perspective decides the nature of criticism and the degree of subjectivity.
- Todorov says that the plot is the principal abstract structure for literary analysis. The abstract structure of a

plot moves from an equilibrium to a dis-equilibrium and again to a new equilibrium.

- He analysed four stories from Boccaccio's *Decameron* using the model of the sentence as comprising a subject, predicate and an adjective.

Exercises

Answer the following questions in 100–150 words.

1) Define structuralist criticism.
2) How is structuralist criticism different from New Criticism?
3) What is the principal abstract structure according to Todorov?
4) What is the common structure among the four selected stories?
5) What is Todorov's conclusion of the structural analysis of stories from Boccaccio's *Decameron*?

Answer the following questions in 250–300 words.

1) Describe the salient features of structuralism.
2) Explain how structuralist criticism is different from other critical approaches.
3) How does Todorov respond to Henry James' criticism of the structuralist approach?
4) How does Todorov prove that structuralist criticism is a scientific method?
5) Elucidate upon Todorov's structural analysis of stories from Boccaccio's *Decameron.*

MARXIST LITERARY CRITICISM

Historical Background

Marxist literary criticism draws on Marxism, a theoretical system that emerged from the political and economic ideas of Karl Heinrich Marx (1818–1883). His was the most influential critique of capitalism and its institutions. His important ideas may be briefly stated as below:

1) *Marxism is a critique of capitalism* – Capitalism stands for a mode of production in which capital in its different forms becomes the principal means of production. Capital can take the form of money or credit for purchase of labour power or stocks of goods. In all its forms it is privately owned by one class. Marx criticised the wealthy class that owned the means of production and caused the ownership of property to be concentrated in a few hands, while excluding the bulk of the population. He termed this class the bourgeoisie and held it responsible for the exclusion and exploitation of the working class—the proletariat.

2) *Marx redefined Hegel's social theory* – G. W. F. Hegel (1770–1831) was a German philosopher associated with the movement of German idealism. He argued that different systems of philosophy undergo cyclic formations in different historical phases. Therefore his proposition was that we can better understand philosophical systems if we examine them in certain historical contexts. All systems work through history and move towards freedom. However Hegel's thought was not completely free from idealistic notions. He formulated his philosophical views by considering the divine spirit as the base and source of all entities. Marx adopted Hegel's dialectical method of history. However he differed from Hegel in that he believed the dialectic of history is motivated not

by any divine spirit but by material forces. He also insisted that the dialectic in history should excite people to revolutionary action.

3) *Marx's model of base and superstructure* – This is the most important metaphor used by Marx to explain the relation between means of production and different forms of social consciousness. The economic structure of a society is its base and social and cultural institutions like political system, morality, art, culture, etc. form its superstructure. Base is the cause of superstructure in the sense the economic structure produces all other forms of social consciousness.

4) *Ideology* – This is the most commonly used term in Marxist analysis. It has come to be differently interpreted and so has as many meanings and contexts. But for Marx it means: the ruling class projects its own interests as the interests of people by employing social institutions like religion, school, media, etc. to indoctrinate the masses into believing that the exploitative structure of society is correct, and even beneficial to them.

Marxism as an economic and socio-political theory developed over a long period in two phases across Russia and Europe. The first phase is called **Soviet** or **Russian Marxism**. It came up immediately after Marx and co-theorist **Friedrich Engel**'s (1820–1895) death and continued to develop through Lenin to Stalin. It consisted of theorists like Georgii Plekhonov and Karl Kautsky. **Georgii Plekhonov** (1856–1918) was the father of Russian Marxism because he developed Marx and Engel's thought into a theory called Marxism. He strongly believed that Marx's idea of economic determinism (that is economic structure shapes all human practices like politics, morality, art and culture) was a coherent and comprehensive world view and there was no need to improve upon Marxism. Like Plekhonov, the German theorist, **Karl Kautsky** (1854–1938) was against any improvement or revision of Marxism. Together they formulated an orthodox version of Marxism. Lenin broadened the base of Marxism and used it as the guiding principle for the 1917 Bolshevik revolution in Russia. Marxism became the official state and party doctrine (a set of guiding principles) during Stalin's (1879–1953) rule. Soviet Marxism gave more importance to material analysis of human history and claimed Marxism as a universal science. As a result Marxism in this phase became rigid and dogmatic.

The second phase is called **Western Marxism**. It started in Europe around the 1920s. It consisted of theorists like **Georg Lukacs** (1885–1971), **Antonio Gramsci** (1891–1937) and **Karl Korsch** (1886–1961). These theorists changed the focus of Soviet Marxism from political economy and state to philosophy, culture and art. They broke away from orthodox Marxism (the rigid Marxism restricted to the consideration of political economy and the role of state) and brought in different issues of culture, class consciousness, subjectivity and aesthetics. This radically different application of Marxism to different fields of knowledge was carried forward by a critical movement called the **Frankfurt School** in Germany during 1930s. It included theorists like Theodore Adorno, Walter Benjamin, Herbert Marcuse, Lucian Goldmann and Jean-Paul Sartre. These theorists criticised both capitalism and Soviet Marxism for their repressive ideologies. They found the ideas of Soviet Marxism narrow and incomplete to deal with the diverse facets of human life. So they tried to improve upon Marxism by referring to other non-Marxist systems of thought. In their attempt at relating Marxism to other disciplines, Western Marxist theorists examined the relationship of Marxism to culture, art and literature. Thus these theorists provided important ideas and frames of analysis to literary studies and helped build the critical approach called Marxist criticism.

Marxist criticism is not a single unified critical approach. It is a collection of various methods of literary/artistic analysis. Marxist critics have taken different positions in their analysis of literature but the central idea that runs through their analyses is that literature is the product of historical, social and economic structures. There are three main versions of Marxist criticism. These are—1) the Hegelian, 2) Structuralist and 3) Gramscian versions.

The **Hegelian version** of Marxist criticism is based on Hegel's idea that a work of art is the expression of a structure that precedes it. This means that a complex social and economic structure produces a work of art. A work of art is not autonomous and free from the dialectic but a part of a historical process. As a result it becomes a secondary activity derived from the reality it reflects. Theorists like Georg Lukacs practised this version of Marxist criticism. Other theorists like Theodore Adorno and Walter Benjamin strongly opposed Lukacs' ideas and enlarged the scope of Hegelian Marxist criticism in their own specific ways. Their main concern was the tension between reality and its representation in art/literature.

The **Structuralist version** of Marxist criticism moves away from the Hegelian notion of reality and its representation through literature. It believes that there can never be an absolute division between reality and its representation because reality is always present in the structure that produces a work of art. However the main focus of the Structuralist version is on the process behind the production of a work of art. It tries to understand the institutional structure that produces a literary work. It treats literary production (text) as a part of general system of social production and at the same time grants a degree of autonomy to it. It treats a literary production as a reality in itself and argues that it cannot be the copy of any external reality. Louis Althusser (1918–90), a French structuralist theorist, was the pioneer of this version of Marxist criticism and it was further developed by Pierre Macherey (b. 1938), a former student of Louis Althusser and an influential contemporary French Marxist critic who redefined Marxist ideas in the light of poststructural notions about language, text and author.

The **Gramscian version** of Marxist criticism, as the name suggests, is based on the ideas proposed by Antonio Gramsci. Gramsci's concept of hegemony became the guiding principle of this version of Marxist criticism. Hegemony is the process by which a dominant class maintains its supremacy by controlling the ideological, moral, and intellectual fields of society. Gramsci, in his analysis of culture, considered literature and other arts as a historical institution. He insisted on the importance of the class function of intellectuals in literary productions. Raymond Williams and Terry Eagleton have interpreted literature differently in the light of Gramsci's views. They have shown the contradictory interrelationships between canonical and non-canonical literary works as they are used in the formation of national popular culture.

It is worth adding a brief note about the important Marxist literary critics. The first and most significant Marxist critic was the Hungarian **Georg Lukacs.** He wanted to build Marxist aesthetic theory and took critical realism as the base for his literary theory. His realism was different from Soviet socialist realism in that it was not as narrow and dogmatic. His realism (if we limit it to literary studies) can be summed up as: Literature should reflect the underlying pattern of contradictions in a society and thus give a concrete understanding of reality. He examined the genre of historical novels and argued that it became prominent because of the increasing historical consciousness of the bourgeoisie (the capitalist class) and various economic changes. He stated that Sir Walter Scott (Scottish novelist famous for his realistic description of the Scottish countryside), Honore de Balzac (French novelist famous for realistic representations of society) and Leo Tolstoy (Russian novelist famous for his realistic portrayal of life) were the greatest realist writers. He disliked the social realistic writing of his time for the sordid descriptions of society and also the naturalistic writing of writers like Emile Zola. He also disliked the Modernist writings of James Joyce, Virginia Woolf and others, dismissing it as decadent and false. He made trenchant attacks on these experimental writers and dismissed Modernism as a bourgeois ideology. He believed that Modernist writers offered their individual subjective concepts of reality and projected them to be objective and universal versions of reality. They offered a false view of society as static and also a false image of life as fragmentary and isolated. He criticised their separation of history and society from literary works. He preferred a coherent form and content in literary works and rejected any kind of experiment with them. Lukacs' other important view was about the content and form of literature. For him content is more important than form because it determines form. This can be seen as a re-statement of the Marxist metaphor of base and superstructure, where content is base and form is superstructure.

If Lucaks had a keen interest in the representation of reality in art, **Antonio Gramsci**, one of the most influential Italian theorists, was interested in revealing the dominant role of the ruling class in society. He proposed the concept of hegemony. He defined it as the strategy adopted by the ruling class to establish and maintain its rule. We can briefly understand hegemony as—force (applied by the ruling class) + consent (tactfully earned by the ruling class from the intellectual people) supported by power (coercion). Political society organises force and civil society gives consent to it. This consent is used as power to establish policies which favour the dominant class. Gramsci applied this concept to literature and analysed it as the class function of intellectuals. He examined literature as a tool in enforcing the hegemony of the ruling class. Literature, according to him, serves the interests of the ruling class by projecting a particular world view. We can find the influence of Gramsci's concept of hegemony on the works of British Marxist theorists, Raymond Williams and Terry Eagleton.

Theodore Adorno was one of the prominent members of the Frankfurt school. He can be seen as the polar opposite of George Lukacs. Unlike Lukacs he defended Modernism and its breaking established norms of formal structure/features of literary works. He criticised Lukacs' realism because it demanded direct presentation of social reality in literary works. Lukacs wanted literary works to reflect social reality directly, whereas Adorno wanted them to do so obliquely. For Adorno, Modernist literary writings actually work in line with the expectations of Marxism. They detach themselves from reality and thus negate the impact of the repressive economic system of capitalism. They also indirectly criticise the works of art (including literature) which submit to the force of the economic system. He supported the experiments of Modern writers with the form of their writing and the so-called non-historical and non-social content of their works. This is because literature is not simply a reflection of reality but also a part of reality. It works within the system of reality and lays bare its repressive patterns. An experimental form and oblique style of writing cut across the deeply entrenched forms of exploitation in the economic system and help Modern writers (like Brecht and Beckett) achieve insights into the workings of social reality.

Walter Benjamin (1892–1940) was a German Marxist theorist who became influential after the Second World War. He was a friend of Bertolt Brecht (1898–1956, the German poet, playwright and Marxist famous for his epic theatre) and of Adorno. Like Adorno, he criticised Lukacs for his traditional way of thinking and his attack on new kinds of writing. He strongly defended Brecht's work against Lukacs' attack and praised new art forms. He welcomed technological developments and new media like photography and cinema and argued that they radically changed the status and role of arts. These new developments shattered the uniqueness and originality of works of art and rescued them from the traditional ritual of posing to be unique and original. However Benjamin was not sure that the new technologies would bring about a revolutionary change in the social system. So he appealed to artists to ensure that they spoke out against hegemonic oppression through their works.

Louis Althusser (1918–1990) was a major French Marxist theorist. His most important contribution to Marxist theory was his reinterpretation of the concept of ideology. It is very difficult to explain Althusser's concept of ideology but it may be phrased as a system of ideas, values and beliefs that keeps people away from true knowledge of society. We are already familiar with Gramsci's concept of hegemony, and how it operates through social institutions. Althusser terms the principle in operation here, *ideology*. Althusser explained his conception of ideology in his essay, 'Ideology and Ideological State Apparatuses'. He proposed that ideology is an imaginary construction that represents the real world and that this representation is so realistic that nobody challenges it. He also posited that ideology always has a material existence in the form of concrete entities or apparatuses. He proposed two key terms to understand this concept—'Ideological State Apparatus' and 'Repressive State Apparatus'. These are the ways through which a state rules over its subjects. 'Ideological State Apparatus' is a means through which the state or ruling institution propagates its ideology. This mode is covert, and works through social institutions like religion, law, politics and media, and produces willing compliance in subjects. 'Repressive State Apparatus' is a more overt mode of control, in which the ruling class suppresses and dominates the working class by force, through state institutions like the army and police.

People are ostensibly free to make their choice, but their choices are unwittingly and influenced in favour of the ruling class. This can be demonstrated with an example. If you visit a big bookshop, you will come across a prominently displayed list of bestselling books. You are then more likely to buy books which feature in the list. The list suggests that the bestselling books are the books that people most want to read, and you unconsciously accept that you are likely to enjoy what so many people before you have already read and enjoyed. We read what others read because that is what is advertised as the standard of reading. If many people read a particular set of books it is assumed that reading those books will help us achieve the standard. Thus the advertisement is at once both choice and compulsion. By extension this is also true for literary texts. They are vehicles of certain ideologies as they express a system of values and beliefs helpful to the ruling class. Althusser's concept can be applied to every text, and is a hugely influential theoretical concept.

Raymond Williams (1921–1988), was Professor of Drama at Cambridge University. After Christopher Caudwell he was arguably the most influential English Marxist critic and the first of his kind in Britain. In the earlier phase of his career he did not take up the popular Marxist principle of ideology for his analysis. He devoted his energy to the study of culture from the historical and materialist point of view. However, in his book, *Marxism and Literature* published in 1977, he clearly stated his position as a Marxist critic. He developed his own theory of 'cultural materialism' and redefined Gramsci's concept of hegemony. He was instrumental in re assessing the premises of culture. He disapproved of the elite class's claims for superiority of the art popular with them, terming it as 'high culture', through a well-reasoned and sustained analysis and laid down the foundations of Cultural Studies in England.

Terry Eagleton (b. 1943) is the foremost Marxist critic and cultural theorist of Britain after Raymond Williams. Eagleton was Williams' student, and assimilated the influence of Marxist theorists from Lukacs to Williams. He wrote extensively on a wide variety of subjects, like ideology and literature, ideology in the works of English novelists, the function of criticism, and the reassessment of structuralist and poststructuralist theories from the Marxist point of view. His work as a Marxist critic can be understood in two phases of his career. In the first phase he was influenced by the structuralist Marxism of Louis Althusser. This was evident in his book *Criticism and Ideology* (1976), where he argued that criticism should renounce subjectivity arising out of ideological positions and become a science. In the second phase poststructuralist theories changed his outlook. He moved away from Althusser's scientific method towards the theoretical positions of Walter Benjamin and Bertolt Brecht. He criticised structuralism for neglecting the fact that language and literature are both forms of the social system and social production, and poststructuralism, for being bourgeois in its approach. He argued that poststructuralist theories do not have political content and that most of their radical ideas have already been expressed by Marxist critics like Adorno and Benjamin. In his subsequent work, Eagleton has mostly followed the Marxist historical materialistic method of analysis. According to him the function of literary criticism is to relate itself to cultural and political issues and to help bring about radical social change.

Fredric Jameson (b. 1934) is an American scholar and distinguished Marxist critic. His Marxist theory covers a huge range of ideas from the early Marxist thought of Lukacs to postmodernism. It is therefore eclectic (drawing on many different sources) and comprehensive. He draws upon the ideas of a wide range of critics, from Lukacs, Adorno and Althusser, to non-Marxist structuralist, psychoanalytic and poststructuralist critics. Jameson worked on Sartre and French literature for his doctoral research. But with the publication of the book, *Marxism and Form* in 1971, Jameson discovered his lifelong subject of study and outlined his position as a Marxist critic. He argued in the book that form is only the working out of content in the realm of superstructure. In the next book, *The Prison House of Language: A Critical Account of Structuralism and Russian Formalism* (1972) he revealed the political and cultural implications of structuralism. Jameson believed that the traditional methods of critical analysis like class struggle and commodity production are not adequate to deal with the changing forms of capitalism in the postmodern period. Therefore he adopted an eclectic method to show the relation between postmodern theories and capitalism in the subsequent books. In his *The Political Unconscious* (1981), Jameson used his method of dialectical materialism to synthesise diverse and often contradictory theories, a few examples being the theories of Althusser, Adorno, Freud and Lacan. According to Jameson the role of the critic is to discover the strategies of the texts to contain and conceal ideologies. The critic should follow dialectical materialism to reveal ideology in a literary text and also in order to transcend it.

Salient Features of Marxist Literary Criticism

1) Marxist criticism studies the materialist and social character of literature. It is influenced by the politics of Marxism, which is essentially a critique of capitalism.

2) It studies literature in relation to its social, economic and historical contexts. It examines the relation between the ideas and values expressed in a work of literature and the ideas and values prevalent in contemporary society. It attempts to study the relation of literature with class struggles and conflicts between social groups for economic and political power.

3) It tries to explain how ideology influences literature, and attempts a critique of ideology. Ideology works to justify unequal social and economic conditions and hide social contradictions using literature.

4) The metaphor of base and superstructure has been frequently used and differently interpreted by Marxist critics. For Marx, base is the economic structure of a society and superstructure is forms of social consciousness like politics, morality, culture and art. In subsequent discussions the relationship between base and superstructure has been variously contested. It has been interpreted and used in the analysis of different art forms.

5) It undertakes an ideological study of literature, in the sense that it examines literature as the direct expression of class interests. Such study is carried out in two ways— a) by showing how certain ideas and values are structurally imposed through a literary work and b) by showing the apparatus of publishing and distribution.

6) Marxism developed in two phases. The first phase can be called Soviet or Russian Marxism, as it was concentrated in Russia, or the erstwhile Soviet Union. Critics

who practiced Soviet Marxism were focused on state apparatuses and political economy, and included Georgii Plekhonov and Karl Kautsky. The second phase can be called Western Marxism. It began in the 1920s in Europe. Critics who practiced this were influenced by Russian Marxist theorists, and included Georg Lukacs, Antonio Gramsci and Karl Korsch. They analysed art, culture and literature from a Marxist lens.

7) Another useful classification for understanding the various strains of Marxist literary criticism is by determining the chief philosophical influence (apart from Marx himself). The three important variants are Hegelian, Structuralist and Gramscian, and have been influenced by the ideas of Hegel, Saussure and Gramsci, respectively.

8) The concept of realism has been central to all versions of Marxist criticism. Realism means the accurate presentation of society and its class conflicts through the use of 'typical' characters. However this concept of realism, valued by earlier Marxist critics like Lukacs, has been challenged by later critics like Brecht, Adorno, Benjamin and Macherey. For Brecht it is important that literature expresses radical and revolutionary content rather than present an accurate portrait of society. For other Marxist critics, literature as per the Lukacsian concept of realism cannot express real contradictions and oppositions in society. On the contrary it hides them and projects false unity in its reflection of the world.

Introduction to Terry Eagleton's *Marxism and Literary Criticism* (Chapters 1–2)

These chapters appear as a preliminary to Marxist literary criticism in Eagleton's book *Marxism and Literary Criticism* (1976). In the first chapter Eagleton opens the discussion with Marx's views about literature. It is often argued that Marx did not write elaborately about literature and therefore he regarded literature as unimportant. Eagleton rejects this argument and provides some information about Marx's treatment of literature. Marx himself was an author in his youth, and wrote lyric poetry, a fragment of verse-drama and an unfinished comic novel. His writings are full of literary concepts and allusions. Marx was greatly influenced by literary tradition, from Sophocles to the Spanish novel. He used to devote an evening every week to the discussion of art and literature and was a regular theatre-goer. He had artistic sensibilities and was sensitive to the questions of literary style. It is true that Marx did not offer a complete aesthetic theory but Eagleton provides enough biographical information about Marx's engagement with art and literature to prove that he regarded art and literature seriously. His views about literature are scattered throughout his writings and are fragmentary in nature. With this opening clarification about Marx's treatment of literature Eagleton moves on to examine the notion of 'sociology of literature'. This notion is very much prevalent in the West. Eagleton defines it as an approach that deals with the means of literary production, distribution and exchange in a particular society. It enquires into the process of the publication of books, the social status of the authors and readers, levels of literacy, etc. Eagleton appreciates the excellent work done by the practitioners of this notion but makes it clear that it is one among the several aspects of Marxist criticism and not the only one. 'Sociology of literature' as a notion practised in the West is not particularly Marxist or particularly critical. This is because it does not address historical, economic, social or literary/aesthetic issues in particular. In its comprehensive sense, 'sociology of literature' aims at explaining the literary work more fully. This includes the study of forms, styles and meaning of literary works. However Eagleton is careful enough to mention that the study of forms, styles and meaning should be done as the products of particular history and not in isolation from historical contexts.

In order to understand Marxist literary criticism one needs to understand the basic ideas of Marxism. Eagleton realises this need and provides the necessary conceptual background. He begins with the discussion of the Marxist metaphor—base and superstructure. Marx's argument was that productive forces and social relations form the economic structure of society. This economic structure was called 'base' or 'infrastructure'. From this base emerges 'superstructure'. It comprises certain forms of law and politics and other forms of social consciousness like religious, ethical and aesthetic consciousness. The ruling class uses these forms of superstructure to legitimise its mode of economic production. In other words the ruling class makes use of one or many forms of superstructure (religious or aesthetic for example) to protect its economic interests. Marx called this strategy of the ruling class 'ideology'. Ideology works to legitimise the power of the ruling class in society. Art and literature are a part of 'superstructure'. They are the products of the complex relations between base and superstructure. Therefore if we want to understand literature we must understand it as a part of the total social process. Literature is not the creation of mysterious inspiration and the author's psychology is not the key to its meaning. It is a form of perception; a particular way of seeing the world. Every age is characterised by a certain worldview, and literature presents the dominant worldview of the time as true, universal and permanent. This is where ideology works through literature and criticism needs to discover it. To illustrate his point Eagleton takes the examples of *King Lear* (a tragedy by Shakespeare), *The Dunciad* (a satire on dullness in three books by Alexander Pope) and *Ulysses* (an experimental novel by James Joyce). He argues that it is not enough to interpret the symbolism in these works, to study their literary history and add footnotes about sociological facts related to them. It is important to study the complex and indirect relations between these works and the worlds they represent. But this is not an easy task because it involves a subtle understanding of contradictory worldviews. It may appear more difficult to students of literature whose study is usually limited to plot and characterisation. In spite of the difficulty of this approach of studying literature, and the confusion it may cause about the purity of the literary approach, Eagleton asserts the importance of the Marxist study of literature. This must not be restricted to socio-economic and historical analysis but must also take into account the artistic/aesthetic aspects. Eagleton takes the example of Joseph Conrad's novel, *Nostromo* (1904) and interprets the famous Placido Gulf scene in it from the Marxist point of view. It is a brief but brilliant piece of Marxist literary criticism. Decoud and Nostromo are shown isolated in utter darkness in the scene, and this is symbolic of pessimism. Eagleton argues that it is not pessimism in the mind of the author but the pessimism prevalent in his contemporary world. It is an ideological pessimism (worldview) transposed into the novel which considers history as futile and cyclic, individuals as solitary and values as relativistic and irrational. This is the worldview of the Western bourgeoisie, of whom Conrad was one. Eagleton argues that Conrad could write the scene not because he possessed an extraordinary prose style but because the historical situation he lived in facilitated this. Being a politically conservative and aristocratic person, Conrad wrote in much the same style that other major writers of the twentieth century like Yeats, Eliot, Pound and Lawrence wrote.

Eagleton discusses the relation between literature and superstructure. He argues that literature may be the part of superstructure but it is not the passive reflection of the economic base. In other words the economic base alone does not influence the superstructure but the superstructure also acts upon the base. This mutual influence causes change in society. However, art on its own cannot cause change in the economic structure of a society and can only contribute towards it. Eagleton refers to Marx's view about the relation between art and superstructure. In this discussion Eagleton deals with the problems that Marx's view raises—the relation of art created in the present with art created in the past, and the relation between base and superstructure. Marx regards art as a part of superstructure and as an example of the complex and indirect relationship between superstructure and base. He points out the unequal relation between art and economic structure, and uses Greek art to illustrate his point. There is no direct relation between the greatest artistic achievements and highest development of productive forces. In spite of its antiquity Greek art holds great appeal in modern times. Marx raises this issue of artistic appeal and states that the Greeks could produce major art because they were living in the undeveloped state of society. Eagleton emphasises this, and says that the modern capitalist notion of division of labour was not known to the Greeks; so they could live in a child-like state of harmony with Nature and could create art without any pressures of demand and supply.

Eagleton then turns to another problem of the relation between base and superstructure. Marx clearly states that the two aspects are not symmetrical and therefore they do not form a composite and equal relationship. Each element of superstructure like art, law and politics has its own way of development and it cannot be reduced to a mere expression of class struggle or the economic state. As Trotsky observed, art has a high degree of autonomy. Yet, in his final analysis, Marx claims that art is determined by the mode of production. In order to explain this discrepancy, Eagleton takes the literary example of T. S. Eliot's poem, *The Waste Land*. He briefly shows how a simplistic Marxist interpretation of this poem may be attempted. It may be argued that the poem is directly determined by ideological and economic factors. The spiritual emptiness and exhaustion that the poem expresses is the expression of the bourgeois ideology that emerges from the crisis of the First World War. But this interpretation does not take into account the many levels that mediate between the text itself and capitalist economy. It does not consider the important factors of Eliot's individual social situation. He had a very ambiguous relationship with English society as an aristocratic American expatriate writer. He was a committed conservative traditionalist rather than a bourgeois-commercialist. The English were largely bourgeois-commercialist, and Eliot, being an émigré, was not used this worldview. The simplistic Marxist interpretation does not say anything about the forms of this English ideology—its structure, content and internal complexity. It is silent about the form and language of the poem. It does not explain why Eliot was an avant-garde (originally a military term which came to designate anti-traditional and experimental artists in the modern period) poet despite his extreme political conservatism and on what ideological basis he selected certain progressive experimental techniques. Eagleton insists on explaining all these factors for a complete understanding of the poem.

In the next part Eagleton discusses the relation of literature to ideology. He defines ideology as the way men live out their roles in class-society. It binds people to their social functions through values, ideas and images and prevents them from a true knowledge of society. In this sense *The Waste Land* is ideological as it shows man making sense of his experience in ways which are false and prevent him from a true understanding. The relation of literature to ideology is therefore not simple and direct. Eagleton mentions two extreme views about this relation: a) all literature is nothing but the expression of ideology and b) literature transcends ideology and shows realities that ideology hides. He rejects both these views as too simple. For a deeper understanding of this relation he refers to the view of the French Marxist theorist Louis Althusser. According to Althusser, ideology and literature both represent the imaginary ways in which men experience the real world. Literature works within the fold of ideology but also manages to separate itself from it. In doing so literature helps the readers to feel and perceive the ideology from which it originates. Literature does not offer us knowledge because knowledge means scientific knowledge to Althusser. It cannot, thus, be acquired through a literary work like Charles Dickens' novel *Hard Times* but through a scientific treatise like Marx's *Das Kapital.* For Eagleton science is the conceptual knowledge of a situation and art/literature is the experience of that situation. Art may not offer knowledge to readers but it allows them to see the nature of ideology and thus leads them to a full understanding of ideology. Pierre Macherey, another French Marxist theorist and colleague of Althusser, elaborates this point of how literature can allow the readers insights into ideology. Macherey differentiates between the two terms, illusion and fiction. Illusion for Macherey is ideology that provides material to the writer. The writer puts this ideological material into a shape and structure called fiction. Thus ideology gets a determinate form and this fictionalised matter gets separated from ideology. This separation offers the readers insights into ideology, its working and its limits. Eagleton does not fully agree with the views of Althusser and Macherey, but he admits that they are deeply suggestive. Literature is essentially a part of ideology and it puts ideology into a certain structure. Significantly by doing this literature distances itself from the ideology of which it is a part and reflection. The role of the critic then is to find out the principle that binds the literary work to ideology and distances it from literary work. Eagleton calls this the finest Marxist criticism.

In the second chapter titled 'Form and Content' Eagleton relates the form of literature to history. He makes it clear that Marxist criticism has not paid any attention to artistic form or formal features of literature. This is because it strongly holds that formal features deprive literary works of their historical significance and reduce them to aesthetic games. Another point is that such technical pursuit reflects the interests of advanced capitalist societies. Not withstanding the extreme Marxist views about 'form', it is curious to know Marx's view about 'form'. Marx himself, Eagleton points out, believed that literature should reveal a unity of form and content. He criticised the extreme use of stylistic techniques but he did not mean to completely disregard the 'form' of literary works. Greek classical art, for example had achieved the unity of form and content or the spiritual and the material that Marx advocated. But this right balance is absent in Romantic art/literature as the spiritual elements dominated the sensual elements and the content completely absorbed the form. Marx was influenced by Hegel's views in his conception of the form and content of art. However both Hegel and Marx believed that forms of artistic works are determined by the kind of content they have to represent. Form changes with change in content. Theoretically they may be different but practically form and content are inseparable. In conclusion it may be stated that Marxist criticism sees a dialectical relation between form and content and believes finally in the primacy of content. Eagleton states that this Marxist view of a dialectical (mutually influencing) relationship between form and content rejects on one hand the formalist view of art and the 'vulgar Marxism' (that altogether dismisses the role of form) on the other hand.

Eagleton then turns to the discussion of the relationship between form and ideology. He maintains that form changes as ideology in society changes. This is evident in the rise of novel in eighteenth-century England. The novel of a particular period acquires its 'form' as per the changing sets of ideology. It may differ in content but it shares certain formal/structural features. Eagleton mentions the views of the literary critic Ian Watt and the Marxist critic Georgii Plekhanov, who argue that forms of literary works change with class interests. For example there was a change in form of the classical tragedy to sentimental comedy in France because there was a shift from aristocratic values to bourgeois values. Eagleton gives another example of the transition from naturalism to expressionism in European theatre around the turn of the century. Expressionism as a changed 'form' crossed the limits of naturalistic theatre and tried to expose the deception and isolation concealed under the label of normalcy. Naturalism as a bourgeois form of ideology dehistoricised reality and accepted the state of society as a natural fact. Eagleton alludes to Lukacs' views on Emile Zola and Balzac regarding naturalism. Lukacs observed that the naturalist writers offered only a surface picture of society and did not go deep to show the complex relations between men and their world. Naturalism presented an alienated vision of reality and made writers clinical observers. Formalism worked in the opposite direction but it also suffered from the loss of historical meaning. The world of Franz Kafka, Robert Musil, James Joyce, Samuel Beckett and Albert Camus projected man as alienated from society and stripped him of history. Both naturalism and formalism lost the dialectical unity between the inner and the outer world. While naturalism became a kind of abstract objectivity, formalism became a kind of abstract subjectivity.

In the next part of the second chapter Eagleton explains the ideas of Lucien Goldmann (the Romanian Marxist critic) and Pierre Macherey. Eagleton elaborates upon Goldmann's critical method called 'genetic structuralism'. He uses the word 'structuralism' because he is less interested in the contents of a particular world vision and more interested in the structure of categories that it displays. Goldmann expects literary works to represent the structure of ideas, values and aspirations of a group of people. It is a collective mental structure, and therefore, two very different writers may be shown to share the same structure. He uses the word 'genetic' because he wants to know how such mental structures are historically produced; that is, the relations between a world vision and the historical conditions which give rise to it. Goldman's critical work on Racine's (Jean Racine, the seventeenth-century French tragedian) *The Hidden God* is a very good application of his critical method. He finds a recurrent structure of categories in Racine's plays—the categories of World, God and Man. These categories change in content from play to play but they retain a particular world vision. Racine's characters live in a valueless world, accept it as the only world and yet protest against it. Their protest against the world they live in suggests their search for some absolute hidden value. Goldmann discovers this absolute value in the French religious movement called Jansenism. Goldmann compares Jansenism to a social group of court officials who were economically dependent on the king but politically opposed to him, and hence were powerless to stop royal absolutism. He thus demonstrates how the mediation of the world vision of a social class changes its social position and how it influences the structure of a literary work. Eagleton finds Goldmann's method interesting but he also finds some faults with it. Goldmann's method fails to cover dialectical conflicts and it remains mechanistic, according to Eagleton.

Eagleton at the end of the second chapter explains Pierre Macherey's concept of 'de-centred form'. Macherey states that the relation of a literary work to ideology is based on what it does not say, more than what it explicitly says. It is in silences, gaps and absences that ideology becomes apparent. Ideology prevents the text from saying certain things and the author is forced to reveal it through gaps and silences. It is through these gaps and silences that the text speaks. Therefore the text is based on difference and not on unity. It always remains incomplete and brings contradictory meanings. For a critic like Goldmann, a work is centrally structured, while for those holding a critical position like Macherey's, it is always 'de-centred'. Eagleton takes Charles Dickens' novel *Dombey and Son* as a case in point. The author uses many conflicting styles like realism, melodrama, allegory and the pastoral to describe the events in the novel. This results in a clash of styles and symbols and the novel becomes ambiguous. The ideological base of this ambiguity lies in the contradictory views of the bourgeoisie (conventional middle class people) and the petty bourgeoisie (people of the lower middle class). While the bourgeoisie admired industrial progress, the petty bourgeoisie were anxious about its disruptive effects.

Key Points

- Eagleton discusses the relation of literature to history in his first chapter.
- Marx did not propose any theory of literature but regards art and literature seriously.

- Eagleton examines the phenomenon of 'sociology of literature', and defines it as an approach that deals with the means of literary production, distribution and exchange in a particular society.
- Eagleton discusses art and literature as an example of the complex and mutually influential relation between base and superstructure. His analysis of Eliot's poem *The Waste Land* shows the complex and many-layered relation between the base and superstructure.
- He differentiates between simplistic Marxist criticism and Marxist criticism proper. Simplistic Marxist criticism regards a text as a direct expression of capitalist economy and ideology, while Marxist criticism proper takes into account historical, social and economic factors and the mediation between the text and the capitalist system, and at the same time, the formal/linguistic structure of the poem.
- Eagleton also discusses ideology, and refers to Louis Althusser and Pierre Macherey. He says that though literature can work as ideology. it can also help readers develop awareness about ideology by distancing itself from ideology.
- In his second chapter, Eagleton discusses form and content. The traditional Marxist stance has favoured content over form, because focusing on form would deprive readers of understanding the historical significance behind events in the text. Eagleton, however, argues that the relation between form and content is dialectical. He points out that the relation between the form of literature changes with a change in ideology; for example the shift from classical tragedy to sentimental comedy in France, or from naturalism to expressionism.

- Eagleton goes on to explain the ideas of Lucien Goldmann's critical method, called 'genetic structuralism', and Pierre Macherey's concept of 'de-centred form', and emphasises the importance of spaces and silences in a text.

Exercises

Answer the following questions in 100–150 words.

1) What is 'sociology of literature', according to Eagleton?
2) Distinguish between base and superstructure.
3) Define ideology.
4) How is simplistic Marxist criticism different from Marxist criticism proper?
5) What are Macherey's two terms regarding ideology and literature?

Answer the following questions in 250–300 words.

1) What were Marx's views on art, according to Eagleton?
2) What is the relation between literature and history, according to Eagleton?
3) Describe the relation between form and ideology.
4) What is Goldmann's critical method of genetic structuralism?
5) Elucidate Pierre Macherey's concept of 'de-centred form'.

POSTSTRUCTURALISM

Structuralism and Poststructuralism: A Comparative View

Poststructuralism is, broadly speaking, a group of theories about language and its relationships with other disciplines like psychology, history, philosophy, sociology and literature. Its orientation is linguistic and textual and its method is disruptive. It challenges earlier theories and reveals many inconsistencies in them, as well as contradictions in what we assume to be commonsense thinking. It raises radical questions about language and other cultural practices but does not lay any claim either to new theories or solutions. It has deeply influenced the course of humanities after the 1970s. It has drastically altered our attitude towards ourselves, our world and the disciplines we study. It is important to know that poststructural theories are not directly concerned with literature as such. Some of the major poststructuralist theorists have attempted to analyse of literary works, in order to better illustrate their ideas. Literary critics, on the other hand, have been heavily influenced by certain ideas from poststructuralism and applied them to literary works. So in the discussion that follows only the ideas pertaining to literature in poststructural theories is taken into account. In this part of discussion the focus is on the relation of poststructural theories to literature.

The introduction to poststructuralism should begin with the term itself. Observe carefully the term 'poststructuralism'. Is there anything special about it? It is 'post-structuralism' and the prefix 'post' creates confusion about its meaning. Does the prefix, 'post' in 'post-structuralism' suggest the continuation of structuralism or rejection of structuralism? Or does it suggest both at the same time? Finally, is it confined to structuralism alone? Poststructuralism addresses the same issues that structuralism talks about, but also goes beyond structuralism. It questions certain structuralist ideas and produces its own methods of dealing with language and other cultural practices. It accepts the structuralist concept of language as a system of signs and its function of signification. But it redefines the concept of sign, reconsiders the relation between language and reality and rejects the idea of determinable meaning. Its criticism of structuralism is only a part of its comprehensive program to re assess Western philosophical thought. It is useful for us to understand the similarities and differences between these critical approaches:

Structuralism	**Poststructuralism**
Structuralism is grammatical in its approach. Like grammar it tries to find out the codes/rules underlying all cultural practices. It tries to find out the rules of a system to know its message.	Poststructuralism is rhetorical in its approach. Like rhetoric, it is persuasive and analytical. It does not try to find out the rules underlying any cultural practice. It shows that the rules subvert the classification they make out.
It sets a scientific aim to its analysis. Its broad aim is to find out basic codes, rules, structures common to all cultural practices. With literature its aim is to find out a set of codes/structure that can define literature and can help understand its meaning.	It does not have any specific aim because it is not definitive. It does not believe in any final, fixed and universal set of rules. It concentrates on the process behind cultural practices like literature and not on their end result; i.e., meaning.
It is against humanist and empiricist (the belief that ideas originate from experience and experiment) theories. It does not consider that the author owns the meaning of a literary text, and challenges the idea that reality exists before its expression and that literature reflects reality.	It is also against humanist and empiricist theories but it is radical in its rejection. It completely dismisses the role of the author as the origin of text and source of meaning. It questions the very idea of 'reality' and its communication.

It studies literature as a sign system like language. It tries to reveal the rules or codes that unite and regulate literary texts. It rejects the traditional view that literature is a unique creation of language.	It shows that the sign system and the discourses of theorists are not free from inherent breaks and discontinuities. It challenges the structuralist claim to scientific study of literary texts by revealing the problems involved in such study. It further removes the distinction between 'literary' and 'non-literary.'
It does not make use of traditional elements like plot, character, theme, setting, tone, etc. It investigates into literary texts as a system based on certain coordinates that reveal the meaning.	It also does not make use of traditional elements. It uses its characteristic terms and methods like 'differance' and deconstruction and explains a literary text not as a stable structure with determinable meaning, but as a piece of writing that constantly undergoes changes.
It believes in 'structure'—a system of codes/rules that are interrelated and that work together. Such interrelated structures are present in all literary texts and the job of the critic is to discover it in a scientific way. It also assumes the presence of a centre that regulates the working of the system and makes it stable and meaningful.	It does not believe in any stable system with determinable meaning. It shows that there is actually no centre that regulates a system. As a result, it does not treat a literary text as a structured unit that contains meaning.
It makes use of the notion of 'binary oppositions.' We know the world and ourselves through 'binary oppositions.' It is through classifications like 'light vs darkness' that we know the state of affairs. Literature is also be studied through systematic observation of binary oppositions.	It shows that 'binary oppositions' are based on unequal and privileged classification. One element in a pair of 'binary opposition' is always thought to be superior and central to the other. However none of the two elements is completely opposite—they share certain qualities and blur boundaries between them. This blurring of boundaries can be traced in literary texts.

It believes that meaning comes out of the arbitrary use of signs and their differential position within a system. Convention and common usage of signs and their difference from other signs offer meaning. Literary texts can be thus examined to determine their meaning.	It does not look for meaning in any text because it is based on the belief that that text does not contain a fixed and final meaning. Every text constantly reverses its hierarchies (like central and marginal, good and evil) and signs constantly postpone and differentiate meaning. Meaning is only provisional and it gives way to another set of meanings.
It tries to discover unity, integrity and wholeness in a text by discovering its structuring rules or codes.	It tries to show ambiguities and disruptions in each text. It dissembles text into different investigable parts to reveal ambiguities in them.
It defines language as a system of signs. Language is not referential but relational and differential. It does not refer to objects in the world but to mental concepts. It works on the difference of one sign from the other and relates signifier to signified.	It criticises the structuralist view of language. Language is not a stable sign system but an endless game of signs. It refers to neither objects in the material world nor mental concepts, but to other signs only. Language is not referential but self-referential.
In structuralist theory, a signifier is linked to a particular signified as a matter of social convention, i.e. users of a language relate a certain word to certain object/meaning due to convention formed out of communal consent.	It rejects the view that a signifier is or can be related to a signified, or the idea of the signified as meaning. Poststructuralists state that signifiers relate to other signifiers and not to any signified. Both Lacan and Derrida proposed this view of the play of signifiers. Poststructuralism is not concerned with discovering meaning but with observing the play of signification.

Historical Background

Poststructuralism covers many different theories like Jacques Lacan's psychoanalytic theory, Michel Foucault's archaeological and genealogical theory, Roland Barthes' semiological theory and Jacques Derrida's deconstruction. But as a movement away from structuralism and as a program of radical re-assessment of Western philosophy, it began with Derrida's theory of deconstruction. The starting point of poststructuralism is generally thought to be the International Colloquium of October 1966 at Johns Hopkins University, Baltimore, Maryland, where Derrida presented his groundbreaking paper 'Structure, Sign and Play in the Discourse of Human Sciences.' This conference was organised to discuss the major concerns of structuralism. But Derrida's paper showed the blind spots in structuralism and expressed the need to reconsider its principles. He challenged structuralist ideas like objectivity, belief in a scientific explanation behind the working of any system and faith in reason. With this, he set the poststructural movement in motion and his method of analysis came to be known as 'deconstruction.' It is different from other methods because Derrida introduces linguistic study of philosophical texts. He examines philosophical texts as constructs of language. Language is rhetorical, fluid and unstable, so any text using language is necessarily fluid, unstable and rhetorical. Philosophical texts thus cannot remain free from or above the rhetoric of language. This textual method has become so influential that it has become almost synonymous with poststructuralism. The influence may be seen in the large following Derrida attracted, consisting of the most illustrious American critics. Celebrated critics like Paul de Man, Geoffrey Hartman, J. H. Miller, Harold Bloom and Barbara Johnson applied Derrida's ideas to literary texts.

Jacques Derrida (1930–2004), was a French philosopher who wrote extensively about the hierarchical construction of knowledge by Western philosophers, from Plato down to Saussure. His first work was *Edmund Husserl's Origin of Geometry: An Introduction* (1962). Husserl was interested in how the geometer, as an individual, could propose the objective laws of geometry. In other words: how can a 'person' propose *impersonal* laws? Husserl's answer was in and through language. He argued that the impersonal objectivity necessary for the laws of geometry could be achieved through language. Derrida's response to this was that language itself is not free from the problem it is supposed to solve. Language is not objective and impersonal and so its use to state objective and impersonal laws is problematic. This was the basic idea that Derrida developed extensively in his later works in the form of serious doubts about the things believed to be pure, original and central. In 1967, he published three books in succession. The first is *Speech and Phenomena* (1967, trans.1973). This is devoted to the study of phenomenology. It analyses Edmund Husserl's theory of signs and the nature of the concepts of voice and presence. It is a seminal work of deconstructive analysis as it explains the traditional philosophical concepts of speech, presence and absence in a new light. The second is *Of Grammatology* (1967, trans.1973). It deals with the Western philosophical approach to language. It analyses the hierarchy of speech and writing and shows that this age-old hierarchy (the traditional belief that speech is superior to writing) can be reversed. In this work, Derrida discusses Saussure's privileging of speech over writing and Rousseau's principles of presence and supplement. The third is *Writing and Difference* (1967, trans.1978). This is a sequel to *Of Grammatology*. It discusses the ideas of major contemporary thinkers like Freud, Michel Foucault, Emmanuel Levinas, Edmund Husserl, Antonin Artaud, Georges Bataille, and Claude Levi-Strauss. This work contains Derrida's epoch-making paper on 'Structure, Sign and Play in the Discourse of Human Sciences'. His next work, *Glass* (1974), shows how texts intrude into one another's space, cross the disciplinary boundaries and create many meanings. Derrida compares Hegel and Genette's texts to show the impossibility of definite meaning and possibility of mutual overlapping. He examines Marx's texts and Marxism in his work *Specters of Marx* (1993).

Derrida does not take any position that is consistent and definite or propose any alternative theory. He does not provide solutions but points out problems in traditional Western philosophy. He discovers patterns of hierarchies in traditional methods of philosophy and criticism. In order to explain such hierarchies, he invents new terms. He challenges traditional boundaries between disciplines like history, philosophy, literature, criticism, etc. He shows how texts of different disciplines intersect with one another—their references cross one another, their styles shade into one another, and so on. He also shows that all types of texts are full of inconsistencies and contradictions. Therefore the aim of philosophy and by extension of criticism should not be to search for the truth, permanent values and definite meaning, but to show inconsistencies and contradictions. Two major aspects of Derrida's deconstructive method may be briefly outlined as below:

a) Derrida explains patterns of hierarchies and terms of opposition in texts. In other words, he shows that texts are not stable, certain and definitive. They are like tissues made of many cells so they do not have a unified structure and definite meaning and they are not original as traditionally claimed.

b) Derrida undermines the patterns of hierarchies and separates terms of oppositions. He reverses the given order of a text and shows that the inferior and unimportant elements can be as important as the given superior elements. Thus he shows that there can be nothing permanently true, fixed and definite in the given pairs of elements because all elements have all the features present in them.

As a matter of common practice we know everything through terms of opposition. For example, we call something white and something else black. We consider that the white object is absolutely and permanently white and the black object is absolutely and permanently black. The white object is white due to some inherent quality in it which the black object does not have. We fail to understand that such classification is deceptive because the white object and the black object are not completely and permanently white and black. The white contains the traces of the black and vice versa. The white depends on the black as it is defined against the black. Every concept consists of and is defined by its opposite concept. The opposition assumed between any pair of concepts or objects is hierarchical and provisional. Derrida applies this logic to language. Language, for him, contains contradictions and oppositions.

Language contains everything—our consciousness, our self, our world. It constructs the world for us. Our experience does not create language but language creates experience for us. This view was proposed earlier by structuralism. It regarded language as arising out of the innate stable structure of the human mind. The structuralist view of language is based on the concept of binary opposition. It considers one element of a pair superior and the other, secondary. This oppositional view gives language a stable, structured and communicable form. In the structuralist view, then, language becomes a well-founded, stable and orderly system of signs. Derrida criticises this view. He shows the internal contradictions and hierarchies in the structuralist concept of *structure*. He argues that this is applicable to the entire Western philosophy. All Western systems of thought since Plato have had a base for their views/theories and have built them around some controlling centre. This centre creates order, unity and logic in the building of a view or theory. While the world changes the centre remains unchanged and our attitude to the world (worldview) also remains unchanged. Derrida says that the modern worldview is based on logocentrism. *Logocentrism* is a belief in one focal point which guarantees stable and fixed meaning in a system. For example, the author is a *logos* that works as the centre or foundation of his/her work. Consequently, any reading of that work starts and ends with the author as he/she composes the work, and is thereby believed to possess the key to its meaning. This can be applied to *phonocentrism* where speech becomes a *logos*. Speech is held as the source of truth and originality and in turn the guarantor of meaning. Speech is privileged over writing, because writing is deemed to be a secondary, imitative and fleeting activity.

Derrida criticises the logocentric worldview which informs all Western systems that falsely offer permanent, stable and definite explanations. This is all very theoretical and somewhat difficult. Let us illustrate the point. Take the example of a tree. How do we know that a tree is a tree and nothing else? We know this by virtue of its central feature that characterises it as a tree. It is important here to know that we do not identify the central feature 'tree' with its individual parts. That is, we do not call a stem or a branch 'tree'. It means that the 'treeness' of a tree is not in its parts but in its totality. It is everywhere, in every part of the tree. But Derrida reveals the contradiction in this assumption. The 'treeness' of the tree is everywhere in the tree and nowhere because 'treeness' cannot be separated from the tree and the observed part of tree. It is due to this contradiction of the presence and absence of the centre that the centre loses its central position.

Traditionally we have been taught that every system has a centre. Structuralism taught us that if we learn about the centre, we can learn everything about the system. Derrida's deconstructive method offers a very different view of the centre. We cannot say that the centre is there, nor can we say that it is not there. We cannot say anything firmly and assuredly; we are merely ambiguous and doubtful. Derrida argues that such contradictions and ambiguity characterise Western thought because of language. Language is by nature contradictory and ambiguous so the thought articulated using language it is bound to be contradictory and ambiguous. Language constantly reverses our order of things, changes our priorities and undermines our intentions.

Derrida analyses two examples to prove his point. His first example is of the French philosopher, Jean-Jacques Rousseau's logic of supplement. Rousseau's logic of supplement establishes a deceptive scheme of pair. Supplement means something that completes or makes an addition to something else. Rousseau uses the word with reference to the dual relation between nature and education. He says that education supplements nature. This creates a very contradictory relation of nature with education. Interestingly the concept of nature is self-contradictory. In the first sense, it is something complete in itself and education is an addition to it. In the second sense, it is something incomplete and education supplements it so that it becomes complete. In Rousseau's logic education is necessary for human beings because it helps them know their true 'nature'. This logic establishes the superiority of nature over education. Nature becomes the central and the *original* term and education becomes the secondary and *external* term. However, education is also an essential and internal part of nature as it helps nature realise itself. Thus the secondary and external is also essential and internal and shows that education consists of all the features of nature and nature consists of all the features of education. Rousseau's logic of supplement thus reverses its own order.

Derrida's second example is of Saussure's prioritising speech over writing. The Western theories of language since Plato have regarded speech as natural, original and direct communication, while writing is seen as imitative, secondary and indirect communication. During the act of speech, the speaker and listener are both present. Words flow as spontaneous and transparent signs from the speaker and the listener can understand them. Writing, on the other hand, is an imitation of speech, a medium to represent speech, a technical device. In writing, the speaker and the listener are absent. It only leads the reader to some thought and does not directly explain it because the speaker is not there to explain it to him/her. These are the traditional views about speech and writing and Derrida calls them 'phonocentrism.' Saussure follows this 'phonocentrism'—superiority of speech over writing. Both traditional thinkers and Saussure believe that writing is characterised by features like distance, absence, misunderstanding and distortion. They think that writing can infect and affect the purity of speech. But Derrida shows contradictions in both the traditional view and Saussure's view of the superiority of speech over writing. He argues that speech cannot maintain its purity and superiority over writing because it is a part of language, along with writing. As a result, speech and writing both inherit all the features of language. Speech is a form of writing. Language, whether in the form of speech or writing, is a play of signs. So if writing is not stable and pure, original and natural, speech is also not stable and pure, original and natural. It has been argued by the traditional thinkers and Saussure that writing takes place in the absence of the users of language (writer/reader) as compared to speech in which the speaker and the listener are present. But Derrida shows that absence is not the feature of writing alone but of speech also. Signifier (word) and signified (meaning) are not present in speech. A signifier in speech does not refer to any particular signified. It does not refer to any particular object or thing and does not refer to any particular image in mind as Saussure argued. A signifier refers to another signifier and this goes on endlessly. Therefore speech is as distant and separated from thought and meaning as writing is. This is how Derrida shows that Saussure's privileging of speech over writing is self-deconstructive. He shows that the marginal element in its marginality becomes the central element. It is important to know that Derrida in his attempt to show the absurdity of the superiority of speech over writing does not claim that writing is superior to speech. He only explains that in any pair of elements, the belief that one element is original and superior to the other element is false. Both elements share the same properties. Thus Derrida, by reversing the hierarchy, treats speech as a kind of writing. He redefines writing as *archi-writing* or *ecriture.* This term covers both speech and writing and it suggests the constant play of language. It contains marking (writing) and articulation (speech). It is characterised by the relations of signs to one another.

Western philosophy and humanities have created certain systems of knowledge. These systems try to establish knowledge of the *self* and knowledge of the *world* in a methodical and scientific way, through opposition of elements like *nature* and *culture.* Such binary oppositions become the source of knowledge. But the differential play of language challenges the attempts of these systems. Language frustrates any intellectual attempt to interpret the self and the world in a systematic and comprehensive way. It undermines any attempt to establish order and hierarchy, and reverses the established order of things. If the order is reversed its claim for stable and sure knowledge of the things becomes futile. Language, thus, disrupts unity, stability and foundation of any system of knowledge. We can briefly understand Derrida's theory of language in the following way:

a) Language is not a transparent medium of meaning or thought.

b) There is nothing outside language. It does not refer to any reality that exists before the moment of utterance of signs.

c) Language used in any form and for any purpose is not free from contradictions. Language in ordinary use and in literary use is equally contradictory and ambiguous. So categories like literary and non-literary language, or creative and everyday language, are illusory.

d) Derrida accepts Saussure's idea of sign and its differential nature. But he extends it to suggest its dual function—differing and deferring. He terms this as *differance.* Difference is one sign being unlike the other and deferal is being delayed or postponed. Each sign differs from the other sign and defers (postpones) its meaning to another sign. Derrida's addition is that a sign carries forward the meaning to other sign and this play of carrying forward goes on endlessly. It is because of this endless play that signs do not refer to a particular signified or meaning. Derrida argues that signs (words) do not refer to any meaning either in the form of the concept or object. This is because signs refer to other signs and thus only pass on the meaning.

e) Derrida's term *trace* is a theoretical advance, and negates the Saussurean concept of sign. This is because the sign finally arrives at a certain meaning in the process of signification. The term *trace* does not refer to anything outside the chain of signs and thus it differs and defers. Unlike Saussure's signified it is not fixed and original. It is only a decentring term that questions the before and after of any binary opposition. It constantly reverses binary opposition (like nature versus culture) and keeps signs under *erasure*—a constant play of undoing/preserving.

With this basic understanding of Derrida's views about language let us briefly discuss how they challenge and change ideas about literature. In the light of Derrida's radical views, the traditional notion of literature as a pure, specific, original and purposeful entity gets challenged. It does not communicate any message and is written with no particular intention. A literary work does not express an experience or a reality that is original and still not expressed, because it is only a reconstruction or rearrangement of words that already exist and have been used before. It is not motivated by anything outside itself, and it does not have any particular meaning. The hierarchy between the literary and non-literary is based on the difference between creative use of language and everyday use of language. If, according to Derrida, all kinds of language reverse the hierarchy and unsettle our understanding, then the idea of literature as a creative and communicative discipline becomes ineffective. In other words, the traditionally celebrated nature and function of literature becomes questionable. A literary work, then, is not a creatively written book with a world view but a text that undermines the given priority of things. A literary work, in the traditional sense, is a unified work with fixed meaning. It is different from and independent of other works. However on deconstructive reading it turns into a text that reveals an underlying reversible order. A text, then, does not have *literariness* (a term used by the Russian formalist critic Roman Jakobson which suggests that the meaning of a literary work lies in the form of the work). It is not different from other texts but is involved with them. Its meaning is always provisional and so it can never be fully and finally determined. So the job of the literary critic is to find out how a literary text disrupts the apparent hierarchy and suggests other perspectives.

Paul de Man (1919–83) was perhaps the most notable practitioner of Derrida's deconstruction theory in America. He had a different style from Derrida but he shared his method of analysis and objects of study with him. He wrote *Blindness and Insight* (1971) under Derrida's influence in which he argued that critics achieve insight into a literary work only through some kind of blindness. He discusses the case of New Critics who were inspired by Coleridge's concept of organic form. The concept was that poetry has unity and coherence like a natural form. The New Critics did not seek unity and coherence of the natural world in poetry but discovered many-sided and ambiguous meanings. This was because they mistakenly believed that the interpretation of the parts and the whole of poetry would reveal its form, characterised by unity and coherence. Instead they were rewarded with the discovery of different layers of meaning. In *Allegories of Reading* (1979) de Man dealt with 'tropes.' Language is full of tropes and because of their shifting nature they destabilise direct or literal meaning. Critics cannot decide between literal and figural meaning and their criticism becomes another exercise in figural language like that of literature.

Michel Foucault (1926–1984) is one of the most resourceful and radical thinkers of the poststructuralist era. He constituted another influential strand of poststructuralist thought that was different from Derrida's theory of language and textuality. He concentrated on the relation between power and knowledge which together give rise to discourse. He did not propose any systematic theory or a set of methodologies but constantly broke away from his own methods. His writings are difficult to classify; however, they fall in certain groups like the earlier *archaeological* and later *genealogical* method of analysis. Foucault extensively dealt with the history of different institutions like madness, prison, medicine and sexuality but his method was anti-historical. He was not interested in the traditional method of historical analysis like the chronology of events, cause and effect, past theory and practice of various institutions and their continuity without any great interruptions. He was interested in exploring power and its role in bringing discontinuities and interruptions in discursive formations. It is obvious then that his approach was interdisciplinary, multi-dimensional and without any aim to establish a particular thesis or methodology. His archaeological method is evident in his seminal work *The Archaeology of Knowledge* (1969), which was an attempt to offer impersonal history—how people come to think and live the way they do and the internal history of social practices—how things work. His genealogical method is used in his masterpiece *Discipline and Punish* (1975), which focused on non-discursive practices and explored the links between non-discursive practices and minor events. He turned away from great and the spectacular events in history to discontinuous, discredited and illegitimate knowledge that have been denied space in history. His approach to language and literature is precisely like his approach to social practices. He criticises the 'classical' status accorded to literary writing and does not expect it to function as a circulator of values and ideals. Literature, for him, works through the stages of selection, sacralisation, and institutional validation. In his important essay *What is an Author?* (1969), he expresses his views about writing and authorship more explicitly. He goes beyond Barthes' announcement of the death of the author and argues that authorship is a more complex issue. Like Barthes, Foucault also rejects the idea of the individual author as the foundation or origin of a literary discourse. The author should not aim at self-expression or to assign a definite meaning to his writing.

Salient Features of Poststructuralism

1) Poststructuralism is a set of theories which examine language, its nature and function.

2) Prominent poststructural theories include Jacques Lacan's psychoanalytic theory, Michel Foucault's archaeological and genealogical theory, Roland Barthes' semiological theory and Jacques Derrida's deconstruction.

3) Deconstruction is an examination of philosophical texts as constructs of language. Derrida demonstrated the unstable, fluid and inconsistent nature of language. He reversed commonly accepted oppositional pairs in language to show that hierarchies are made and are not inherent, and proposed that no element from the binary opposition is marginal and/or central. His radical views about language can be summed up in the following points— a) language does not merely communicate one meaning, b) it does not lead its users to meaning but to another set of words, c) language is not just differential but self-referential as well

4) Paul de Man argued that the critic's awareness of the multidimensional nature of language was necessary to destabilise established meanings and hierarchies.

5) Michel Foucault, who proposed the archaeological and genealogical method, argued against classical status being bestowed upon a work of literature or an author

Introduction to J. H. Miller's 'Derrida and Literature'

J. Hillis Miller, one of the important practitioners of the Yale school of deconstruction (The Yale school of deconstruction was an influential group of American critics that consisted of J. H. Miller,

Paul de Man, Geoffrey Hartman and Harold Bloom. These critics offered a characteristically American version of criticism which was different from both Continental and Anglo-American criticism. These critics were heavily influenced by Jacques Derrida's theory of deconstruction and became the most prominent practitioners of deconstruction in America) explicates Jacques Derrida's ideas of literature and his method of literary criticism in his essay, 'Derrida and Literature'. He supports his explanation with a wide variety of references to Derrida's work and to other philosophical and literary works. Miller's task is a difficult one, that of explaining the complex meeting of literary and philosophical ideas. Derrida's deconstruction is generally supposed to be a language-oriented theory and analysing his ideas, terms and strategies is considered to be an intensive exercise into philosophical matters. Miller convincingly reveals the seriousness and sincerity of Derrida's consideration of literature and also substantiates his claim that Derrida is one of the great literary critics of the twentieth century. The explanation is lengthy and heavily illustrative. But we can sum up the essay in three broad points— 1) Miller interprets Derrida's idea of literature in contrast with the speech act theory of J. L. Austin and John Searle, 2) Miller discusses Derrida's ideas about literature like 'iterability', literature as 'invention' (and not essence) and the association of literature with democracy and freedom of speech, 3) Miller brings out the characteristic features of Derrida's practical literary criticism.

Miller assembles all the important details of Derrida's consideration of literature and develops them into a coherent and convincing argument. This is evident from the very opening of the essay as it begins with a quotation by Derrida in which he states that literature is his most constant interest. Miller carries forward the key point of the quotation—literature—and argues that Derrida, apart from his other distinctions, is also one of the great literary critics of the twentieth century. Derrida is a great literary critic not because he proposed a literary theory but because he provided brilliant and insightful readings of literary works by major authors ranging from the French poet, Stephen Mallarme, to the novelist, Marcel Proust.

Miller mentions that Derrida's speech act theory can help us understand his consideration of literature and elaborates this point. Derrida's speech act theory is based on the criticism of J. L. Austin and John Searle. J. L. Austin (1911–1960) was a famous British philosopher of language who developed a theory of speech acts. Austin found that language was invariably tied to making statements and these statements were often understood as true or false. In other words, speakers used sentences only to describe some state of affair or to state a fact, which must be either true or false. Utterances were assertions cut off from the actions they described. He changed this focus on the linguistic aspect to 'performative utterances'. His central argument was that utterances are not just assertions or statements but actions also; that is, utterances in certain conditions can bring about changes in some institutional state of affairs. For example, if someone says 'You're fired' it may mean that someone is dismissed from his/her job and if someone says 'I second' it may mean that a motion is placed before an assembly and it is seconded by the speaker. Austin made it clear that there is no direct relation between the action (here either the dismissal from a job or the seconding of the motion) that the words describe and the actual completion of the action. He proposed another important point in his famous book *How to Do Things with Words* (1962) that actions are communicated on different levels and with different intentions. He offered three levels or acts of uttering words. These are the locutionary act, the illocutionary act and the perlocutionary act. They can be explained with an example. A boss of a private company may utter the words: 'There will be a meeting of the employees at 11 a.m. in the Central Hall.' This utterance itself is a locutionary act. The illocutionary act is that it is an order or notification and the perlocutionary act is that through this utterance the boss causes the employees to assemble at a certain time and at a certain place. The perlocutionary act mobilises words into action. Austin distinguished between the conditions under which performative utterances could become successful or could fail. This is his 'doctrine of the Infelicities'. Derrida criticised this doctrine in his last essay 'Signature Event Context', in the book *Margins of Philosophy* (trans. 1982). He rejected Austin's argument of the ideal speech situations and tried to prove literature as a felicitous act. This debate with Derrida was carried further by one of Austin's former students, John Searle (an American philosopher of language).

Austin and Searle drive literature out of the domain of felicitous speech acts on the ground that it is iterable. Iterability is a term taken from the Sanskrit word 'itara', meaning 'other' or the Latin 'iter', meaning 'again'. Derrida uses this term to suggest at least three things in relation to the analysis of speech acts: 1) to suggest difference, 2) to suggest decontextualisation or removal of context and 3) to suggest recontextualisation or association of contexts. These suggestions are against Austin's speech act theory because Austin insists on contexts and even distinguishes between ideal conditions and non-ideal conditions. To further explain the term 'iterability', we can take the example of language. When we use certain sounds we do not invent them but take them from an already available common pool of sounds. Sounds produce different meanings each time we use them. Even repeatedly used sounds produce different meanings. The term also means 'differance'. 'Differance', a French portmanteau word means both *difference* and *deferral* or postponement. Derrida's argument is that we cannot express or find meaning in its pure form because we have to take the help of language. We cannot express the meaning inside us as it is because the expression is an outside act and done through the medium of language. In such cases, we express outside of ourselves and enter into the play of language where everything related to meaning goes beyond our control. As a result meaning does not remain pure and intact. Austin calls literature infelicitous, non-serious and etiolated. Derrida, on the other hand, makes iterability a point of contention and calls it an intrinsic feature of language. He contends that iterability should be taken into account in the analysis of every speech act or sign.

This feature of iterability is present in both repeated utterances and in utterances used only once. It (Miller calls it the structure of repeatability) always internally divides or multiplies all types of utterances. For Derrida, literature is the possibility for any utterance, writing or mark to be iterated (repeated) in many different contexts. The utterance or writing is able to function in the absence of an identifiable speaker, context, reference or hearer. This does not mean that language does not refer to anything or anyone. It means that language refers to many possibilities of referents or meanings. Miller gives the example of Kate Croy, a character in Henry James' (1843–1916, an American novelist) novel, *The Wings of the Dove* (1902). A reader will never know the real referent for Kate Croy; that is, a reader will never find the real Kate Croy. The description of the character of Kate Croy in the novel will give the reader the impression that Kate is an actual person, in real life, but she is only fictitious. It means that Kate Croy refers to many Kate Croys and not to a definite, real Kate Croy. Derrida argues that any piece of language, oral or written, can be taken as literature. This is so because the possibility of being taken as literature is intrinsic to literature. In other words literature depends on the possibility of separating language from its firm social or biographical context and allowing it free play as fiction.

Miller criticises the usual university-based institutionalised attempts to study literary works as social, historical or autobiographical documents. He points out that this kind of institutionalised study of literature suppresses and ignores what is properly literary in literature. To further explain the point, Miller quotes Derrida's definition of literature. But before we go to Derrida's definition of literature it is sensible to know two terms that Derrida uses: *transcendent* and *non-transcendent*. By *transcendent*, he means going beyond the interest for signifier or language and in search of the referent or meaning. By *non-transcendent* he means taking interest into finding out the signifier or language in the study of an oral or written text. 'Transcendent' is search for meaning and 'non-transcendent' is search for play of language. For Derrida, literature has no pure originality and so it should be studied in a non-transcendent way (that is concentrating on its language play). He also argues that philosophical, scientific or journalistic texts can be studied in a non-transcendent way. We know that we read non-literary texts not for the sake of its language but for the sake of meaning, but Derrida's insistence here is that we should study them as linguistic constructions. According to Derrida, there is no text that is literary in itself. Therefore literarity (quality of being literary) is not a natural essence or an intrinsic quality of even a so-called literary text. After explaining this initial part of Derrida's definition, Miller turns to its relation to phenomenology. He explains that Derrida borrows terms like 'transcendent', 'noematic' and 'noetic' from Edmund Husserl's phenomenology. He also explains that Derrida's view of literature as a phenomenon is different from Husserl's. Husserl gives more importance to the reader's perception of a text as a literary text. Derrida, on the other hand, argues that it is the reader's choice to follow a transcendent or non-transcendent method of reading a literary text. This is because the possibility of the text being taken as literature is not in the mind of the reader but in the text. Thus Derrida shifts Husserl's focus on the reader's perception to the text. Miller illustrates another important aspect of Derrida's consideration of literature. Derrida observes that when we consider a piece of language as a literary work, it not only involves intentionality (the reader's perception) but also a complex set of conventions, rules, institutions and historical features. This complexity is present both within the text and the reader's mind. It is not the private, subjective perception of the reader that influences this perception, but also the rules and conventions within the text. We, as readers of the text, do not act as private egos. The rules and institutions of our cultural community act through us. Thus our understanding of a text as a literary text is an interactive, intersubjective act.

Miller proceeds to further spell out Derrida's point on rules, conventions and institutions, and how they characterise a text as a literary text. According to Derrida, literature as an institution in the West is linked to democracy and freedom of speech. This means that literature has a short history and it emerged with Western-style democracies in the late seventeenth century. Continuing this point Miller quotes another passage by Derrida in which he argues that literature is a modern invention and not an essence. Derrida associates literature with democracy and freedom of speech because literature is given the right to free speech and it can afford the possibility of non-responsibility. This is where the contradiction between literature and democracy becomes apparent. In democracy an individual is held responsible for his/her actions or speech whereas there is absolute freedom of speech in literature and an author is not held responsible for his/her actions/speech. This means that an author is free to write anything and s/he is not responsible for his/her writing. S/He need not respond to any questions related to his/her work and explain his/her position or views. This non-responsibility of the author is supported by the common assumption that the narrator of a novel must not be identified with the author. Miller refers to the Russian novelist Fyodor Dostoyevsky's (1821–81) novel *Crime and Punishment* (1866). In this novel Dostoyevsky separates himself from the axe-murder and explains that he is just an author, has imagined an axe-murderer and has told a story about him.

Miller extends this discussion of the non-responsibility and non-responsiveness of the author to Derrida's notion of the 'ideality of the literary object'. This refers to Husserl's transcendent phenomenology and it accounts for the non-responsibility and non-responsiveness of the author. Derrida calls a literary work an object. It is not, however, a material object like a stone or a jug.

It is an object that the mind perceives and an object bound to language and limited to its form. It is not free from cultural or historical determination like the mathematical objects of number, algebra and graphing. In spite of such dissimilarity between mathematical objects and literary works, Miller points out the similarity between them. The similarity between a triangle and a literary work is shown, as an example. Like a triangle, a literary work is an ideal object. A triangle is an ideal object because its existence does not depend upon any actual/particular triangle. The ideal triangle will exist even after the actually inscribed triangles disappear. This is true with a literary work as well. The reader can have access to Henry James' novel *The Golden Bowl* (1904) only through its reading. And even though every single copy of this novel is destroyed it will still exist as an ideal object. Thus, because of the ideality of literary work, the author refuses to respond and becomes non-responsible.

Miller explores the convincing justification for the author's non-responsibility and non-response with another of Derrida's concepts, called 'invention'. He regards literature as an invention and not an essence. In order to explain this concept Miller refers to Derrida's analysis of a short poem of eight lines, 'Fable' by the French poet Francis Ponge (1899–1988). Derrida distinguishes between the two forms of invention. The first is the ordinary sense of invention in which invention paradoxically invents nothing. This is because it is a statement based on known facts. The second is the invention that produces a new aspect of an event through a merging of chance and destiny. Derrida shows the possibility and impossibility of both meanings. The literary object is ideal in the sense of having been there all along. It is accessible only through the words in the work but it was always already there. This is one form of invention of the possible, of what already exists there. The other is an invention of the impossible, the invention of what is not there. This invention creates space for 'the other' (which is apparently not there in the text but enters it when a place is created for it). It is done by destabilising the language of the text. Derrida applies this destabilising strategy to Ponge's poem and shows how it allows 'the other' to intervene. He states that this 'other' is not singular but plural in nature. It defines 'we', a community of human subjects with all the features of society, contract, institution, and so on. This invention of 'the other' creates new rules that imply a new 'we', a new community. It produces multiplicity of meanings and resists any single, determinate and fixed understanding of the poem.

Miller returns to Derrida's association of literature with freedom of speech and non-responsibility. He justifies the author's non-responsibility and non-response in the light of Derrida's concept of 'the secret'. The secret makes the comparison between the ideality of literary object and the actual literary work impossible. It is through the words that we can have access to the ideality of the literary work. We can know only what the words say. We can never know the unsaid by any means. The unsaid remains an impenetrable secret. As an example, Miller refers to one of the incidents in James' *The Wings of the Dove*, where the dying Milly Theale writes a letter to Densher but Densher can never read it because Kate Croy throws it unread in the fire. Significantly the reader can never know about the content of the letter. It remains a permanent secret Milly takes to her grave. Derrida's comment is very revealing in this regard. He considers literature as a possibility of saying everything about the secret without touching upon it; that is, that the reader can have many hypothetical meanings but cannot have access to the secret. Miller thus explains that Derrida's concept of the secret helps to know the non-responsible and non-responsive state of the author. The author himself does not know the secret so he cannot tell about it and cannot take personal responsibility for it.

With this elaborate explanation of Derrida's theoretical arguments and concepts about literature, Miller proceeds to the last part of his essay. In this part he clears up the nature of Derrida's practical criticism of literary texts and its features. The first feature is that we cannot have a uniform understanding of Derrida's literary criticism because he has not built a unified method of criticism. On the contrary he explores different sets of ideas, terms and techniques with every new text. The second feature is Derrida's complex association with the French method of close reading called 'explication de texte'. This method is different from the American New Critical method in that it not only pays great attention to grammatical, rhetorical and syntactical aspects of a given text but also considers historical and biographical contexts. Derrida was trained in this method of textual analysis which insisted on close reading, attention to linguistic details and utmost care in citations. But he does not practice this method strictly within its specified limits. He practises it in such a manner that he bends its norms and shows its limits. The third feature is the effect of his preparation for oral explication of his criticism. Derrida prepared his literary criticism for oral presentation in conferences and seminars and so factors like limits of time and space and elaboration of the selected topic influence his criticism. Miller cites the example of Derrida's essay, 'The Law of Genre', which was prepared for oral presentation. In the midst of the essay he says that he has many more things to say about the 'interpretative alternatives' and the 'particularly rich combinatory of possibilities' of the two sentences he had begun by *uttering*. The fourth feature is Derrida's unending creativity. Derrida is so innovative and productive that his search for new reading strategies never ends. This can be observed in his characteristic style of writing, which is curiously neither an established and repeatedly-used mode by Derrida himself nor easily imitable for others. Miller points out that his essays are 'exuberant' (lively and energetic), exorbitant (elaborate), excessive, iterative (repetitive) and hyperbolic (extravagant). In spite of being too long and elaborate, his essays leave many things unsaid or only hinted at. He does not offer a passive description of a text but analyses multiple and contradictory aspects that the text holds up to him. He explores the possibility of 'the other' in the text (this includes dissembling the text in unusual ways and revealing many contradictory layers of meaning even in the obviously straightforward expressions). The fifth feature is that Derrida demonstrates that the parts of a text are greater in importance than the whole. He builds his analysis on an apparently insignificant aspect of a text (or an insignificant text of a great writer), like a single word or phrase, and interrogates it at length. He assumes that in literary criticism, it is better to concentrate minutely on parts than to make generalisations about the whole.

Miller mentions certain doubts that Derrida's views about literature and practice of literary criticism might raise. For example Derrida chooses literary texts that fit his assumptions about literature. But the fact is that he was invited on several occasions to deal with specified authors like Paul Celan (1920–1970, French poet and translator) and James Joyce, and so he chose specific texts. Another doubt is related to his juxtaposition of literary works with philosophical, anthropological, psychoanalytical and other non-literary works. He juxtaposes the French poet Charles Baudelaire with the sociologist Marcel Mauss, the French novelist and playwright Jean Genet with the philosopher Hegel, the novelist Franz Kafka with the philosopher Immanuel Kant, the poet Edgar Allan Poe with the psychoanalyst Jacques Lacan and so on. But he has himself asserted that he analyses literary work for its own sake and not for the sake of comparison. Literature for him is an exemplary place that brings into the open the wholly other, the secret. Therefore his method of criticism takes on the verbal structure of the given text, teases its apparent unity and coherence and creates space for other, subversive elements of the text. Derrida's literary criticism helps the readers know breaks, inconsistencies and the possibility of several referents in the given text.

Key Points

- Miller's essay can be divided into three parts—a) his interpretation of Derrida's idea about literature in contrast with the speech act theory of J. L. Austin and

John Searle, b) a discussion of Derrida's ideas about literature—iterability, invention and association of literature with democracy and freedom of speech, and c) an explanation of Derrida's practical literary criticism.

- Miller begins by discussing two contrasting viewpoints on the nature of literature. Austin calls literature infelicitous, non-serious and etiolated. Derrida's counter-argument that literature is iterable.
- Literature offers the possibility for any utterance, writing or mark to be iterated (repeated) in many different contexts.
- Derrida associates literature with democracy and freedom of speech because literature assumes the right to free speech and it can afford the possibility of non-responsibility. The author is free to write anything and is not responsible for his writing.
- Derrida has a non-transcendent method of examining literature.
- Miller explains Derrida's notion of the 'ideality of the literary object'.
- Literature is seen as an invention and not as essence.
- The author does not know 'the secret' of literary creation so he cannot speak about it or take personal responsibility for it.
- Miller states that the chief features of Derrida's literary criticism are— a) no uniform, singular critical method, b) complex application of close reading method, c) show the effect of preparation for oral presentation in conferences and seminars on his literary criticism, d) Derrida's

unending creativity in innovating new strategies for reading literary texts, e) Derrida's demonstration that the parts of a text are greater than the whole

Exercises

Answer the following questions in 100–150 words.

1) What is iterability?
2) Why does Derrida link literature to democracy?
3) Why is literature invention for Derrida?
4) What is the secret of the author's non-responsiveness?
5) State any two features of Derrida's literary criticism.

Answer the following questions in 250–300 words.

1) What are the features of poststructuralism?
2) How do you justify Miller's claim that Derrida is one of the great critics of the twentieth century?
3) Elaborate upon Derrida's argument that literature is not an essence but an invention.
4) What relation does Derrida observe between literature, democracy and freedom of speech?
5) Explain Derrida's method of literary criticism.

PSYCHOANALYTIC CRITICISM

Historical Background

Taking a psychological approach to literature is not new to literary criticism. Aristotle in his classic definition of tragedy mentioned the emotions of pity and fear responsible for catharsis. Philip Sidney in his defence of the moral effects of poetry outlined the psychological process behind poetic creation. The Romantic poets Coleridge and Wordsworth proposed psychological theories of imagination. In the beginning of the twentieth century, I. A. Richards' analysis of poetry as a process of psychological communication offered a different perspective to literary studies. It may be argued that almost every literary critic has been concerned at some time or the other with the psychology of writing. In the psychological approach, the psychology of the writer and/or the psychology of the characters is examined. In the twentieth century this approach came to be associated with a particular school called psychoanalysis. It was developed by the Austrian-German psychologist **Sigmund Freud** (1856–1939). Psychoanalysis is different from traditional psychology and psychiatry. Psychology is a broad science that examines the observable phenomena of human behaviour. Psychiatry is a kind of therapy that deals with serious mental disorders. Psychoanalysis, on the other hand, tries to reveal the common disturbances and desires that lie under the surface of the human mind. It is the discovery and understanding of man's unconscious mind.

It is interesting to know how Freud came to propose the revolutionary theories of psychoanalysis, which included the psychology of human sexuality and interpretation of dreams. In the early period of his medical practice Freud worked as an assistant to the great neurologist Jean-Martin Charcot in Paris. It was during this period that he took a keen interest in the treatment of neurosis (psychological disorders like hysteria, depression, phobia, and compulsive and obsessive disorders) and learnt that psychology and not neurology was important in the treatment of neurosis and hysteria. He used the technique of hypnosis in the treatment of the neurotic patients. In this technique the patient was asked to recall original incidents related to certain symptoms. Freud with his friend Josef Breuer published his observations in a book titled *Study on Hysteria* (1895). However Freud began to think hypnosis was inadequate as a treatment method, and developed a new technique called 'free association' in which he asked neurotic patients to freely express their thoughts or fantasies. He neither interrupted them nor censored the flow of their free expression. This technique worked much better than hypnosis because hypnosis required complete submission of the patient to instructions and a doctor's authority. Free association was free from external influences and was a kind of self-help treatment where the patient could better understand and solve his/her problems. This was a revolutionary development and the beginning of psychoanalysis. The years between 1887 and 1902 were perhaps the most fruitful and creative period in Freud's life in which he developed the most significant ideas of psychoanalysis and established it as an independent discipline.

The next stage was Freud's study of dreams, which resulted in his publishing his theory about dreams and how to interpret them in *The Interpretation of Dreams* in 1900. Freud argued that dreams are disguised fulfilment of repressed wishes. They fulfill repressed childhood wishes and also present-day wishes. This wish fulfilment is disguised through symbols, which the psychoanalyst helps the patient interpret. Freud carried this enquiry further and asserted that dreams can help in solving neurotic problems. Most neurotic problems originate in repressed wishes of early childhood and analysis of dreams can take the analyst to the root cause of such problems. He divided the content of dreams into two parts—the *latent* and the *manifest* part. The manifest part is the dream itself and the latent part is the hidden meaning of the dream which can be discerned only after careful investigation.

Freud proposed a theory about the structure of human mind. He divided the mind into three parts—id, ego and superego. The *id* is the unconscious, primitive, dark and inaccessible part of the mind. It is chaotic and unorganised and does not follow the categories of time and place. It is ruled by libido—repressed sexual urges and desires. It works towards the satisfaction of fulfilling repressed desires and constantly seeks pleasure. Freud called the id the pleasure principle. The *ego* works as an intermediary between the id and the external world. It is the conscious, secondary and accessible part of the mind. It is well-organised and follows the categories of time and place. It regulates and controls the drives of the libido, balancing it against the demands of the external world. Freud called it the reality principle as opposed to the pleasure principle of the id. The *superego* works at a higher level than the ego. According to Freud as the child grows, he/she becomes independent of his parents, acquires cultural and moral ideas and norms of behaviour. These ideal norms of behaviour are internalised, and form the superego. The superego regulates the ego so that all behaviour and conscious thought is in accordance with societal standards. Essentially, the superego is the mind's moral guardian.

Freud studied how libido—the primitive energy of the sexual drives—works in human beings. He made two important observations in this regard. The first observation is that sexuality begins in early childhood, and the second is that the adult sexual function is the result of several earlier stages. The first stage of sexual function is called the *auto-erotic stage*, during which the infant gets pleasure through oral and anal parts of his/her body. During this stage the object of desire for the infant is his/her mother because she is the closest person to him/her. The infant outgrows this stage by overcoming what Freud called the Oedipus Complex. The libido of every infant is directed towards his/

her mother, but boys and girls overcome this in different ways. Boys view their fathers as competition and grow hostile to them. The father is a more powerful figure, however, and the threat of castration forces boys to give up their desire for their mothers. They then begin to identify with their fathers, in the hope of attaining a woman like their mothers someday. This process is more complicated with girls. Though as infants, their libido is directed towards the mother, they cannot hope to fulfill this urge, as they discern that they lack a penis. Girls then develop 'penis envy', and develop hostility towards their mothers for depriving them of a penis. They cannot identify themselves with either their mothers or fathers. They re-direct their libidos towards their fathers, which begins the process of identification with their mothers, and their identity formation as women. What follows is a stage called *latency*, where no sexual activity occurs and the emphasis is on cognitive and social development. At puberty, the individual concentrates his/her sexual energy on his/her genitals and links them with reproduction, marking the transition to stable sexual and emotional relationships with the opposite sex. The libido and how it develops as an individual grows informs the development of the human mind. Failure to develop appropriately during any of the psychosexual stages results in neurosis.

Psychoanalysis developed as a discipline due to the group of followers Freud had in Vienna. Notable names among these include Dr. **Alfred Adler** (1870–1937), Dr. **C. G. Jung** (1875–1961) and **Otto Rank** (1884–1939). Freud, with these friends and followers, developed the Viennese Psychoanalytic Society. Adler is known for his discovery of the 'inferiority complex'. He argued that self-assertion and struggle for power dominate human behaviour and that everyone in the world suffers from an 'inferiority complex'. He did not agree with Freud's theory of sexuality and the theory of Oedipus complex and soon withdrew from the group. Jung was a Swiss psychiatrist who applied psychoanalytic principles to the study of schizophrenia. He worked as a close associate of Freud from 1907 to 1913. He then left the Psychoanalytic Society and established an independent school of thought called 'Analytical Psychology'. He differed from Freud on the matters of the unconscious and sexuality. He proposed the term '*collective unconscious*' in place of Freud's individual unconscious. He argued that the collective unconscious works as a racial memory wherein archetypes (images, rituals and beliefs of a society) pass from generation to generation through genes. He disagreed with Freud on sexuality (libido) and claimed that libido is not purely sexual.

Freud's method of psychoanalysis had a far-reaching impact on literary studies. Freud, himself a gifted writer, wrote extensively about art and literature and analysed some literary texts in the light of his ideas. His views on Sophocles' *Oedipus Rex* and Shakespeare's *Hamlet* are quite famous. He offered a psychoanalytic examination of the novella *Gradiva* by the German writer Wilhelm Jensen. He also wrote a paper on Dostoevsky's novels by the title, 'Dostoevsky and Parricide' (1928) and claimed that Dostoevsky depicted so many violent and murderous characters in his novels because he himself suffered from similar tendencies. 'Creative Writers and Day-Dreaming', a paper written in 1907, outlines his views on literature and literary creation from a psychoanalytic lens. He argued that writers write in order to satisfy their unsatisfied sexual drives. In other words creative writing is the wish fulfilment of its author. When writers do not find means to satisfy their repressed desires they turn away from reality and engage in 'phantasy'—their creative writing.

Freud's revolutionary psychoanalytic ideas opened up new ways to interpret literary works. But the relation between psychoanalysis and literary criticism was firmly established by the writings of the British psychologist, **Ernest Alfred Jones** (1879–1958). He examined famous literary works in the light of Freud's ideas and ably demonstrated the application of psychoanalysis to literary studies. He wrote monographs on Keats' poems, and two of Shakespeare's plays, *Hamlet* and *Oedipus*.

The second phase of psychoanalysis begins with the French psychoanalyst **Jacques Lacan** (1901–81). He is the most influential psychoanalyst after Freud because he reinterpreted Freud's views in the light of the changing intellectual scene and enlarged its scope and applicability by adding his own theories. Apart from Freud, Lacan was also influenced by Roman Jakobson, Ferdinand de Saussure and F. J. Hegel. Contemporary theories of language attracted Lacan's attention because his study of the unconscious had given him ideas similar to those used in language theories. He tried therefore to re-state his interpretation of the unconscious in linguistic terminology. Saussure's structural linguistics was perhaps the most important influence on Lacan and he extensively references it to express his views on the unconscious. Lacan states that there are three orders of the mind—the imaginary, the symbolic, and the real. The imaginary order is a pre-Oedipal stage in which the infant finds himself and his mother as a single body. He cannot distinguish himself from his mother or other objects in the world. In other words the infant cannot conceive his own self and the 'other.' This is followed by the symbolic order wherein the infant becomes aware of himself and the world around. This order separates him from his mother and brings him into the world of social categories, gender differences and the play of language. The entry of the child into the symbolic order is in fact entry into language. Language defines his position in the social setup, and Lacan calls this the subject position. If the child is to become a part of society, he must know the system of signification called language. In order to speak the child must differentiate 'I' from 'you'. The child thus identifies his position with the first person singular pronoun 'I' and continues to know himself in other positions like 'he', 'she', 'boy' and 'girl'. The subject position changes when 'you' (the other) speaks to 'I' (the self). 'I' becomes 'you' and 'you' becomes 'I'. Such reversal of subject position does not allow for a fixed and permanent position to the subject and it remains in flux. In Saussurean terms, the subject, like the signifier, always keeps changing its position and its meaning (subjectivity/identity) and the signified remains unattainable. (It is important however to know that unlike Saussure, Lacan does not believe that the two terms of the subject/signifier and the object/signified can represent reality under certain circumstances. He strongly believes that reality escapes the efforts of both—the subject and the object. This view of incompleteness is very much like poststructuralist scepticism.) Lacan believes that the unconscious is structured like language. It works very much like language in which the repressed desires express themselves in the hope of fulfilment but remain unfulfilled like the signifier that tries to represent the signified/meaning but fails to do so in entirety. As language disrupts any attempt at definite meaning the unconscious also disrupts consciousness. Lacan never really deals with his third order of the real. He considers it impossible because it is beyond the reach of signification.

Freud and Lacan's theories about human psychology, self, sexuality and the unconscious have greatly influenced many theorists and critics. The most notable among them are the French feminist critics Julia Kristeva and Luce Irigaray, who were influenced by Lacan's writings on female sexuality. Kristeva and Irigaray both reconsider the Freudian theories of Oedipus complex and female sexuality from the feminist point of view and reject the patriarchal thinking implicit in them. The Slovenian critic **Slavoj Žižek** (b.1949) is probably the most influential psychoanalytic critic in the poststructural period after Lacan. He applied psychoanalytic theory to social and cultural topics. For example he made an engaging study of Marx and Hegel's theories from the Lacanian point of view in his book *The Sublime Object of Ideology* (1989). In the succeeding book *Looking Awry* (1991), he offered a Lacanian interpretation of popular culture including the films of Alfred Hitchcock.

Salient Features of Psychoanalytic Criticism

1) Psychoanalysis is a systematic analysis of the human mind, especially of the unconscious.

2) Freud's general proposition was that creative writing is the product of the unconscious and that the object of psychoanalytic criticism is to discover the operation of this process.

3) Literary work is interpreted as a substitute for the author's unconscious desires and drives, and the job of the psychoanalytic critic is to explain this process of substitution.

4) Psychoanalytic critics study the linguistic and symbolic patterns in the text and attempt to reveal the subconscious motives behind the surface description.

5) Psychoanalytic critics following Freud's lead examine literary works in the light of the concepts that he proposed, like libido, dream interpretation or the Oedipus complex. These and many other concepts are applied to factors like the author, text, readers and characters to determine the workings of the unconscious behind the creative process. Critics follow different strategies to examine these factors but they do so with the common intention of unravelling the unconscious.

6) Apart from Freud's method of psychoanalysis Carl Jung's concept of 'collective unconscious' is also applied by psychoanalytic critics. This method explores the relationship between the literary work and the collective unconscious, which, according to Jung, is the racial memory through which the human spirit expresses itself.

7) Jacques Lacan's psychoanalytical theories, heavily influenced by concepts from linguistics, are also extensively used by psychoanalytic critics. Lacan stated that the unconscious was structured like language. His linking of the unconscious and language, his three orders of the mind and various other concepts influenced later theorists like Julia Kristeva, Luce Irigaray and Slavoj Žižek.

Introduction to Frederick Feirstein's 'Psychoanalysis and Poetry'

This essay is written with the purpose of clearing the misconceptions about psychoanalysis. It also shows the resemblances between the working of psychoanalysis and poetry. Feirstein takes the working of the unconscious part of the mind as the common basis of psychoanalysis and poetry and shows how it expresses itself in a particular order and form. The narrative elements work as a medium to express the workings of the unconscious in both psychoanalysis and poetry.

In the very opening sentence Feirstein refers to the abandonment of the Formalist notion of poetry—its techniques of metre and rhyme as well as conventions such as the linear narrative structure. (Formalism was a literary movement prevalent in Russia during the 1920s and '30s. The essence of this method is summed up in Shklovsky's definition of literature—'the sum total of all stylistic devices employed in it [literary text]'). The most prominent critics of the movement were Viktor Shklovsky, Jan Mukarovsky and Roman Jakobson. The important features of the movement were a) search for a scientific basis for the theory of literature and interest in method, b) study of aesthetic effects produced by literary devices, c) seeing the literary work as an organic unit where formal devices are more important than content, d) study of verbal organisation of literary texts including the technical ability and skills of the writer, e) formal devices (both structural and textual) considered more important than content, f) literature being regarded as a special use of language; so literary language must be different from non-literary language, g) distinction is drawn between plot and story: plot is strictly literary whereas story is raw material that needs artistic arrangement. He finds the origin of this in the misunderstanding about the unconscious in psychoanalysis. The unconscious was misunderstood as totally 'free'. Feirstein argues that this misunderstanding emerged with the early Modernist artists. With the passing of time it became the standard assumption. Literary critics/theorists used this wrong assumption to attack the use of 'form' in poetry. It was treated as an artificial imposition on the unconscious processes thought to be the source of creativity. However, recent work in neuroscience and dream research shows that the unconscious is not lawless. It has its own rules and with proper training we can observe it working in a particular order. Feirstein calls these rules the 'primary processes' of displacement (a process in which the emotion associated with one idea or experience is detached from it and attached to another one) and condensation (a psychological process in which two or more thoughts/ideas in the unconscious merge into one symbol). These rules about the working of the unconscious are also the rules that inform the metaphors of poetry and action metaphors of narrative and drama.

Feirstein holds the academia responsible for the misleading interpretation of both the unconscious and the Formalist notions of narrative poetry. Psychoanalysis is essentially a narrative, because it is the story of a person's life traced back to its origin. Like Greek tragedy, psychoanalysis works from effect to cause. To explain his point, Feirstein gives the example of psychoanalytic treatment. During this treatment the analyst interacts with and interchanges roles with the analysand (the person who undergoes psychoanalysis). The analyst acquires different roles/selves and becomes the significant other of the analysand during the clinical treatment. Through the narrative and key metaphors the analyst gradually comes to know about the motivations of various selves that the unconscious of the analysand takes on. The analysand also realises that he/she is living a double life—one is the conscious life and the other is the fantasy life. The fantasy life causes many selves in the mind of the analysand (that is, the analysand assumes the role of other personas) and creates plots and subplots in his/her mind. The analysand's mind uses fixed but often false plots to organise unconscious fantasies and all this is done in response to his/her forbidden wishes and traumas.

This is very much like a poet who uses stock plots to organise his/her poem. During the course of the gradual unfolding of the analysand's unconscious the analyst traces the origin of certain fantasies to the analysand's childhood. Both come to know that certain fantasy plots are fixed and appear repetitively. Such stock plots may be the Oedipus Complex or the fantasy of anal birth or the Cinderella fantasy. These are called 'personal myths' and they control large parts of our behaviour. We construct such personal myths for survival and growth. We continue to do so throughout our lives because we want pleasure and we need to change according to the situation. Likewise some of us reproduce these personal myths in the form of narrative art. Just as we create new versions of personal myths (fantasies) for pleasure and adjustment, the maturing writer also explores plots, themes and patterns of imagery. This exploration of fantasies helps the writer find out solutions to inner conflicts and also discover further themes. Feirstein points out that if such inner conflicts do not get symbolic representation (like some people find in their artistic expression/writing) they lead to self-mimicry and despair. As a result we feel blocked or boringly repetitive.

Personal myths are based on stereotypes or universal myths. Therefore when the writer offers his personal myths or fantasies they become identifiable with the audience/readers' personal myths. Such identification creates a trance-like condition in the mind of the audience/reader. This condition takes the reader/audience into the writer's myth and gives comfort to his mind. Feirstein argues that we all have experienced such trance-like states with a writer's myth in our adolescence. The pre-conscious part (that part of the mind connected both to the unconscious and to waking reality) of our mind becomes active during such trances, completing our identification with a writer's fantasy. Writers and psychoanalysts both commonly experience such pre-conscious states. The analyst enters the personal myths of the analysand, experiences his/her fantasies and yet remains attached to real world. During the treatment the analysand repeatedly uses one or two central metaphors and they appear in his comments about the self, reality or dreams. The metaphors represent instinctual wishes and can reveal the unconscious to the analyst. The mind uses a single metaphor to express the experience of several traumas (emotional shocks producing lasting harmful effect). This is very much like the poet writing a sequence of lyrics by using a key metaphor. Such metaphors appear repeatedly in the first session of the treatment as clichés (this term is generally used in literary contexts and it refers to words which have lost their meaning because of repetitive use. Feirstein deliberately uses it here to suggest the resemblance between the poetic and the psychoanalytic process). This happens because the pre-conscious does not allow the cliché to turn into a true metaphor. When the analyst becomes successful in turning the cliché into a metaphor he uses it differently to reach to the analysand's unconscious. Feirstein gives the example of an analysand who, in his first session of treatment, described that he often felt he was 'a car in neutral'. He reported that he was in an old sports car that he could not start up. There were many dreams of cars throughout the treatment and they represented different versions of his self. By the final session the analysand found a change in his unconscious. He found the metaphor of a sports car to be very pleasant because he was driving a white BMW car after winning it in a contest. Feirstein further explains that the analysands's dreams are not logically connected in the beginning and they do not have characters and action. But during the treatment such dreams find missing links, characters and action.

Feirstein highlights the resemblance between the art of the psychoanalyst and the poet. According to him psychoanalysts often use metaphors, symbols and narration in their treatment, and they also use form. This is like a 'formal poet' who uses rhyme and metre to create a work of art. These devices—metre and rhyme—do not constrain the poet but rather help create a trance-like state and take him to deeper levels of his mind. Rhyme, for example, leads us to connections of meaning which are otherwise not available to us. He calls such rhymes to be primitive poems because they refer to forgotten fantasies. In continuation of this argument Feirstein refers to the views of the author Theodore Thass-Thienemann. This author had proved that etymology (study of the history of words) is another road to the unconscious. He had argued that association of sounds leads to association of meanings. Sound associations like rhymes originate from the earliest layer of language. They are a part of the forgotten and unknown language of fantasies. Thass-Thienemann and many other psychoanalytic writers like Susan Den, Laurence Kubie, Henry Krystal and Joyce MacDougall have used terms from poetry to explain the working of the mind. Den, for example, explained that the health of the artist depends on the free flow of symbols. Feirstein shares another example of a soldier who had come to him for treatment. He was not able to give the right responses to people because he did not understand their emotions, and the reason for this lay in the absence of rhythm in his speech.

Feirstein refers to another psychoanalytic writer, Joyce McDougall, and shows how her use of narration and symbolisation help recover the health of her patients. He particularly refers to her two books, *Theatres of the Mind* and *Theatres of the Body*. McDougall uses the metaphor of the theatre to understand failure in the symbolisation process and to describe the journey of her patients and herself into the unconscious. She argues that the theatre persona or self repeatedly plays roles from the past and reproduces the same tragedies and comedies; pain and pleasure. Roy Schafer, another psychoanalyst, calls psychoanalysis 'a dialogue' in his book, *The Analytic Attitude*. He regards it as a narrative in which the confused and conflicting story about the self is actively re-experienced in the transference of roles. Feirstein concludes on the note that the goal of psychoanalysis is to cure patients and this can only be achieved by becoming narrative poets.

Key Points

- This essay is Feirstein's attempt to explain the misconceptions about the unconscious and the resemblance between psychoanalysis and poetry.
- The element common to psychoanalysis and poetry is the narrative.
- Formalist techniques of poetry like metre, rhyme and linearity of narrative have been abandoned by modern artists and critics, in favour of freedom of creative expression.
- Such abandonment is a result of a misunderstanding about the unconscious. The unconscious is misunderstood as completely free from all Formalist notions.
- Feirstein argues the unconscious is not free and lawless; proper training can reveal its rules to the investigator.
- He regards the primary processes of displacement and condensation as the chief controlling factors of the unconscious.
- The art of psychoanalysis is essentially narrative and the unconscious works from effect to cause.
- His analysis of the psychoanalytic treatment given to an analysand acts as an illustration of the element of narrative.
- The analysand realises that he lives a double life during the treatment—the conscious life and the fantasy life.
- Poets use stock plots to organise their personal fantasies. These are called personal myths, and are based on stereotypes or universal myths.
- A pre-conscious Pre-conscious state (the state of mind between fantasy and reality) characterises both the poet and the psychoanalyst.

- Metaphor has a central place in the narrative (retelling of past life) of the analysand. It is the instinctual wish that repeatedly appears in the analysand's mind.
- Repetition of a certain metaphor is indicative of a certain instinctual wish.
- Like poets, psychoanalysts also make use of metaphors, symbols and narrative in their treatment of the unconscious.
- The Formalist features of poetry are equally applicable to psychoanalysis—they are not constraints but ways to create a new work of art and to negotiate with the fantasies of the unconscious.
- Rhyme and rhythm expressions are the fantasies of forgotten or suppressed language and are used by both poets and psychoanalysts.

Exercises

Answer the following questions in 100–150 words.

1) Why, according to Feirstein, is the unconscious misunderstood?
2) What is the common element between psychoanalysis and poetry?
3) Describe the metaphor of the analysand taking treatment under Feirstein.
4) Describe the double life of the analysand in short.
5) How are rhymes and rhythm useful to the poet and psychoanalyst?

Answer the following questions in 250–300 words.

1) What are the salient features of psychoanalytic criticism?
2) Summarise Feirstein's argument that abandonment of Formalist principles is the result of the misconception of the unconscious.
3) Explain narrative as the common element between psychoanalysis and poetry.
4) What does Feirstein prove through the description of the relation between the analyst and the analysand?
5) How does metaphor help understand the resemblance between psychoanalysis and poetry?

READER-RESPONSE CRITICISM

Historical Background

Reader-response criticism as a critical approach to literature can be seen in part as a reaction to Formalism and New Criticism. It brings forth the importance of the reader in the meaning-making process of literary works. Critics neglected the role of the reader for a very long time in the name of objective and impersonal analysis. Such classical notions of fixed meaning and objective interpretation kept readers and contexts away from the process of meaning-making. It was only during the period of Romanticism that contexts and readers were taken into account in literary analysis. But it was short-lived and limited in scope. From the mid-nineteenth century onwards, the focus shifted back to objective and disinterested analysis, as advocated by Matthew Arnold's literary theory, Eliot's literary theory in the early twentieth century, and the strictly textual analysis practised by New Critics. Reader-response theory, contrary to the dominant critical stance held for several decades, showed the role of readers in the act of interpretation and thus the relevance of contexts in the meaning-making process.

Reader-response criticism is based on ideas drawn from phenomenology and hermeneutics. Phenomenology is the study of how we understand the world and hermeneutics is a theory of textual interpretation, especially those texts dealing with human acts, products and life. They are interrelated and involve mainly the analysis of perception and interpretation of the world and human life. Phenomenology deals with psychology and social theory. As a movement in philosophy, it began in the late nineteenth century and the founder of this movement was the German theorist **Edmund Husserl** (1859–1938). Husserl proposed that the real aim of philosophical study is not to examine the external objects in the world but the process by which the objects appear to the mind (consciousness) of a perceiver. He stated that the objects in the world are as they appear and the perceiver gives meaning to them. Thus in Husserl's philosophy, the perceiver's role is very important in determining the meaning of objects. It leads to a simple view that the human mind is the centre and origin of all meaning. **Martin Heidegger** (1889–1976), German philosopher and Husserl's student, rejected his view that the perceiver alone projects meaning onto the things of the world. He made it clear that while the perceiver's mind (consciousness) projects the things of the world, the world also affects his mind. It is not a one-sided process; the mind (consciousness) affects and is affected in turn. He further explained that consciousness is situated in a certain place and time and this situatedness always affects our understanding of the world. Therefore we can never have a view of the world free from these references of time and place. Heidegger's theory influenced another German theorist, **Hans-Georg Gadamer** (1900–2002). He applied Heidegger's situational approach to literary theory in *Truth and Method* (1975). He argued that literary works do not appear in the world with one final meaning. The meaning is decided by the historical situation of the interpreter. Gadamer thus denied that literary works had an inherent meaning and brought the interpreter and his historical situation in focus. This literary application was carried further and elaborated upon by succeeding critics. The first important critic to formulate a theory based on the role of the reader in the act of interpretation was **Hans Robert Jauss** (1921–1997). He was influenced by Gadamer. He combined the insights of Russian Formalism (that simply focuses on literary text and ignores history) and social theories (that focus on history and ignore literary text). He proposed his concept of 'horizon of expectations' as a set of criteria that readers use to judge literary texts. This concept implies that readers bring many contexts to literary texts and interpret them accordingly. But such interpretations change as contexts change with time. Literary works are not universal in their appeal and their meaning is not fixed forever. Juass made contextualisation and historicisation necessary to understand the meaning of literary works.

Wolfgang Iser (1926–2007) is another seminal critic who practised reader-response theory. He was also influenced by Gadamer and the phenomenological aesthetician, Roman Ingarden. Iser's efforts ensured that reader-response theory acquired a full-fledged form of literary theory and a perspective different from the earlier perspectives of Gadamer and Jauss. He followed the phenomenological approach of Gadamer and identified the important role of the perceiver/reader in the act of interpretation. But it is important to note that Iser was not completely carried away by the role of the reader. His approach was not entirely subjective or based on the impressions of the reader. He was careful enough to keep his focus on the text and not on the historical situation of the reader. He is the very opposite of Jauss on this point. He removes contexts and history from the act of interpretation and brings the text and the reader in close exchange. However, he is not a Formalist either. He does not consider that there is only one fixed meaning and all interpretations should try to get at that. He argues that there are possibilities of many meanings and they can be discovered through the interaction between the text and the reader. In his key work, *The Act of Reading: A Theory of Aesthetic Response* (1978), he builds his theory of interpretation. He does not conceive of the text as a closed, self-sufficient structure with a fixed meaning but as a site open to all kinds of interactions and possibilities. The readers' experiences rewrite the text and the text's effects redefine their perceptions. Iser's argument is that the text contains 'gaps' or 'blanks' (that is, it does not tell everything) and the readers must fill in these gaps so as to build meaning/s. He divides the readers into two classes—'implied reader' and 'actual reader'. The implied reader is in agreement with the text, in the sense that he/she reads the text in the way the text dictates him/her to read it. The actual reader gets certain impressions from the text but at the same time he/she brings his/her own experiences to bear on the impressions received from the text. In his discussion Iser assigns a central role to the reader's experiences in the act of interpretation and asks the critic to explain the effects of the text on the readers.

The American critic **Stanley E. Fish** (b. 1938) in his pursuit of reader-response criticism offered a new technique called *affective stylistics*. He improved upon this technique at a later stage and proposed the concept of 'interpretive community.' In the early stage Fish argued that meaning is not something inherent in a literary text, waiting to be extracted. It should be negotiated by readers. It is in the negotiation process that some kind of meaning is evolved. Readers play an important role in this meaning-making process. But Fish's readers are not ordinary readers. They are 'informed readers' who know literary conventions and who are ready to change with the changing appeal of the text. During this stage Fish focused both on the text's strategies to deceive readers and to lead them to different meanings, and readers' important role in constructing meaning. But later, he offered more space to readers in the process of interpretation. In his *Is There a Text in This Class?* (1980) he modified his position and held that readers recreate the text they read. This happens because readers bring their strategies to the text. We can observe that Fish does not give the decisive role to the text in this revised view. In this landmark work, he proposes his theory of interpretive community, which states that informed readers (those who have linguistic competence and who are aware of literary conventions) form interpretive communities. These communities share certain common assumptions about texts and they recreate texts when they use these assumptions in their reading. It means that readers share the same or similar interpretive strategies and become members of the same interpretive community.

Salient Features of Reader-Response Criticism

1) Reader-response criticism is an investigation into the readers' participation in the act of literary interpretation and a reaction to all traditional and modern approaches that dismiss the consideration of reader-oriented analysis, like Formalism and New Criticism.

2) In traditional criticism, the author was at the centre of literary interpretation and in modern criticism, the text became the central factor. In counter-approaches like Marxism the social, economic and political contexts became important in literary interpretation. In all critical approaches the reader was never seen as important. The German theorists first brought the reader at the centre of a literary discussion. However, the discussion of the readers' role in the literary interpretation has undergone successive changes from Edmund Husserl to Stanley Fish.

3) New Criticism believed that the literary text was a closed text which can only be understood by understanding its internal structure. The text offers important clues to the reader and the reader has to construct his response based on them. This means that the reader is passive and at the receiving end. The author, the text and sociopolitical contexts are factors in literary interpretation that constantly replaced each other but the individual reader as a factor was largely ignored.

4) New Criticism as a theoretical lens can be said to have begun with Edmund Husserl, who focused on perception of the world rather than observation; so the perceiver's (reader's) role assumed importance.

5) Martin Heidegger, another important critic, differed from Husserl's view, stating that perception is not one-sided; if the perceiver perceives the world, the world also affects

his perception in turn. Hans-Georg Gadamer follows Heidegger. For him the literary work does not have a final meaning. Meaning is formed by the interpreter and his historical position.

6) Hans Robert Jauss combines the Formalist focus on text and the socialist focus on history in the meaning-making process. Jauss proposed the concept of 'horizon of expectations', which stated that readers bring many contexts to literary texts and interpret accordingly but the meaning changes with the change in contexts.

7) This view also changed with Wolfgang Iser and Stanley Fish's versions of reader-response criticism. Iser proposed reading to be a collaborative activity between the reader and the text. He explained that during the reading process the text creates gaps and invites the readers to fill them and thus helps formulate certain responses. Fish is more radical in his argument. He argues that the reader, through his reading, brings his individual contexts to the text and thus rewrites the text.

Introduction to Wolfgang Iser's 'Interaction between Text and Reader'

Wolfgang Iser's approach to literary work is more practical and pedagogical than most other reader-response critics'. He distinguishes literary work as a repository of both the text and the reader. He avoids taking an extreme position in his analysis and justifies a compromise between the Formalist theory of literature and reader-based theory. Formalism assumes literature to be a stable object of study and regards text to be the source and site of interpretation. Reader-response theory, on the other hand, rejects the exclusive focus on the text, and strongly advocates the role of the reader in the act of interpretation. Iser draws on the significant ideas of both the approaches and makes his own method more practically useful. The text is like a script of performance. Just as the script guides actors but the actors perform it in different ways, the text guides the reader but the reader interprets it differently at different times. The interpretation of a text is neither subjective nor objective. It is always a result of the dynamic interaction between the text and the reader. Meaning is not static but dynamic. It changes with the reader because the reader brings different sets of perspectives to it and the text provides its own set of perspectives.

In the opening statement, Iser outlines the importance of the interaction between text and reader in the act of reading. He points out that the literary work has two parts—the artistic and the aesthetic. The artistic pole is the author's text and the aesthetic pole is the reader's realisation of the text. It means that the work is neither entirely the author's text nor the reader's subjective understanding. The work is situated between the reality of the text and the reader's realisation. The reader passes through various viewpoints offered by the text. He relates these viewpoints with one another and also to his individual experiences and viewpoints. Iser insists on taking into account both aspects of literary work—the author's techniques and the reader's psychology. With these preliminary remarks about his approach Iser turns to the process of interaction between text and reader. He interprets this interactive process in terms of communication. Communication between the text and reader goes both ways—the reader receives the message of the text by re-composing it. However there is no common code between the text and reader based on which the communication can take place.. A common code may be discovered during the course of interaction. Iser refers to certain types of communication from psychoanalytical research which can provide common codes that can govern the interaction between text and reader. He refers to the Tavistock School (a British school of psychology influential during the 1960s and 70s) and the view of one of its important psychologists, R. D. Laing. In interpersonal relationships, others' views about us cannot be called pure perception (that is, others' views about us cannot be genuine and true). They are the result of interpretation. Laing observes that we cannot experience the experiences of one another. We interact with one another on the assumption that we know what others think of us. But there always remains a gap in such interaction. This gap can be filled in by interpretation. If we do not know with certainty what others' views about us are, we interpret them and form our reactions accordingly. Interpersonal relationships, thus, are not based on *perceptions* of one another but on *interpretations* of one another. This can serve as a starting point to Iser's succeeding discussion about the nature of interaction between the text and the reader. Much like interpersonal relationships, the interaction between the text and the reader depends on mutual understanding.

Iser differentiates between the interaction between the text and the reader and other social interactions. Reading is not a face-to-face interaction. The text never tells the reader about the accuracy or inaccuracy of his views of the text. Another difference is that there is no certain or fixed context which can regulate the process of the interaction between text and reader. On the contrary, the codes or the contexts which can make this interaction possible are fragmented in the text. For any kind of possible interaction between text and reader, these contexts need to be put together. However the absence of such common codes/contexts leads to the creation of gaps between the text and the reader. Iser argues that these gaps (the lack of corresponding points between text and reader) give rise to communication in the reading process because the reader fills in the gaps and enters into an interactive relationship with the text. But this is a bilateral process so Iser cautiously points out that for such communication the reader's activity of filling the gaps must be controlled in some way by the text. He quotes Virginia Woolf's observation about Jane Austen. Woolf states that for a better understanding of Austen's novels it is important to relate the trivial aspect (unimportant) to the significant aspect of the text. Iser calls this the act of 'filling the blanks'. The readers fill the blanks by linking the things said in the text with unsaid things, or linking the explicit things with the implicit. Iser argues that blanks and negations control the interaction between text and reader. The blanks encourage the reader to bring together various perspectives and patterns in the text and to build a referential field or context to arrive at the meaning. The various types of negations evoke familiar and determinate elements (Iser calls these elements 'knowledge') in the reader's mind. These elements only serve to cancel out one another and thereby bring the reader into the right relation with the text. Blanks help the reader to become active within the text and also control his activity.

Iser explains the functions of the blank. The blank as an empty space between the perspectives helps them come together. It makes the organisation of a referential field (the contexts that help understand the meaning of the text) of interacting textual perspectives possible. Secondly, it enables the reader to create a determinate relationship between the perspectives. Lastly, the blank helps create a structure where a perspective (like the narrator or characters) becomes the theme. As another perspective takes on the earlier perspective, another theme also takes on the earlier theme. Due to a range of alternating themes the reader is able to establish his interaction with the text. Blanks thus excite and guide the reader's activity. The reader fills the blanks in the text and the structural qualities of the blanks bring together the reader's wandering responses.

The act of the reader is to connect the segments and patterns of the text. There are several patterns and perspectives (Iser lists out the four most prominent perspectives) and the reader has to correlate them in order to establish a meaningful interaction with the text. According to Iser, the story is the most basic form of the pattern of the text. The narrative structure of the story undergoes many changes on the level of characters and events and the reader has to find out the link lost during and due to such changes.

Iser argues that the text contains a variety of perspectives. These perspectives outline the author's view and also the reader's response.

He explains four main perspectives of a narrative text: the narrator, the characters, the plot and the fictitious reader. These perspectives do not tell us the meaning of the text on their own or in isolation. They should be understood collectively in the reading process. Iser shows how a collective understanding of all perspectives in the text can be achieved by contrasting with their counterparts in the text. He takes the example of Henry Fielding's (eighteenth-century English novelist and playwright) novel, *Tom Jones*. In his novel, Fielding portrays each character's perspective of eighteenth-century English society. Characters are each assigned a specific character trait and are often contrasted with one another; for example, the character of Allworthy who represents benevolence, is contrasted with Squire Western and Miss Western, who represent lust for wealth and power. The hero of the novel, Tom Jones, in his interactions and negotiations with these contrasting characters, is really negotiating with the norms of contemporary social systems. The reader is engaged in a similar interaction with the text, and arrives at a meaning by piecing together the links between the thought systems informing the novel.

Key Points

- Iser's approach is a more practical version of reader-response criticism, and avoids taking an extreme position.
- He combines the ideas of Formalist criticism and reader-response criticism.
- He considers the text and the reader equally important in the act of interpretation.
- The text guides readers during the course of reading but readers interpret it differently.
- Meaning of a literary work is the result of the interaction between text and reader.

- Interaction between the text and the reader brings the artistic and aesthetic parts together.
- Both aspects—the author's techniques and the reader's psychology—are important.
- The act of reading is a two-way communication between text and reader.
- The British psychologist R. D. Laing's views about interpersonal relationships can serve as a prototype for the interaction between text and reader.
- There is a difference between text–reader interaction and other social interactions. Absence of any common codes or contexts between the text and reader creates gaps in communication. The reader fills in the gaps but his/her activity is controlled by the text.
- These gaps or blanks activate the interaction between the text and the reader.
- The blanks encourage the reader to bring together various perspectives and patterns and form certain responses to the text.
- Various types of negations also activate the interaction between the text and the reader.
- Negations are the elements in the text that cancel each other out and bring the reader into the right relation with the text.
- The story is the most basic form of the patterns that motivate the reader to fill the blanks.
- Functions of the blank— a) brings various perspectives together, b) enables the reader to create a determinate relationship between the perspectives, c) helps create

a structure where a perspective (like the narrator or characters) becomes the theme.

- There are four major perspectives to take into account in the reading process—the narrator, the characters, the plot and the fictitious reader.

Exercises

Answer the following questions in 100–150 words.

1) Why does Iser take a middle path in his discussion of the interaction between text and reader?
2) What is meaning, according to Iser?
3) Which two parts does the interaction between text and reader bring together?
4) What are the differences between text–reader interaction and other social interactions?
5) What are the four major perspectives, according to Iser?

Answer the following questions in 250–300 words.

1) Write a short historical account of reader-response criticism.
2) Elucidate the salient features of reader-response criticism.
3) How do you justify the statement that reader-response criticism is a reaction to New Criticism?
4) Do you agree with Iser's view that the blank in the text guides the reader's activity?
5) Explain the functions of the blank.

FEMINIST LITERARY CRITICISM

Historical Background

Feminism is a socio-political movement for the freedom and equality of women that began in eighteenth-century Europe. Feminist literary criticism is based on the ideas and worldview of feminism and emerged in Europe and America in the 1960s. It is a movement which advocates equal economic, political and social rights for women, and seeks to dismantle patriarchal structures (Patriarchy is a network of systems created by men to overpower women through control of homes, education, marriages and creative outlets like art. It is based on a male-centred worldview and it works to subordinate, marginalise and inferiorise women in all fields). But feminist criticism can be traced as far back as Chaucer's time, to fourteenth-century medieval England. Medieval women were not feminist in the present-day sense of the term and they did not have the freedom and authority to be writers and critics. However the study of their representation in literary works and the effects such representation had on their attitude to the world and their lives could offer great insights into the conditions of medieval women.

Feminism and feminist literary criticism have been interdependent and have derived ideas, views and practices from each other. It is therefore very natural that any discussion of feminist literary criticism should also discuss feminism as a socio-political movement. Notwithstanding the common goals of women's liberation and assertion of their rights, feminism has taken on different forms all over the world due to different cultural contexts. Therefore, we now talk of feminisms, and not of feminism as a single all-encompassing movement. We shall therefore study its thematic concerns, rather than attempting a chronological survey. It would be useful to understand the emergence and growth of feminism, and feminist literary criticism as a corollary, as a movement in three stages, or *waves*. Feminist critics and scholars have used different models to study the development of feminism and feminist criticism. It has, for example, been studied along nationalistic and cultural lines, such as British feminism, American feminism and French feminism where the contribution of female activists and theorists of the respective nations has been elaborated. The other model for mapping the history of feminism and feminist criticism has been provided by American feminist theorist Elaine Showalter. She proposes three phases of women's literary development. The first is the **feminine phase** (1840–80) in which women writers mostly followed the established tradition. The second is the **feminist phase** (1880–1920) in which women protested against inequality and repression and fought for their rights. The third is the **female phase** (1920–present) in which women have changed their focus from highlighting the misrepresentation of women in male texts to discovering women-oriented texts written by women. The orientation in this phase is towards self-discovery. This model studies literary works in the light of viewpoints provided by various critical approaches, and has given rise to approaches like Marxist feminism, psychoanalytic feminism, gender studies and minority feminist criticism. This kind of study adopts a certain theoretical position and examines accordingly the representation of women in literary texts.

The first wave of feminism began with **Mary Wollstonecraft** (1759–97). It initiated the feminist analysis of the representations of women in literary and non-literary works. Wollstonecraft was a political activist and a woman of firm radical views. She started a school and wrote a book titled *Thoughts on the Education of Daughters* (1787). She took issue with Edmund Burke for his idea of femininity and his attempt to defend the old order of male domination. Burke, in his work *Philosophical Enquiry* (1757), had claimed the qualities of the sublime to be strength, masculinity and pain, and the qualities of the beautiful to be weakness, femininity and pleasure. This classification was biased as it privileges men over women. Wollstonecraft wrote *A Vindication of the Rights of Men* (1790) as a reply to Burke's prejudiced argument. She argued that Burke was creating a false image of woman and an incorrect aesthetic so that women would submit to the categories of the old order. In her next work, *A Vindication of the Rights of Woman* (1792) she argued for rejecting old traditions and constructing a new, more liberal model of living for all of humanity. She pointed out that women were led into the trap of placing a high value on the social constructs of beauty and femininity. Her solution to this problem was to create a society free from gender classification as men and women.

Wollstonecraft's revolutionary thought was carried forward in the eighteenth century by social thinkers like **John Stuart Mill** (1806–1873). Influenced by the views of his wife, Harriet Taylor, Mill championed the cause of liberation of women from the patriarchal structure and their entitlement to intellectual and social rights. He presented the bill of the right to vote for women in the parliament in 1866 and argued for women to be seen as equal in marriage and society in his essay, *The Subjection of Women* (1869). Mill's active support to the cause of women's liberation gave spirit and force to the movement and worked as a link between Wollstonecraft's thought and twentieth-century feminism. The first wave or phase of feminism in the mid-eighteenth century was explicitly political in its pursuits and was focused on the issue of women's suffrage (the right to vote).

Virginia Woolf (1882–1941) was active as a feminist and was a part of the suffrage movement. She strongly pleaded for autonomy and equal status for women and criticised the representation of women by male writers. She wrote *A Room of One's Own* (1929), a classic work now part of the canon of feminist criticism. The matter for the book came from what were originally lectures given by Woolf to women students at

Cambridge. The central argument of the book is that women should have money and space (room) to write fiction. She insisted that women should be allowed economic and social liberty so that they can realise their aspirations. She wrote *Three Guineas* (1938) as a sequel to *A Room of One's Own* and insisted on the emancipation of women. Woolf pioneered the British version of feminism and feminist criticism and proved to be an enduring inspiration to many British feminist critics. British feminists are typically inclined towards a Marxist-feminist stance while analysing women's literary works. For example **Juliet Mitchell** (b. 1940) in her book, *Women's Estate* (1971), criticised patriarchy in the Marxist terms of production and private property. In her next work *Psychoanalysis and Feminism* (1974) she tried to integrate Marxist and psychoanalytic ideas in her analysis of patriarchy. The other important British critic is **Michèle Barrett**. In her *Women's Oppression Today* (1980) Barrett tried to apply the Marxist method of class analysis to her study of the representation of women in literary texts.

Simone de Beauvoir (1908–86) was a French novelist and philosopher. She was one of the most significant and influential feminist theorists, with whom the second wave of feminism began. Her classic work, *The Second Sex* (1949), provided a theoretical base to feminism. It offered great insights to feminists, literary critics, philosophers and historians and opened up a whole new range of feminist interpretations. Beauvoir's work influenced Euro-American feminist writers and critics like Betty Friedan, Kate Millett, Juliet Mitchell, and Germaine Greer to the extent that they adopted her views about the cultural construction of the identity of woman as the base of their study. The work argued that women have been assigned a secondary role in relation to men and this subordination has been maintained through the ideologies of femininity. These ideologies have long projected men as the self, the subject and the dominant category and women as the other, the object and the submissive category. Men have achieved great physical and intellectual prowess whereas women have become slaves meekly carrying out their reproductive and maternal duties. She pronounced 'one is not born, but rather becomes, a woman.' It means that the category of woman is not natural but culturally constructed by men. She made the significant differentiation between sex and gender and argued that gender is a socially constructed concept by men for their benefit. She provided a theoretical base and orientation to feminist criticism so that it could examine more subtly the working of the male ideology.

Woolf and Beauvoir laid the foundation of feminist criticism and offered various positions to examine the repressive male ideology and biased projection of women. The feminist movement later branched out in different directions in different parts of Europe and America. The direct influence of Beauvoir's radical views about femininity could be seen reflected variously in the critical writings of American feminist critics. **Betty Friedan** (1921–2006) wrote a highly influential book *The Feminine Mystique* (1963). In this book Friedan shows her deep concern for the repression and subordination of middle-class American women. She explains how patriarchal modes restrict women to the private, domestic life and deny them entry into the public space. Other feminist critics also produced critical works of great impact around this time. **Mary Ellman** (1921–89) wrote *Thinking About Women* (1968), **Kate Millett** (b. 1934) wrote *Sexual Politics* (1969), and **Germaine Greer** (b. 1939, an Australian theorist) wrote *The Female Eunuch* (1970). Millet, in her powerful book, examined the representation of women and handling of female sexuality in the works of Henry Miller, Norman Mailer, Jean Genet and D. H. Lawrence. She connected gender to the concept of politics and power (as the title of her book suggests) and discussed literature as a place where such sexual politics takes place. Literature, according to her, creates and maintains sexual politics and therefore it is necessary to analyse literary works. She thought that feminist analysis of literary works would liberate women from their subordination.

She distinguished gender from sex, arguing that sex is a biological category whereas gender is a cultural construction.

Elaine Showalter (b. 1941) is one of the most influential American feminist theorists. She wrote her significant book *A Literature of Their Own* (1977) in which she introduced many forgotten and neglected women writers, hoping to build the female literary tradition. She described three phases of women's literary development—feminine, feminist and female, and interpreted them as a successive progression from imitation of the established tradition in the first phase to the opposition and demand for freedom in the second phase to self-discovery in the third phase. Her most important contribution to feminist literary criticism is her model of 'gynocriticism.' She proposed this model in order to build an autonomous and self-referencing female tradition. It changed the focus of study from male-authored texts to female-authored texts. In this shift, the reader, author, character(s) and critic are all women and together they form a literary tradition different from the male tradition.

Sandra Gilbert and **Susan Gubar** have carried forward Showalter's model of gynocriticism. In *The Madwoman in the Attic* (1979) these critics offered a detailed examination of nineteenth-century women's works and explained women writers' struggle against the patriarchal structure for their self-assertion.

The French version of feminist criticism has been interdisciplinary, multivalent and poststructural in its theory and practice. The French feminist critics have drawn ideas from sources as different as Jacques Lacan's structuralist concept of the unconscious, Jacques Derrida's deconstruction, Roland Barthes' semiology and Michel Foucault's concept of power. French feminist criticism is synonymous with three important feminist theorists— **Hélène Cixous**, **Julia Kristeva** and **Luce Irigaray**. The critical works of these theorists radically differ in theory and practice. The only thing common to them is that they have been influenced by poststructural ideas in their analyses and they offer strong critiques of *phallocentrism* (the view that privileges the phallus [at a conceptual level] as the signifying source of power and treats femininity as secondary and derivative).

Hélène Cixous (b. 1937) is an Algeria-born French theorist and a highly prolific writer. In the long span of her meditations, from her influential 'The Laugh of the Medusa' (1975) to *Three Steps on the Ladder of Writing* (1990), she strongly criticised the patriarchal structure behind Western philosophical traditions. Under the influence of Derrida's philosophy, Cixous deconstructed the symbolic practices of phallocentrism which create hierarchical binary oppositions like nature/culture and man/woman. Writers, according to her, should write to exceed these binary oppositions. This view came to be known as *ecriture feminine* (feminine writing). It is an alternative model of writing that opposes dominant phallic model of communication and expresses the feminine consciousness. This kind of writing can be practised by anyone who occupies a feminine space in culture and not necessarily by women alone. All this means that writers should not fall into the trap of male structures of 'important' and 'unimportant' and should write to express freely the feminine consciousness.

Julia Kristeva (b. 1945), a Bulgarian-French feminist theorist, was initially interested in linguistics but later took up psychoanalysis as her main area of study. She was influenced by the diverse ideas of Marxism, structuralism, and the theories of Roland Barthes and Jacques Lacan. In her landmark work, *Revolution in Poetic Language* (1984), she interpreted language as a signifying process that is mobile and fluid and that produces symbolic meanings. Further, she combined linguistic and psychoanalytic ideas to propose her famous theory of 'the semiotic and the symbolic.' These are the two interrelated aspects of language. The semiotic aspect is pre-Oedipal, pre-verbal and rhythmic whereas the symbolic is social, cultural and rule-governed. Interpreted from the feminist point of view the semiotic aspect becomes the mother-centred expression and the symbolic aspect, the expression of the Law of the Father, socio-cultural rules.

Luce Irigaray (b. 1930) a Belgium-born theorist, completed her doctorate at the University of Paris and has ever since lived in France. She is different from the other two French feminist theorists in the sense that she does not directly say anything about literature. She criticises the other feminisms and Freud and Lacan's psychoanalysis. She is also critical of the liberal feminism of the nineteenth and early twentieth centuries and Beauvoir's existential feminism. According to her these feminisms regarded men and women to be fundamentally the same, because they sought to remove the inequality between them. Her argument is that in place of sameness, sexual difference must be emphasised. The difference that male tradition creates between men and women is a negative difference, that is, it characterises women as inferior and incapable of the activities specified for men. For example, women are presumed to be weaker than men, less intelligent, and so on. But Irigaray's concept of difference is not negative. She insists on sexual difference because she wants women to be free from the excluding/enclosing activity of the male tradition. The male tradition excludes women from full human status enclosing them instead in the same tradition, as subordinate members. Her two works, *Speculum of the Other Woman* (trans. 1985) and *This Sex Which is Not One* (trans. 1985), made a great impact in the English-speaking countries.

Black feminist criticism emerged in the late 1960s and early 1970s in America. The three important events of the time—the Civil Rights Movement, second wave American feminism dominated by white women and the Black Power and Black Art movement dominated by black men—were variously responsible for the rise of black feminist criticism. Like white feminist critics, black feminist critics tried to discover black women writers of the past and establish a new literary canon. They studied the machinery of dual oppression, via race and gender. This brand of feminist criticism is characterised by creative writers—African American poets, novelists and dramatists—writing critical essays and texts. The year 1970 was very crucial for this movement because it saw vitally important publications such as Toni Morrison's novel *The Bluest Eye*, Alice Walker's novel *The Third Life of Grange Copeland*, Maya Angelou's memoir *I Know Why the Caged Bird Sings* and Toni Cade's anthology *The Black Woman.* These texts show how African American women are oppressed by both white racists and by black men. Barbara Christian's *Black Women Novelists: The Development of a Tradition* (1980) was another landmark critical study of African American women's literary tradition. Black feminist criticism is concerned with the economic empowerment of black women, the battle against the ills of racism and sexism, and self-recovery and self-expression.

Postcolonial feminist criticism is an important critical approach developed mostly by Third World feminist critics. It has separated itself from the universalising and totalising theories of Western feminist critics and studies women's oppression from the historical, social and cultural point of view keeping in view the differences and specificities of the indigenous culture. It has addressed a wide variety of themes like differences of class, race, sexuality and geographical location of the Third World women, gender-based analysis of colonial history and the relationship between colonialism and patriarchy. Postcolonial feminist critics have derived ideas from seminal postcolonial texts and from poststructural theories to make their analyses interdisciplinary and comprehensive. The works of postcolonial theorists like Frantz Fanon (*The Wretched of the Earth*), Edward Said (*Orientalism*) and Homi Bhabha (*The Location of Culture*) and the poststructural theories of Jacques Derrida and Michel Foucault along with Jacques Lacan's psychoanalysis have provided postcolonial feminist critics with many contesting issues and methods to deal with the complex field of postcolonial feminism. **Gayatri Chakravorty Spivak**'s work has been instrumental in bringing forth many important debates in postcolonial feminist criticism. Her 'Can the Subaltern Speak?' (1988) is a seminal essay in the sense that it discusses the discourses of the West and the possibility of the subaltern woman's speaking. Her *A Critique of Postcolonial Reason: Toward a History of the Vanishing Present* (1999) brings colonial and postcolonial issues face to face with the Western theories of Marxism, deconstruction, feminism and discourse analysis. Spivak is critical of Western feminism for its neglect of the socio-cultural differences and historical specificities of women in the decolonised countries and its totalising theorisation. Another feminist critic **Trinh Minh-Ha** writes on the same lines as Spivak. She argues in her work, *When the Moon Waxes Red: Representation, Gender and Cultural Politics* (1991), that Western feminist critics ignore the dominant patriarchy within the native cultures of Third World women and also neglect the fact that the Western gaze objectifies them as the Other. due to their ethnic identity. **Anne McClintock** in her *Imperial Leather: Race, Gender and Sexuality in the Colonial Context* (1995) draws on diverse disciplines like psychoanalysis and social theories and produces a cultural critique of showing that sex, class and gender work hand in glove and that discourses like patriarchy and colonial rule redefine them in new modes of oppression. **Chandra Talpade Mohanty** in her *Third World Women and the Politics of Feminism* (1991) edited with Ann Russo and Lourdes Torres remarks on the projection of Third World women as victims of male domination and cultural practices by Western feminist critics. She argues that Third World women are as much historically and culturally produced subjects as Western women are but also have as much of a voice as Western women do. She expresses the need to understand Third World women in their historical and cultural contexts.

Kumkum Sangari and **Sudesh Vaid** (eds.), in their *Recasting Women: Essays in Indian Colonial History* (1990), attempt to locate women in colonial and postcolonial conditions. They assert the need to examine the historical processes to know how patriarchy is reconstituted in the colonial period. For them historical and cultural study is important in understanding the constitution and working of patriarchy.

Another comprehensive attempt in this direction has been made by **Susie Tharu** and **K. Lalita** in their *Women Writing in India* (1993). They argue that texts authored by women in the early nineteenth and twentieth century are in fact documents of their engagement with the world they lived in. They assert the importance of knowing the contexts in which women wrote and how contexts like class, gender and empire influenced their worldview and lives.

Salient Features of Feminist Literary Criticism

1) Feminism is a socio-political movement that fights for the social, economic and political rights and for the cultural place of women. It examines women's marginalisation from different points of view like historical, philosophical, psychological, etc.

2) Feminist literary criticism re-examines the past and the present literary works by women writers in the light of new feminist theories.

3) It studies literary texts as the expressions of patriarchal ideology. The feminist critic tries to discover whether a literary text expresses a particular patriarchal ideology or challenges it.

4) It examines the patriarchal view of male critics, publishers and the socio-economic conditions of women writers.

5) It protests the marginalisation of women in the literary canon and shows a powerful orientation towards the

writings of women. It attempts to redefine literary theory in the light of the feminist consciousness.

6) Other concerns are re-discovering the significance of female literary texts neglected in the past, examining the public reception of female texts and the author's role in writing and her style.

7) Certain themes like reproduction, representation and sexual division of labour recur in feminist literary criticism. It assigns more importance to women's personal experiences as it believes that the personal is political. New concepts are proposed to reveal the oppressive nature of the traditional mode of thinking. These are *sexism* and *essentialism*. Sexism is the social structure based on sexual distinction and essentialism is the tendency to attribute certain characteristics to women as biological or inborn tendencies.

8) Feminist criticism can be studied in three phases—feminine, feminist and female.

9) Though feminist literary criticism began in the 1960s in England and America, it has since taken on several new forms. It has borrowed from other critical approaches like Marxism and poststructuralism. There are also models of feminist criticism based on nationality and culture.

Introduction to Simone de Beauvoir's 'Woman's Situation and Character' (Chapter VI) from *The Second Sex* (1949)

In the chapter 'Woman's Situation and Character' Beauvoir argues that the conditions created and practised by men in society are responsible for the faults and problems of women. Woman's condition has not changed radically and the situation created for her by men has hindered her progress. She is the product of her situation. The faults and weaknesses attributed to her are not 'natural'. They are not the result of her hormones or a result of the predetermined structure of her brain. Her faults and weaknesses are determined by her situation. Beauvoir uses the words 'situation' and 'character' in the larger context. 'Situation' means the economic, social and historical conditions created by men. 'Character' means women's behaviour and their faults. Beauvoir emphasises the point that women live in a world created, ruled and dominated by men. They do not have their own space and voice. They submit to the dictates of the male world. This supports the point that the environment is male-dominated, which is why women behave differently. Beauvoir opens her discussion with the argument that there is nothing like the 'world of women' because women have never built a closed and independent society of their own. They have always been an integral part of the male world but are given a subordinate place in society. They are treated as inferior and dependent. As a result they remain passive and submissive and do not know ways to resist male domination. They lack technical training like men and do not deal with practical matters. These things keep women distanced from reality and do not allow them to learn. Therefore Beauvoir calls them to be 'eternal children'. Such lack of exposure and experience is further reinforced by women's household activities. Women being restricted to the kitchen, for example, makes them patient and passive. The kitchen teaches them to obey the fire, the water, wait for sugar to melt, for the dough to rise and so on.

Beauvoir convincingly argues that routine and repetitive work kills elements of creativity and newness in a woman's life. She experiences the world only through words and mental pictures. So she mutely accepts masculine authority and never tries to see things clearly or challenge the dictates. Beauvoir further explains that a woman becomes obedient and shows respect to heroes and laws of the masculine world. It is her ignorance and ineffectiveness that forces her to worship masculine heroes and respect masculine laws. Man, according to Beauvoir, can develop different institutions, a new ethic, a new law and can make a new history. Woman cannot do any of this because she takes no part in the making of history. She clings to past idols created by man and tries to arrest the flow of time.

Beauvoir argues that women have no understanding of the world of men because their mode of living does not teach them to use logic and technique. Contrary to this there is a huge world of feminine experience that is beyond the reach of men. Women know that men can never know about their world of experience (Beauvoir calls it to be magical, mysterious, obscure and still complete) and they cannot apply their force in this domain of life. Woman is capable of challenging man, his idols, codes and laws but she cannot do so because man forces her to accept his views. She wants to revolt against masculine authority but her inability to reconstruct a different society brings her back to slavery. Beauvoir explains with examples the duplicity and deception of man. She points out that man believes in ethical rules but that is only on an abstract universal level. When it comes to his private individual life he believes that he is entitled to desire and pleasure. There is a great difference in man's relation with other men and with woman. This can be seen in his public appeal for high birth rate and private concern for minimum number of children. He appreciates the loyalty and faithfulness of wives but wants his neighbour's wife to commit adultery. To further reveal the duplicity of man, Beauvoir explains man's attitude towards prostitution. Men publicly condemn prostitution but privately indulge in it. They want woman to be chaste and loyal but at the same time they secretly want her to be easily available to them. They publicly idealise her but personally wish her to be disloyal to her husband. Woman thus lives as a parasite. She offers the service of sex to man and earns dignity, livelihood and procreation in return. In this deal man wants her to be the other—the object of his passion.

Beauvoir then turns to the illustration of woman's ambivalent attitude towards masculine authority. Woman accepts masculine authority and yet she does not accept it as it is. She knows that man's world depends on the premises he has chosen for his interests and it will exist as long as she agrees with it. She understands that masculine principles, values and morality are all a form of deception.

Beauvoir analyses two other aspects of woman's ambiguous attitude towards man. Woman lives in her domestic domain surrounded by the masculine world. But she makes it important for man by establishing herself as the prototype of Love. Another aspect of her ambivalence is her consideration of her body. Her body is a burden for her. It does not help her get a grip on the world and does not become a source of pleasure for her. It displays reactions which she wants to hide. In spite of all this, she feels proud looking at her body in the mirror. She considers it as a promised happiness, a work of art and/or a living statue. She makes it attractive and puts on a show for men.

Beauvoir examines the role of religion in the repression of women. It can be observed in the authority given by God to man to dictate the terms of life and define the rules of conduct. God endorses the laws that man writes and woman has to accept these laws in the name of God. Man has been the master by divine right and such supremacy is apparent in the Jews, Mohammedans and Christians. The fear of God represses any impulse of revolt in woman and she submits to masculine authority. Beauvoir makes it clear that in ancient times religion was a matter of compulsion, but in modern times it has acquired the form of deception. Man has shrewdly declared the equality of the sexes in the name of God—woman is not inferior but equal in status to man. By this gesture woman is encouraged to believe in the power of God. Her strong faith in God brings salvation to her and transforms her into a sister of angels. Her faith helps her overcome her inferiority and she becomes the creature of God—neither male nor female. She is deceptively drawn out of her consciousness as a woman and encouraged to forget her femininity. This not only reinstates the authority of man but removes any possible threat from woman. Beauvoir gives examples of female saints like St. Bridget and St. Catherine of Siena, who had unshakable faith in God and did not live by the rules of the masculine world. But the underlying fact is that man forces woman into the refuge of divinity and weakens any possibility of resistance to his authority. The woman is not required to do any practical or theoretical work like man. She only has to tell beads and live close to God. Her salvation lies in her nearness and obedience to God. On the other hand, woman also finds that by submitting to the power of God she can gain authority over the masculine world. Her words become sacred and commanding when she speaks in the name of God. She realises this and uses religion to satisfy her desires. Religion gives woman the guide, the father, the lover and above all confirms her social status. Beauvoir thus points out the complicity between woman and the Church and also the hostility of the Church to women's emancipation.

Beauvoir thus substantiates her argument that situations created by man determines woman's character and that man's self-interest, duplicity and dominating tendencies are responsible for her 'faults' and 'follies'. Woman's convictions, values, wisdom, morality, tastes and behaviour can only be explained in the light of the situation created by man.

Key Points

- Conditions created and practised by men are responsible for faults and problems of women.
- Woman is the product of the situation that she lives in. Women's 'faulty' behaviour and their faults are the result of the economic, social and historical conditions created by men.

- Women's lack of technical training and inability in dealing with practical matters and reality keep them from resistance.
- Exposure to household activities makes women submissive and passive, and the routine work involved in running a household kills women's novelty and creativity.
- Man's duplicity is apparent in his public and private life. He has duplicitous attitudes towards the faithfulness of woman. Prostitution is given as an example to illustrate this attitude.
- Woman offers sex to man in return for dignity, livelihood and procreation.
- Woman has an ambiguous attitude towards man and his world. She is unable to establish a counterworld of her own, however, and sets herself up as a prototype of love in man's world. She displays her body as a promised happiness and a work of beauty in order to gain some power and agency, but this is illusory.
- Religion is a repressive ideology and a deception used by men.
- Woman is deceptively drawn out of her feminine consciousness by man through various insidious social and cultural mores.

Exercises

Answer the following questions in 100–150 words.

1) What, according to Beauvoir, is responsible for woman's character?

2) What does household work do to woman?
3) Describe man's duplicity in short.
4) Why is woman's attitude towards man and his world ambiguous?
5) How does religion work as a deception?

Answer the following questions in 250–300 words.

1) Write in detail the salient features of feminist literary criticism.
2) Comment on the various strains of feminist literary criticism.
3) How does Beauvoir explain the statement that woman's situation is responsible for her character?
4) Explain the role of religion in curbing a revolutionary reaction in women.
5) What, according to Beauvoir, are the strategies of men that force women into submission and passivity?

POSTCOLONIALISM

Historical Background

Postcolonialism represents several historical, political, economic, racial, literary and linguistic perspectives outside and against the Western systems of knowledge that intersect one another. The correct usage of the term 'postcolonialism' has excited debates, and it has been variously written with a hyphen as *post-colonialism* or simply *postcolonialism*. Each of these variants indicates a specific position. The hyphenated term *post-colonialism* denotes a particular historical period that comes after the end of colonialism. It is often equated with the period after independence of a colonised country. Without the hyphen, *postcolonialism* denotes disparate forms of representations, reading methods, and values that move across past and present (that is, the discourses subsumed under the term *postcolonialism* examine conditions both in the period before and after colonialism).

Postcolonialism has given rise to many theoretical approaches that draw on Marxism, poststructuralism, feminism, and psychoanalytic criticism. Broadly speaking, it is a critique of imperialism and colonialism. It deals with complex issues like suppression, slavery, race, gender, cultural identity, cultural clashes and ways of resisting imperial (European) power. It also examines the issues that have emerged after the end of (political) colonialism. Postcolonial critics share the following concerns—a) the colonisers not only acquired the land of the colonised people but also dominated their cultural practices and interpreted them to suit their colonial agenda, b) the after-effects of colonisation—social, political, economic and educational effects—still hold sway over the minds of the formerly colonised people, c) postcolonial studies analyse the decolonised peoples' modes of resistance to the Western views of non-Western worlds and Western efforts to dominate such studies.

The term postcolonialism came into active use around the 1950s. Some pioneering theorists and texts provided the necessary frameworks to postcolonial studies for explorations into selected fields. Historically speaking, the Algeria-born French theorist **Frantz Fanon** (1925–1961) was the earliest postcolonial critic. Fanon wrote two seminal texts, *Black Skin, White Masks* (1952) and *The Wretched of the Earth* (1961). These books provided the necessary foundation to postcolonialism as a field of enquiry. In *Black Skin, White Masks*, Fanon was concerned with the miserable conditions of black people under French colonial rule. He used psychoanalytic theory as a model to investigate the conditions of the black people. He argued that the French rulers (the coloniser) forced black people (the colonised) to speak the French language and coerced them into accepting the collective unconscious of the coloniser. This coercion (forced acceptance) made black people lose their cultural specificity (cultural characteristics) and self-esteem. Blackness came to be identified with evil and sin, and whiteness with purity and righteousness. In *The Wretched of the Earth* Fanon offered a Marxist analysis of the hierarchical system of a colonial and post-colonial society. He strongly argued on the side of the 'proletariat' or 'the wretched of the earth' (black people) and expressed the need to topple down such a system. Fanon provided later postcolonial theorists with much of the critical vocabulary (for example, 'otherness') and frames of analysis (for example, psychoanalysis) through his writing.

Edward Said (1935–2003), a Palestine-born American critic, can be rightfully credited with establishing postcolonialism as a field of enquiry in literary studies. Said used many of the ideas of French theorists like Foucault and Derrida in his analysis. His key work, *Orientalism* (1978), firmly laid the foundations of postcolonial theory. It provided not only useful terms but perspectives to undertake a critique of the Europe-sponsored projection of non-European people and cultures and discover space for self-identity and self-assertion. He elaborately examined the Western construction of the 'Orient' and illustrated how the Western power forms views about the 'Orient,' authorises these views through discourse, and uses these constructions to rule over the Orient. Said argued that the Western rulers represented Eastern people as inactive, thoughtless, immoral and unreliable. These negative stereotypes were intended to highlight the inability of the Eastern people to rule over themselves and justify the supposedly civilised and civilising rule of the Europeans. In his next work *Culture and Imperialism* (1993), he maintained this focus on the power relations between the West and the East. He explained the complicity between colonisation and imperialism and the consequent view that the colonised people need to be ruled over. He pointed out the binary opposition between the West as the Self and the non-West as the Other and emphasised the need to abolish this construction. He insisted on the actual experience of a culture and region for its representation and asked writers and critics to develop a historical view towards the Orient so as to understand the variety of and differences between human experiences.

Homi K. Bhabha (b. 1949), an India-born postcolonial theorist, has held teaching positions in various English and American universities. He was influenced by the ideas of Frantz Fanon, Michel Foucault, Jacques Derrida and Jacques Lacan and this reflected in his varied methods of analysis. In his first book, *Nation and Narration* (1990), he discussed the issues of nationalism and nationality. He revealed how different theorists challenged the Enlightenment-era essentialist and universalist conception of nationalism and nationality. In his next seminal work, *The Location of Culture* (1994), Bhabha developed his most important concepts of 'unhomeliness', 'mimicry' and 'hybridity.' He explained the unhomely condition of the colonised person thus: the colonised looks at the world and at himself through two distinctive perspectives, his own perspective as a subject and the coloniser's perspective as a colonised object. This duality places the colonised person in limbo and he feels like a foreigner in both the cultures (his own culture and that of the coloniser's culture). Bhabha called this feeling of homelessness as 'unhomeliness.'

His other famous term is 'mimicry' which is based on Lacan's notion of subjectivity. In the act of mimicry the colonised people follow the colonisers' dictated terms and policy even in their resistance. Bhabha frames the act of mimicry as a unique form of resistance in itself, however, as the colonised subject acquires some characteristics of the coloniser through this act, thereby undermining the latter's colonial authority. While advancing the concept of 'hybridity' he explained the ambivalent nature of the meeting of two cultures. The meeting of two cultures creates a new culture which in turn influences both the cultures. He called this dynamic cultural interaction as 'hybridity.' 'Hybridity' as a cultural process takes place at a social, and not an individual level. So it consists of both struggle against the authority and revision of the authority.

Gayatri Chakravorty Spivak (b. 1942) is one of the leading postcolonial theorists and feminists today. She has been eclectic and pluralist in her approach and analysis. She makes use of diverse approaches like Marxism, feminism and deconstruction to examine postcolonial issues like class, gender, race and politics. She describes herself as a practical Marxist-feminist-deconstructionist-postcolonial critic. Her work has addressed— a) the politics of the academy and the politics of imperial powers like the United States of America, b) the marginalised voices of minority groups like the working class and women, and c) the literary conventions and academic theory of the West that dominate the cultural texts of the colonised people. She became famous with her publication of the English translation of Jacques Derrida's *Of Grammatology* in 1976. She was an active member of the Subaltern Studies Group (also known as the Subaltern Studies Collective) based in Delhi. She used a historiographical approach to explain the repression of women and lower classes and their ideological representations in narrative texts. Her brand of feminism is demonstrated in essays like 'The Woman's Texts and a Critique of Imperialism' (1985) and 'French Feminism in an International Frame' (1987). Her theoretical feminist stance can be briefly summed up as—a) her demonstration of the failure of the Indian nationalist movement to free lower-class subaltern women, b) her criticism of Western feminism for their neglect of class, religion, language and nationality differences and their totalising attempt at creating a universal feminist theory, and c) her awareness of her being a 'Third World' woman speaking on behalf of subaltern women and her prestigious position in an American academy. In her most famous essay, 'Can the Subaltern Speak?' (1988) she dealt with the issue of *sati*, and demonstrated that both Hindu cultural practices and the British imperial program serve to repress the voice and agency of women. She interpreted the history of Bhuvaneswari Bhaduri, a young, middle-class, Indian woman who committed suicide in 1926. She was working as a revolutionary for Indian independence and was given the task of political assassination. She felt unable to commit murder, but recognising that she had failed those who put her in a position of trust, committed suicide. The cause for her death, however, was attributed to be an illicit love affair. Spivak interpreted this act as an attempt to hide Bhuvaneshwari's involvement in the anti-British movement by showing her suicide as the modern example of the ancient Hindu practice of *sati*. This resulted in the removal of her real historical identity as a freedom fighter from the official male-centred records.

Spivak offered a Marxist-deconstructive reading of Western philosophy, especially of the eighteenth-century German philosopher Immanuel Kant's views, in her *A Critic of Postcolonial Reason* (1999). She showed that Kant's theory represented and authorised the educated, bourgeois and masculine human subject. Kant was exclusive and narrow in his treatment of humanity and his theory justified the imperialist program of the Europeans. She continued to demonstrate that even the institution of English literary studies spread the idea of English imperialism through texts like Charlotte Bronte's *Jane Eyre* and Daniel Defoe's *Robinson Crusoe.* Her translations and interpretations of the Bengali writer Mahasweta Devi, on the other hand, revealed the patriarchal repression of the unwritten histories of tribal and subaltern women.

The theoretical and practical framework of postcolonial discourse and resistance was firmly established by the seminal text *The Empire Writes Back: Theory and Practice in Post-Colonial Literatures* (1989). It was written by three Australian critics **Bill Ashcroft**, **Gareth Griffiths** and **Helen Tiffin**. These critics succeeded in establishing postcolonialism as a justifiable alternative to the earlier term 'Commonwealth literature' and as an academic discipline. They interpreted postcolonial literature as challenging the value systems of the colonisers and offering new modes of representation of postcolonial issues. They argued in favour of differences, new values and identities. They discussed at length the issue of the use of English (the language of the colonisers) by postcolonial writers. They explained that English functioning at the colonial centre (England) is different from what is used in the colony (for example, India) because so many varieties of English have outgrown the colonial influence and have violated all colonial rules. The writers of the ex-colonies have reworked English into 'englishes' (note the small 'e' in the word and its plural. The word 'englishes' at once suggests the fallen status of the English empire and the many ways in which English language is creatively used) in order to resist the colonial value structures. The critics insisted on studying postcolonial literary texts from a historical and geographical point of view.

Gauri Viswanathan (b. 1950), Professor of English and Comparative Literature, Columbia University, is one of the leading Indian postcolonial critics. She has written extensively on education, religion and culture. Her major argument is that the modern study of English literature emerged from British colonial practice in India. In her highly influential book *Masks of Conquest: Literary Study and British Rule in India* (1989) she illustrates how the British rulers diplomatically used English literary study to perpetuate their rule and to impose cultural hegemony upon the natives.

As a point of departure some critics based in the academic institutions in postcolonial countries have offered critiques of postcolonial theory. **Aijaz Ahmad** (Professorial Fellow at the Centre of Contemporary Studies, Nehru Memorial Museum and Library, New Delhi) critiques the non-differential perspectives and methodologies of the postcolonial critics based in Euro-American universities. Ahmad is critical of the relation between postcolonial theory as an academic project and its place of production. For him most postcolonial theory is metropolitan theory, in the sense that it is produced by the critics who live in the First World. They do not pay attention to the locations (the ex-colonised countries) and the context of their intellectual arguments. In his seminal work, *In Theory: Classes, Nations, Literatures* (1992), Ahmad emphasised the importance of the themes of cultural specificities and local differences in postcolonial studies. He argued for the use of Marxism with internalised nuances. Another critique was offered by **Meenakshi Mukherjee** in *Interrogating Post-colonialism: Theory, Text and Practice* (edited with Harish Trivedi, 1996). She argued that the term 'postcolonialism' and the concepts of postcolonial theory originated in American universities and could not adequately fulfil the requirements of countries with colonial histories like India.

There are many important enquiries carried out into the themes of resistance to colonialism, class and gender differences, diaspora and migration by critics like Paul Gilroy (*The Black Atlantic: Modernity and Double Consciousness,* 1993), Rey Chow (*Writing Diaspora: Tactics of Intervention in Contemporary Cultural Studies*, 1993), Anne McClintock (*Imperial Leather: Race, Gender and Sexuality in the Colonial Contest*, 1995), Neil Lazarus (*Nationalism and Cultural Practices in the Postcolonial World,* 1999) and many others.

Salient Features of Postcolonialism

1) Postcolonialism is a blanket term given to differently positioned approaches to textual analysis. The common assumption among them all is that literature, culture and history all affect each other in significant ways.

2) Postcolonial critics argue that colonialism was the source of suffering and exploitation and it did not end with the exit of the colonisers. It continues to affect culture and literature insidiously and subtly even today and therefore should be resisted.

3) Postcolonial literatures and criticism rose during and after the struggle for political independence in the colonies of Asia, Africa and Latin America.

4) Postcolonial theorists/critics believe that they cannot avoid subjective and political interpretations in literary studies. This is because criticism and theory must address the real issues in society.

5) The important objectives of postcolonial criticism are to re-consider the history of colonialism from the viewpoint of the colonised, to reveal the economic, political, and cultural impact of colonialism on both the colonised peoples and the colonising powers, to analyse the process of decolonisation, to explore modes of domination and to articulate political and cultural identities.

6) Postcolonial criticism among other pursuits deals with multiple identities created by gender, ethnicity, class and race.

7) Frantz Fanon can be considered the earliest postcolonial critic. He used psychoanalytic theory to investigate the conditions of black people.

8) Edward Said is another influential postcolonial theorist. His landmark text, *Orientalism*, established postcolonialism as a field of socio-cultural enquiry. He explained the Western construction of the 'Orient', with the West being seen as the self and the East as the 'Other'. He critiqued the European projection of negative values on the non-European world.
9) Homi Bhabha is another important figure in postcolonial theory. He proposed three important concepts—
   a) *unhomeliness:* the feeling of homelessness that produces duality in the mind of the colonised person for both the parental and foreign culture
   b) *mimicry:* a double-edged concept wherein the colonised imitates the coloniser's attitudes, undermining his own culture, but also the coloniser's authority over him
   c) *hybridity:* ambivalent nature of the meeting of two cultures; the meeting creates a new culture that influences both cultures
10) Gayatri Spivak is also an important postcolonial theorist. Her main concerns are: a) the politics of the academy and of neo-imperial powers like America, b) the marginalised voice of minority groups, c) the domination of Western literary conventions and theory over those of non-Western literatures.
11) Other important postcolonial critics include Bill Ashcroft, Gareth Griffiths, Helen Tiffin, Aijaz Ahmad, Gauri Viswanathan and Meenakshi Mukherjee.

Introduction to Gauri Viswanathan's 'The Beginnings of English Literary Study in British India'

Gauri Viswanathan presents a very interesting and insightful account of British colonial rule in India and how it made use of literature and literary studies to stabilise their government and ensure military and mercantile benefits. She uses Antonio Gramsci's concept of hegemony to analyse the education policy of the British in India. She convincingly argues that English literary study in India was not introduced with the noble intention to improve the native people but to perpetuate British rule. She justifies her claim through several references to documentary evidences and practices carried out by the British in colonial India.

The passing of Charter Act in 1813 brought about two major changes in the British policy towards Indian people. The first change was that Britain took on the responsibility of native education and the second was a relaxation in control over missionary work in India. It is notable that before the Charter Act, the British government in India was neutral in its religious policy. Scriptural teaching, including that of the Bible, was not allowed in India. The Act allowed for missionary activity in India. The missionaries hoped for official support from the government for their mission of converting the natives to Christianity. But contrary to their expectations, the government did not extend support to them and instead placed checks on their activities. The rulers were afraid of offending Indians' religious sentiments as this would threaten their rule. Thus, they did not openly support missionary activity. It is interesting to know that the British adopted a dual policy in this matter. The members of the British parliament publicly demanded that large-scale religious conversions should not be carried out in India. However privately they knew that the activities of the missionary people would be very beneficial to them.

The British government's policy towards education of Indians suffered from similar internal contradictions. The government encouraged Oriental study as a part of its duty towards the native people but this only served to expose the Hindus and Muslims to their respective religious faiths and frustrated the British purpose of moral and intellectual improvement, the former objective being especially linked intimately to the Christian ethos. This created a tense situation for the British rulers—their increasing involvement in Indian education did not allow for a neutral approach towards religion. The tension was resolved by the introduction of English literature, infused with Christian imagery. English literary study proved a breakthrough for the British when neither the existing policy on education nor missionary activity proved conducive to their rule in India. The provision for literary study was made in the section 43 of the Charter Act. However the provision did not clearly mention which literature was to be studied—Oriental or Western. This ambiguity was cleared after twenty years by Lord Macaulay who interpreted it as Western literature. The early curriculum of English literary study was primarily devoted to the study of language and not to literature. The English Education Act of 1835 made the study of English literature officially mandatory. In the early stage, English education did not take over Oriental studies; it was taught alongside it. But there were attempts to establish separate colleges for English study and even when it was taught within the same college, the English course was kept separate from Oriental study. The purpose behind this policy was to keep English separate from other languages like Persian, Urdu and Sanskrit, and to teach English as a classical language, much like Latin or Greek were taught as classical languages in England.

The missionaries, however, asserted that English literary study carried out in a secular environment would certainly pose a threat to English ethics and morality. The experiment of teaching English literature in India in a secular or non-religious environment would take the natives away from English ethics and morality and would turn them into rebels. The missionaries also believed that for the study of English literature a high degree of moral and mental cultivation was the first requirement. The British had a similar experience in their homeland where they found that they could not secure control over the lower classes without their submission to moral law or the authority of God. Secular texts would not help them rule over the common British people. It was around this contentious time that Charles Grant (an officer of the East India Company) took on Western literature and Christianity in

India, in his famous essay, 'Observations on the State of Society among the Asiatic Subjects of Great Britain' (1792). Grant made two important observations about English literary study and Christianity. In the first place he observed that by insisting on the moral aspect of English literary study, the Indians could be kept away from English liberal thought (which Grant feared would lead Indians to rise against British rule). Secondly he noted that historically Christianity had never been associated with bringing down the government (that is, the introduction of Christianity would not cause any problem to British rule in India because it is free from any revolutionary potential and the missionaries would ensure that it would not develop any such potential). Grant's justification for this was that Christianity was more concerned with the internal condition than the external condition of man.

Viswanathan provides useful information about educational development in England which served as a background to educational policy and implementation in India. The literary curriculum in educational institutes in England remained largely centred around classical study for the upper class and religious study for the lower class. It was not until the last quarter of the nineteenth century when the English middle class challenged the structure of curriculum that alternative English literary study was introduced. The British educational policy and its application in India were by and large similar to the educational policy and its application in England. They were aware that the learned Indians would strongly criticise the incorporation of the religious texts meant for the lower classes in England into the Indian curriculum. But at the same time they were worried about the continuation of their rule over India in the absence of moral law or the authority of God. They were therefore in search of a social institution which would not offend the religious feelings of the natives and yet cultivate their mental and moral attitude and the sense of God's authority sanctioning British rule in them. This was to be done in the apparent absence of a religious institution like Christianity because the British feared religious provocation; yet the moral refinement of the natives was necessary to ensure the natives' complete obedience and submission to their rule.

It was at this point when they faced equally undesirable choices that the British administrators discovered a friendly associate in English literature. It would support their colonial agenda without provoking unfavourable reactions from the natives. In order to reveal the vested interests of the British rulers in introducing English literary study in India, Viswanathan refers to the minutes of the proceedings before the British parliament's select committee in 1852. The proceedings reveal the material interests of the British rulers. They were determined to project Western literary knowledge as objective, rational and universal and to promote their interests through it. The first step in this direction was their announcement of the structural conformity between Christianity and English literature. Missionaries had long emphasised the shared history of Christianity and literature. Their proposition was that Western literature was different from all non-Western literature because it was connected to religion and this connection had helped the Westerners in their material and moral progress. However the British administrators did not directly sponsor the teaching of the Bible. They ensured that the selected literary texts would reflect the Christian faith and would serve all the purposes of the rulers.

Viswanathan analyses this process in the light of Gramsci's concept of hegemony. She reveals how the British were successful in making the natives believe in the wisdom of the Western culture. They were able to show that English texts were the repository of knowledge and they benignly made them accessible to all. This was a 'master–slave' relation structure and it was conveniently argued that the masters' knowledge could redeem the slaves. English literary study thus became instrumental in removing the unfavourable presence of the British rulers from the fraught scene of religious faith in India and yet protected their interests from being overtly known and challenged. It kept the British interest in economic exploitation, military expansion and administration veiled and served the purpose of unopposed and prosperous rule in India.

Key Points

- Viswanathan, in her essay, documents how literature was employed as an instrument to stabilise British rule in India and to seek military and mercantile benefits.
- Viswanathan uses Gramsci's model of hegemony for her analysis of the British introduction of English literary study in India.
- English literature was introduced in India with the passing of the Charter Act in 1813.
- Viswanathan points out the complicity between English literary study and missionary work.
- Two reasons that held the British back from introducing English literary study in India at the initial stage were—a) English literature taught in a secular environment would take the natives away from English ethics and morality and would turn them into rebels, b) belief that a high degree of mental and moral cultivation was necessary for the study of English literature, which the natives lacked.
- The British rulers were worried about the absence of moral law and/or the authority of God which would ensure their rule in India. But introduction of Christian texts into the Indian curriculum would create strong opposition from learned natives.
- The British rulers were thus in search of a social institution that a) would not provoke religious feelings of the natives, b) would cultivate their mental and moral attitude.
- The British policy of education was contradictory in nature. Promotion of Oriental study would not lead to what they believed was the natives' moral improvement;

Christian values were a necessary accessory for this to happen. However, introducing Christianity would interfere with their neutral religious policy.

- The introduction of English literature, rich in Christian symbolism and imagery, acted as an intermediary between the educational aims of moral improvement and the neutral religious policy.
- Lord Macaulay led the initiative in launching English literary education in India.
- Separate colleges were established for Oriental study and English literary study.
- The early curriculum was language-based and not literature-based
- Charles Grant's policy towards Christianity and English literary study in India can be summed up as follows—a) insistence on the moral aspect of English literature rather than on liberal thought, b) Christianity is concerned with man's internal condition and so would not threaten British rule in India.
- English literature thus emerged as a social institution and proved an instrument for the British to consolidate their rule in India.

Exercises

Answer the following questions in 100–150 words.

1) What was the religious policy of the British rulers in India?
2) Why was early English education in India language-based?

3) What was Charles Grant's argument about English literary study and Christianity?
4) Why did the British not introduce religious education in India?
5) What kind of social institution did the British rulers expect?

Answer the following questions in 250–300 words.

1) What are the important features of postcolonialism?
2) What are the contributions of Said, Bhabha and Spivak to postcolonial theory?
3) Why were the British afraid of introducing religious education in India?
4) What was the role of the missionaries in introducing English literary study in India?
5) According to Viswanathan how did English literary study become an instrument to consolidate British rule in India?

CULTURAL STUDIES

Historical Background

Cultural Studies is a relatively new field that took root towards the last quarter of the twentieth century in England. It is a name given to varied approaches that initiate intellectual enquiries into different socio-political and cultural forms and practices. It makes available certain ways of thinking about and understanding culture and of producing knowledge about it. Critical theory and practice in Europe was influenced by the work of Antonio Gramsci, Theodor Adorno, Walter Benjamin, Louis Althusser, Jacques Lacan, Michel Foucault, Julia Kristeva, Jacques Derrida, Roland Barthes, Pierre Bourdieu and many others. This heterogeneous and often radical legacy was carried forward by theorists and critics like Stuart Hall, Tony Bennett, Paul Gilroy, Lawrence Grossberg, Meaghan Morris and Paul Willis. These and many other critics derived ideas from critical theory and applied them to different aspects/areas of society.

Cultural Studies draws on various fields and yet does not completely identify with any of those fields. It blurs the boundaries between itself and other fields and thus is eclectic, pluralistic and multivalent in its subjects and methods of analysis. It has no specific methodology and therefore no fixed frame of analysis. It is decidedly against any kind of description that characterises it in traditional terms. It defies any attempt at institutionalisation. It is not definitive in its claims and arguments and does not regard its analysis of cultural practices like literature and language as final and fixed. Owing to its comprehensive range and interdisciplinary nature it is difficult and undesirable to attempt a clear definition of Cultural Studies. However theorists have offered commentaries on the configurations of Cultural

Studies which can provide insights into its complex nature. For example, Stuart Hall defines Cultural Studies as 'a cluster (or formation) of ideas, images and practices, which provide ways of talking about, forms of knowledge and conduct associated with a particular topic, social activity or institutional site in society'. Hall's observation carefully and skilfully indicates the debatable and dialogic nature of Cultural Studies that contests the given absolutes of both thought and behaviour.

Though many practitioners of Cultural Studies have objected to its institutionalisation with an attempt at establishing its historical account and fixed objectives and methodology, a host of introductory books which offer an account of its development have been written. These accounts have been produced to introduce this new field to students and teachers and interested readers. The Australian critic Graeme Turner wrote the first historical account of Cultural Studies, titled *British Cultural Studies* (1990), which had several editions over the years. It is at present considered to be the best explanation of the concepts and controversies in Cultural Studies. Other critics like John Storey (*Cultural Consumption and Everyday Life,* 1999), Nick Couldry (*Inside Culture: Re-imagining the Method of Cultural Studies,* 2000), Chris Barker (*Cultural Studies: Theory and Practice*, 2000) and John Hartley (*A Short History of Cultural Studies*, 2003) have offered interesting accounts of the historical development and the peculiar analytical ways of Cultural Studies. For a better view of this field we shall also provide a brief account of its history.

Cultural Studies as a field originated in England, when various English scholars proposed alternative modes of thinking about culture. This was a reaction to the earlier conception of culture proposed by idealist and essentialist theorists of the Victorian era, notably by **Matthew Arnold** (1822–88), who was largely responsible for reading culture with an idealist and essentialist lens. He wrote a book in 1869 explaining his model of culture, titled *Culture and Anarchy,* in which he distinguished between internal and external culture and favoured the internal model of culture. The internal model aimed at cultivating the inner self and eschewing the material aspects of life like amassing wealth or indulging in competition. Thus the model was based on internal purification, integrity and abstinence as opposed to material prosperity and external affluence. The internal culture, he felt, was corrupted and made impure by the advent of industrialisation. He was against commercial, material and competitive enterprise because that only focused on the external aspects of culture and distracted people from following a path of moral and mental purity and integrity. He defined the essence of culture as 'sweetness and light'. This essence advocated the pursuit of beauty and wisdom, and moral and social passion for doing good to others. Arnold's model was very much in tune with the traditional assumption of culture as a process of human development. It emphasised cultivation of refined behaviour, mind and society. He regarded culture as a passage to perfection, beauty and wisdom. The attainment of culture was possible only by persons with high tastes, standards and interests. His concept of culture therefore was elitist, exclusive and against ordinary people. He restricted high tastes and cultural interests to a minority group of social elites. This minority culture was against mass culture and so it was anti-democratic, reactionary, feudal and divisive. Arnold criticised the growing demand among the working class for socio-political rights and equality, stating that this deviated from what was ideal moral conduct. They posed the threat of anarchy (absence of the established order that controls and regulates the social and moral conduct of people) and so there was an urgent need to civilise them into accepting the authority of the ideal culture. Arnold expected the state/government to take charge of the deteriorating situation, to curb the personal liberty of people and force them to abide by the 'right' way. In pursuit of this he championed the values and standards of the elite.

Arnold's model was further elaborated upon and reinforced by another influential British critic **F. R. Leavis** (1895–1978). Leavis, like Arnold, held ordinary people responsible for the falling standards of culture and social conduct. He dismissed popular culture as stereotypical, anonymous and deficient in human experience. He complained against the corruption of tastes and public behaviour by mass media, technology and advertising. He strongly advocated for educational institutions to counter the influence of popular culture. He expected them to create a discriminating and highly trained intellectual elite who will be entrusted with the task of preserving the culture of the English people and tradition of English literature. He emphasised the significant role of this small minority in the cultivation of refined tastes and morally appropriate behaviour. In short Leavis continued with Arnold's emphasis on the minority culture of the elites, with expectations from public functionaries like educational institutions to create high standards of moral behaviour and to exclude popular culture from society.

The cultural critics in Britain challenged this classical, exclusivist and anti-democratic conception of culture and inaugurated the new field of Cultural Studies. The pioneering critics are Richard Hoggart, Raymond Williams, E. P. Thompson and Stuart Hall. They can justifiably be called the four founding fathers of Cultural Studies. All of them were adult educators working outside mainstream university education and taught working class students. They had strong sympathies with the working class. They were all deeply influenced by Marxist thought and actively participated in left-wing politics. Such similarities among these critics collectively contributed towards the establishment of this field as a mode of thinking and practice. It became an academic practice that dealt with both academic and non-academic topics. These critics carried out their studies in different areas and with different analytical methods but their objectives were similar. They took traditional high culture to task and exposed it to a series of deep and exhaustive investigations. As the enquiries moved into different socio-political fields, a whole range of critical ideas and models (emanating from poststructuralist and postmodernist theorists like Derrida, Foucault, and Jean-Francois Lyotard) became available to the practitioners of Cultural Studies. As a result the operative range and interpretive strategies multiplied.

Richard Hoggart (1918–2014), a professor of English at Birmingham University, was the first cultural critic who laid the foundations of Cultural Studies as a field of intellectual inquiry. His book *The Uses of Literacy* (1957) and his establishment of the Birmingham Centre for Contemporary Cultural Studies (which was established by him using the royalty he received on his book) in 1964 made him a prominent figure and brought his ideas into public discussion. His chief concern was to advocate expressions of working class life and consciousness. He persuasively described popular culture and the meaning and values of working class life. He interpreted working class life as an energising experience that could strengthen people to face the difficulties of life. He argued that the everyday activities and rituals of the working class were not trivial and debased but enriching experiences that made them strong and adaptable to changing conditions. His task was to replace the old minority culture with mass culture but he feared that consumerism and mass consumption would make his community hedonistic (pursuing the pleasures of life) and passive.

Another prominent critic who greatly contributed to establishing the academic and theoretical parameters of Cultural Studies was **Raymond Williams** (1921–88). He became Professor of Drama in Cambridge University after working as an adult educator. His early books *Culture and Society: 1780–1950* (1958) and *The Long Revolution* (1961) presented revisionist cultural history in the light of Marxist thought. He developed his own theory, called Cultural Materialism and re-examined the English canonical literary texts from the materialist cultural point of view. Williams criticised the ideological role of the English education system and literary texts in preserving the minority culture and excluding the culture of a large section of society from any kind of serious consideration. He offered a sustained critique of both the canonical literary tradition and high culture. In a nutshell, Williams' contributions can be summed up as follows:

a) He examined the English literary tradition from Edmund Burke to George Orwell to explain contemporary socio-political changes and to define modern, democratic industrial society,

b) He provided a historical basis for understanding culture,

c) He defined culture not as a fixed, universal category but as a complex and dynamic process,

d) He categorised culture into three divisions—dominant, residual and emergent culture.

E. P. Thompson (1924–1993) was an influential British social historian and political activist. He was a devoted Marxist and was against any kind of unmindful and ideological exercise of power. He re-interpreted the concept of class and argued that 'working class' is not a descriptive label but a historical phenomenon that developed over time. His most influential work was *The Making of the English Working Class* (1963) in which he presented a historical analysis of the working class community. This work was Thompson's great contribution to British Cultural Studies because by presenting a historical study of the working class community, it opened up a new field of study called social history.

Stuart Hall (1932–2014) was a cultural theorist and sociologist who contributed significantly to the theoretical setup of Cultural Studies. He can rightfully be called the father of Cultural Studies in the sense that he not only contributed radical new perspectives to the field but brought many areas considered unfit for academic study under the purview of Cultural Studies. He started his career as an adult educator but joined the Centre for Contemporary Cultural Studies at the University of Birmingham in 1964 on Hoggart's invitation. He became the director of the Centre in 1968. He moved to the Open University in 1979 as a professor of sociology until he retired. He was a committed Marxist but he never became a member of the Communist party. He was a founder member of the New Left group of intellectuals influenced by Marxism but was critical of Soviet Russia. Hall's work is wide-ranging, interdisciplinary and collaborative. His approach was pluralistic and dynamic. He along with his colleagues at the Birmingham Centre dealt with subjects as varied as politics, racism, ideology, ethnicity, gender, press, television broadcasting, photography, violence, crime and law. Hall was influenced by Gramsci's notion of hegemony and analysed cultural practices from this point of view. He examined power, subjectivity and identity as important perspectives to understand the complex working of culture, and introduced new topics like multiculturalism, immigration, exile, and diaspora in the domain of Cultural Studies.

American Cultural Studies is different from the British strain in many important respects. The British strain emerged out of sociological and materialist studies of culture whereas Cultural Studies in the US was concerned in its early phase (from 1950 to 1980) with the historical analysis of political parties, anti-traditional figures and economy. The British version was acutely conscious of being British whereas the American version was more international in its approach. The British version struggled against the 'minority culture' that represented the high culture of the elite group of the society whereas the American variant found a new voice in minority scholars like Edward Said and Gayatri Chakravorty Spivak. Unlike British cultural critics American critics have not paid as much attention to tracing the genealogy of Cultural Studies in America. (An illustrative and convincing account of Cultural Studies in the USA is provided by Michael Denning, however, in his book *Culture in the Age of Three Worlds*. London; New York: Verso, 2004). These differences of course did not deter the scholars working in the field of Cultural Studies in the USA from drawing their motivation and topics from British cultural critics like Williams and Hall. James Carey, influenced by Stuart Hall's British cultural model of mass communication, practised it in the USA. Lawrence Grossberg wrote in favour of popular music and the politics of youth in the USA. From within American Studies, George Lipsitz has written extensively on topics like urban culture, inequality, the politics of popular culture, and Whiteness Studies. Michael Denning offers a comprehensive view of the historical development of Cultural Studies in the USA. He reveals the left-wing intellectual tradition in American Cultural Studies. He traces the beginning of Cultural Studies back to the Popular Front intellectuals of the thirties. These were heterogeneous groups of anti-fascist and communist intellectuals and activists who claimed to represent the popular will. The US pragmatist thinker John Dewey (1859–1952, a psychologist and educational reformer) was also decisive in bringing serious attention to culture and social justice. This was further developed by Marxist sociologists like C. Wright Mills (1916–1962, a sociologist who wrote the influential book *The Sociological Imagination*). He analysed the issues of class and power and popularised the term 'elite' by focusing on mass culture. Betty Friedan (1921–2006) was a leading American feminist writer and activist whose book *The Feminine Mystique* is credited with having sparked off the second wave of feminism in the USA. She was part of the labour movement of the 1960s and was instrumental in ushering new issues into American Cultural Studies. African-American critics like W. E. B. DuBois (1868–1963, a sociologist and civil rights activist) raised issues of race, ethnicity, socio-political rights and equality. Another important direction in American Cultural Studies is studies carried out in multiculturalism, race and power by minority scholars like Edward Said, Gayatri Chakravorty Spivak and others.

Australian Cultural Studies became prominent in the late 1970s. Several conditions were responsible for its emergence like the renewed interest in Australian culture and history around the 1960s, the development of a nationally focused tradition of media and film studies and the opening up of a publishing market for Australian Cultural Studies. But the most important impetus was provided by the British intellectual émigrés who came to Australia in search of jobs in the late seventies and early eighties. These include Tony Bennett, John Fiske, John Hartley, Colin Mercer and David Saunders. Because these critics came from Britain their orientation and methods of analysis were influenced by the Birmingham Marxism of Hoggart and Hall, and at the same time by European theories like Ferdinand de Saussure's semiotics and French poststructuralism. They applied the interdisciplinary approaches of European critical theory and British Marxism in their cultural analyses. Due to an academic and highly theoretical orientation the movement remained largely university-based for a long time. The Australian version focused on the representation of Australian culture in different forms and the effects such representation produces on the perceivers. A parallel movement to this more academic version developed in a local tradition of film and media analysis around 1970s. Initially this tradition was under the impact of nationalism and anti-imperialism but gradually it became less fastidious and provincial and began exploring the connection between film and culture and the cultural politics of the film text. In the succeeding years this tradition of film and media studies dominated the scene of Australian Cultural Studies. These two traditions in the Australian Cultural Studies—studies of Australian culture and film and media studies—were not very complementary to each other. However they diversely contributed to the establishment of Cultural Studies as an important field of enquiry in Australia. More recently Cultural Studies has taken the form of cultural policy studies. John Fiske (b. 1939) and John Hartley (b. 1948) in particular have contributed to the rise of this form of Cultural Studies. The main purpose of this form is to contribute towards the training of would-be arts administrators, policy consultants and project managers.

African and Asian varieties of Cultural Studies have been as diverse and complex as Anglo-American forms. But they have been markedly different from them in one very crucial respect—the process of colonisation has had a huge impact on their development. The factors that differentiate the Afro-Asian form from the Anglo-American form are: a) the colonisation of many Afro-Asian countries by European rulers, b) intervention into native cultural practices, c) deliberate representations of the colonies as inferior and uncivilised locations, d) the consequent freedom gained by the colonies from their masters, e) the postcolonial conditions that situate colonies in an uneasy and conflicting space of colonial effects and post-colonial socio-political systems, and f) more recently, globalisation pushing ex-colonies into an entirely new world order.

Post-colonial discourses have mostly been sites of resistance to Europe on one hand and an examination of the internal history and socio-political conditions of the new nation-states on the other. The issues of immigrants, multiculturalism, race, gender and identity have become major concerns of Afro-Asian intellectuals. European Cultural Studies provided important perspectives and modes of analysis to Afro-Asian critics. They have drawn extensively from critical theorists like Gramsci, Althusser, Barthes and Foucault. The history of Afro-Asian Cultural Studies is not separate from the histories of postcolonial intellectual movement/s. It may be seen emerging from the writings of Frantz Fanon, and consolidated and elaborated in new directions by Edward Said, Gayatri Chakravorty Spivak and Homi Bhabha. Cultural Studies has been and continues to be diversely practised by critics like Benita Parry, Stephen Slemon, Trinh T. Minh-ha, Aijaz Ahmad, Arjun Appadurai, Gyan Prakash, Romila Thapar, Dipesh Chakraborty and many others. These and other critics have dealt with almost all areas of cultural practices from nationality to ethnicity to gender politics and identity crisis.

Salient Features of Cultural Studies

Cultural Studies, as a discipline, is so diverse, complex and eclectic that it is very difficult to bring out common features that characterise all its variants. Many of them are inflections on nationalities; others are driven by perspectives as diverse as ethnicity, race, media and communication and globalisation. But for the sake of our understanding (and running the risk of taking a reductionist and essentialist view that Cultural Studies practitioners have so strongly opposed) some common features of Cultural Studies are outlined below.

1) Cultural Studies as a discipline originated in the UK. Some of its earliest practitioners included Richard Hoggart, Raymond Williams, E. P. Thomson and Stuart Hall. These theorists are now referred to as the founding fathers of the discipline.

2) Cultural Studies is frequently studied as two categories—Anglophone, consisting of the British, American and Australian strains, and Non-Anglophone, consisting of the African and Asian strains. These categories are by no means exclusive, and are frequently influenced by one another.

3) Cultural Studies is not definitive in nature. It does not appropriate or deal with universals (the assumptions that certain characteristics are universally applicable) or absolutes (fundamental, unquestionable and perfect characteristics or ideals) and therefore does not propose theories and modes of analysis that are complete, fixed and final. It may therefore be called dynamic, easily prone to change and resistant to any attempt at canonisation.

4) It does not provide answers to philosophical/cultural problems of the contemporary global world. It has caused debates and dialogue over problematic and contestable issues and has helped us understand the undercurrents of cultural systems.

5) It is against any kind of traditional mode of thinking characterised by coherence and unity. It does not follow a traditional modality of standardisation; that is, it does not aim at its own definition, or outlining its scope, methodology and history. This is because it is anti-institutional, interdisciplinary and critical of all traditional systems of knowledge.

6) Cultural Studies is a series of intellectual inquiries into different areas that are both academic and non-academic.

It draws on different critical approaches like Marxism, poststructuralism, postmodernism, postcolonialism and feminism, and makes use of their insights and concepts in its analysis. It defies identification with any one discipline and school of thought, however. Cultural Studies has traditionally been resistant to traditional norms and institutionalisation.

7) It examines all those traditions, systems and institutions through which particular values, beliefs, competencies, routines of life and habitual forms of conduct are inculcated in society.

8) Its major concerns are power, identity, subjectivity and meaning. It explores different forms of power like gender, race, class, colonialism, etc.

9) It does not consider culture as a fixed, universally true, unchangeable, idealistic and essential category. Culture is dynamic, changeable, complex and full of contradictions. Cultural Studies understands culture as indicative of a society's whole way of life in which the relations of power and gender, pleasure and pressures of consumption and fantasies and desires through which social relations are carried out are performed in the name of cultural activity.

Introduction to Stuart Hall's 'Cultural Identity and Diaspora'

This essay is an explication of cultural identity. Stuart Hall discusses the nostalgic tendency of Afro-Caribbean diasporic artists to discover their identity in the remote past and the ever-multiplying nature of their present identity characterised by diversity, hybridity and difference. He convincingly argues that the cultural identity of Afro-Caribbean diaspora is not in the essentialised (the characteristic features out of which identity is formed) past but in the play of different aspects that make and remake it. His concern in the essay is with the representation of the cultural identity of the Afro-Caribbean people in emerging Caribbean cinema and black British cinema. But the analysis is so comprehensive in range and appeal that it embraces almost all other cultural factors in its fold. The immediate reference is to the then-emerging Caribbean cinema which is different from African-Caribbean cinema of the diasporas of the West. It is at this point that Hall problematises the issue of representation of cultural identity. His argument is that the practice of representation suggests the positions from which it is done. Hall refers to enunciation as a source of the positions that so radically influence the practice of representation. The French linguist **Émile Benveniste** (1902–1976) proposed this theory of enunciation in his book *Problems in General Linguistics* (1971). He distinguished between the *énoncé* (statement) and the *énonciation* (utterance), or between what is said and how it is said. Pushed logically further this means that the 'I' of the statement is not the same as the 'I' of the utterance. The result of this is that the 'I' is always the 'other'. Hall refers to this theoretical proposition and argues that knowledge of the position of the representation is very crucial in determining the cultural identity. This leads to the problematic construction that the speaker and the subject who is spoken of are never the same and are never exactly in the same place. Identity therefore is not transparent and unproblematic. It is not an accomplished state but a production that is always in process and never complete. It is always constituted within representation itself.

Hall claims that we all write and speak from a particular place and time, from a history and from a culture; that is, our speech is always grounded in some kind of context and so we are always in some position or the other. He gives his own example to substantiate his claim. He comes from a lower middle class Jamaican family, that he has spent all his adult life in England and has lived in the shadow of the black diaspora; this places him in a particular position of the diaspora experience and informs his writing as a narrative of displacement.

Hall explains two categories of thinking about cultural identity. The first one is the Caribbean culture of the blacks. It is a collectively shared unified culture that covers many divisions and identities. It is based on common historical experiences and shared cultural codes. The essence of this culture that holds the Caribbean people together is 'Caribbeanness'. Hall notes that this concept of cultural identity (one, unified, essentialist Caribbean culture) motivated most of the post-colonial struggles and related creative and critical writing. Artists who believe in this kind of cultural identity imaginatively cross over the present state of misery and self-contempt and create a beautiful era in the remote past. The Caribbean cinema that Hall refers to at the beginning of the essay is an example of this kind of imaginative rediscovery. He cites another example, of photographic representations of such cultural identity. The photographs of the visual artist Armet Francis, a Jamaica-born photographer who has lived in Britain since the age of eight and whose photography extensively depicts black people living in Britain and his home country, try to recreate the underlying unity of black people which was disturbed by colonisation and slavery. Hall argues that such representations of cultural unity and oneness are attempts to impose an imaginary coherence on the experience of dispersal and fragmentation. All diasporas tend to recreate such imaginary worlds through their writings.

The second category of cultural identity is fluid, changing and full of breaks and discontinuities. It splits 'the Caribbean uniqueness' of 'one culture' because it is subject to the continuous play of history, politics and culture. It is in this sense that cultural identity is a matter of becoming as well as being. It is not eternally fixed in the essentialised past. It belongs to the future as much as to the past. Hall argues that it is this second category of cultural identity (dispersed, fragmented, plural and anti-essential) that can offer a proper perspective for the examination of the present status of Caribbean culture. Western colonial regimes not only constructed Caribbean people as the Other through their knowledge categories as Edward Said (the famous US-based

Palestinian critic) argued but also made them see and experience themselves as the Other. Hall develops his analysis along this line of thought and makes use of Michel Foucault's notion of 'power/knowledge' (Foucault's proposition is that power relations play a decisive role in the formation of knowledge). The second category of cultural identity is constructed through memory, fantasy, narrative and myth. It does not relate people directly to any kind of essence (since there have been breaks and discontinuities) but to a position. There is always a politics of identity, a politics of position. This identity does not proceed from a fixed origin in a straight, unbroken line so that we can clearly understand its formation. It is complex and intersecting. We can understand it only through an eclectic approach. Hall provides two axes to examine black Caribbean identities: the axis of similarity and continuity, and the axis of difference and rupture. The examination of cultural identity should take into account the interrelations between these two axes. The first axis relates the investigator with the past and makes him aware of the continuity of the past. The second axis makes him aware of the difference that breaks and discontinuities have brought to the Caribbean people—slavery, transportation, colonisation and migration. Hall warns that these breaks and continuities were not the source of cultural and social difference among black Caribbeans. They were already different from one another. Their different countries, tribal communities, villages, languages and gods had already introduced several differences among them. So with the continuity of past traces of Caribbean culture, differences brought about by several intervening factors also continued. The Caribbean cultures have changed and continue to change and the differences among them are easily observable. However all Caribbean cultures appear 'the same' in comparison with the West because they are the marginal, the underdeveloped and the 'Other' to them. Thus similarity and difference work together. African cultural identities like Jamaican, Haitian, Cuban, Gaudeloupean, Barbadian, etc. have similar histories, yet they are differently positioned. Hall carries further this idea of the play of difference and explains that it suggests instability, permanent unsettlement and the lack of any final resolution. The doubleness of this play is present in Caribbean music and other forms of representation. Keeping in view this complex and dispersed form of Caribbean culture, Caribbean cinema cannot represent it as a simple, binary view of 'past/present' or 'them/us'. A simplistic binary view cannot address its complex multi-faceted form. Hall refers to Martinique as an example of this double play. Martinique is an island in the Caribbean seas and an overseas region of France. Officially it is an integral part of France. But it is both part of France and not part of France. It is a part of France, because it is a department of France and this can be observed in the lifestyle and cultural practices of the inhabitants of the city of Fort de France. The city of Kingston, on the other hand, also apart of Martinique, is comparatively poor and less fashionable.

Hall analyses the play of difference by using Jacques Derrida's notion of differance. Meaning (in the present instance, representation) thus remains either over or underdetermined, either an excess or a supplement. Hall applies this play of differance to the positioning and repositioning of Caribbean cultural identities. He investigates the configurations of Caribbean cultural identities and argues that they are not made up of a singular, unified, coherent essence but of three different aspects—the African, the European and the American.

He elaborates on the African aspect of the Caribbean cultural identities—Africa has remained the site of the repressed people who suffered slavery for a long time and who were silenced by this transforming experience. It has remained an unspoken and unspeakable factor of Caribbean culture. Hall points out that it was not until the 1970s that the Jamaican people discovered that they were black and Africans. Thus the Jamaican people who were living on the periphery found their Afro-Caribbean identity. But this discovery of Afro-Caribbean identity did not come to the Caribbean people unmediated. He argues that events like the several post-colonial revolutions, the civil rights struggle and the culture of Rastafarianism (a religious movement in Jamaica which worships Haile Selassie, the former emperor of Ethiopia and is based on the belief that the black people will return to 'Africa') and the music of reggae (popular music from Jamaica that combines native styles with rock and soul music) made a great impact on the process of the formation of Afro-Caribbean identity. Africa has become the origin of all Caribbean people even though they come from a different ethnic background. Hall argues that displacement, dismemberment and transportation have long cut off the Caribbean people from Africa, which used to be the origin of their identity. The present gesture to revisit Africa as the origin makes no sense because it is no longer present in its earlier form. He refers to many literary texts and music that feature such homeward journeys. This journey is not in search of the Africa in the essentialised past but the Africa re-imagined and creatively reconstructed by the Caribbean diasporas in the present time through politics, memory and desire.

Hall then discusses the second aspect of the formation of the Caribbean cultural identities, the European aspect. Europe introduced a new power dynamic, altering the whole discourse of Caribbean culture. This was done through colonialism, underdevelopment, poverty and the racism of colour. The play of politics introduced by the Europeans places the Caribbean people as the 'Other' instead of the Caribbean people placing Europe as the 'Other'. This was a result of strategies of exclusion and imposition adopted by the Europeans, which induced feelings of racial inferiority in the Caribbean people. Notably it excites both similarity and difference in them at the same time. Thus the European aspect is always present in the Caribbean cultural identity. Hall substantiates his argument with a reference to Caribbean film-making and writing where Caribbean filmmakers and writers have very complex and multifarious relationships with the Western filmmakers and writers.

The third aspect of the Caribbean cultural identity is the American presence in the mode of thinking and behaviour of the Caribbean people. The American presence that Hall calls the 'New World' is the juncture where many cultures meet. This 'New World' is both the place where creolisations, assimilations and syncretisms are negotiated and the place of the many continuous displacements of cultures. In order to explain his point, Hall traces the origin of the word 'Jamaica' by referring to Peter Hulme's essay. According to Hulme the word is the Hispanic (originally from an area where Spanish language is spoken and especially referring to Latin America) form of Arawak (one of the indigenous groups that lives along the coast of Guyana). But the original word and its significations are nowhere present in present-day Jamaican cultural and social life. For example the indigenous 'Arawak' is not represented in the emblem of the Jamaican National Heritage Trust. In its place the figure of Diego Pimienta (an African who fought for his Spanish masters against English invaders in 1655) was chosen. This shows the deferred and metonymic representation of Jamaican identity. It shows both the displacement of the so-called African identity and assimilation into the 'New World'. Thus the cultural collisions and assimilations between America and Africa have informed the cultural identity of the Caribbean people. According to Hall the American presence has introduced diversity, hybridity and difference in the African-Caribbean people.

Diaspora for Hall is not a term that refers to the scattered tribes whose identity can only be confirmed by relating them to some sacred past. Hall calls such attempts an imperialistic and hegemonic form of ethnicity. His definition of diaspora is not essence and purity but heterogeneity and diversity. Diasporic identities constantly produce and reproduce themselves through transformation and difference. Hall refers to the nostalgia prevalent among Afro-Caribbean diasporic writers, artists and critics to return to their lost origins. But it is only an imaginary return. Thus Hall explains the multifarious nature of Afro-Caribbean identities and evidently shows that any reductionist approach would fail to recognise their ever-multiplying identities.

Key Points

- Hall's immediate concern in the essay is the representation of Caribbean cultural identity in the then-emerging Caribbean cinema and British black cinema.
- Representation is the result of positions taken by the speaker and the subject.
- Identity is not transparent and unproblematic but opaque and complex; it is a construction in process and not an accomplished fact.
- There are two categories of cultural identity—a) the Caribbean culture of the blacks: a collectively shared unified culture with many divisions and identities, and b) the dispersed fragmented, plural and anti-essential category of culture constructed through memory, fantasy, myth and narrative.
- The search for a cultural identity entails locating multiple positions people take, and not limiting it to an all-encompassing essence.
- Black Caribbean identity can be understood on two axes— a) the axis of similarity and continuity, and b) the axis of difference and rupture.
- The Caribbean culture and people cannot be read as one homogeneous entity, because there are many social and cultural differences among them.
- Hall uses Derrida's notion of 'differance' to explain how the play of difference activates the multiple layers of Afro-Caribbean cultural identity.

- According to Hall, Afro-Caribbean cultural identity is made up of three different aspects: the African, the European and the American.
- Diaspora, according to Hall, can be understood only when there is an acknowledgement of its heterogeneous and diverse nature.

Exercises

Answer the following questions in 100–150 words.

1) What is representation, according to Hall?
2) What is the nature of identity?
3) Describe the two categories of cultural identity described by Hall.
4) What are the two axes through which Afro-Caribbean cultural identity can be studied?
5) What are the three aspects that make up Afro-Caribbean cultural identity?

Answer the following questions in 250–300 words.

1) Elucidate the salient features of Cultural Studies.
2) Describe in detail the historical development of Cultural Studies.
3) What is Hall's concept of cultural identity?
4) How does Hall apply Derrida's concept of differance to Caribbean identity?
5) Why does Hall argue that the original Africa is an imaginary land for the Caribbean diaspora?

DIGITAL HUMANITIES

Historical Background

The title contains two terms—digital and humanities. It combines the traditional and modern modes of critical understanding. Humanities in its traditional avatar consists of various text-based disciplines which study classics, literature, philosophy, performing arts, media and communication and cultural studies. Digital humanities is a new variant which uses informational technology as a method of research in traditional humanities disciplines like literature and the performing arts.

As a field of study digital humanities has cut across disciplines and has provided not only tools but new methods of research and analysis. It has moved beyond preservation of physical artefacts (like images, manuscripts, texts, etc.) and has gone to the extent of creating new artefacts like digital archives. We may very briefly define it as a combination of the methods of traditional humanities disciplines like philosophy, linguistics, literature, art and archaeology with computational tools like information retrieval, data visualisation, data processing, data mining, multimedia and digital publishing.

The history of the origin and development of digital humanities is well-documented. It begins with the painstaking efforts of an Italian Jesuit priest Father Roberto Busa (1913–2011, a pioneer in the application of computers to linguistic and literary analysis). Father Busa began to write an *index verboratum* (originally a Latin term that means preparation of an index of words or terms used in a book) of all the words in the works of St. Thomas Aquinas (1225–1274, an Italian theologian and philosopher) and other related authors. The index went up to eleven million Italian words. Busa thought that a computer, still a new technology at the time, could help him complete his huge task. He went to visit Thomas J. Watson (1874–1956, an American businessman who served as chairman and CEO of IBM) at IBM (International Business Machines Corporation is an American multinational company) in the USA. With the help of IBM technocrats Busa was able to slowly transfer the entire text to punched cards. This was perhaps the first ever attempt to combine humanities with computation. Two other activities helped digital humanities develop further. The first was the launching of a new journal, *Journal of Computers and Humanities* in 1966 under the editorship of Joseph Raben. It was a journal exclusively devoted to the study of how computers could be used in humanities. Raben made the journal a vehicle for the circulation of new experiments and developments in computing humanities. The second event was the establishment of centres dedicated to the use of computers in humanities around the 1960s, an example of which is Roy Wisbey founding the Centre for Literary and Linguistic Computing at Cambridge in 1963.

In the next period, the 1970s and 80s, a series of conferences on the application of computers in the humanities was organised, first in England and then in the USA. Later these two national groups entered into a collaboration with each other and founded The Association for Computers and the Humanities in 1978. Such attempts to encourage the involvement of humanities with computation were supported by archives like the Oxford Text Archive (OTA), set up in 1976. It provided electronic texts and references to researchers and tried to preserve them. During this period courses on computing humanities were also introduced in computing centres. The courses were mostly based on vocabulary, stylistic analysis and linguistic applications.

The period from the 1980s onwards was a time of important developments in computing humanities. Personal computers (PCs) became available to people working in the humanities and the texts on screen (that later came to be known as hypertexts) came as a great advantage to them. By this time the facility of electronic mail which was limited to computer scientists and researchers was made available to researchers working in computing humanities. John McCarty (an American researcher in digital humanities who coined the term *artificial intelligence* and conducted seminal research in the field) started the journal *Humanist* in 1987. It was pivotal in making electronic communication possible among people working in computing humanities. It has maintained high standards ever since and is an excellent site for electronic discussion lists.

The period from the 1990s onwards saw great changes in the computing humanities, both in terms of development in electronic communication and in the variety of experiments and versions of multimedia, software and hypertext. The most important events of this period were the arrival of Internet and the World Wide Web (WWW). These two electronic modes made things easier, faster and quickly accessible. They freed users from the traditional constrains of time, space, exposure and institutional hazards of printing books. Scholars in computing humanities made an enormous amount of material including references, texts, biographies and other information available to the common users. There are countless benefits of these electronic media and millions have used them since their arrival. Texts being turned into hypertexts not only lead to greater reach and ease of access, but also provide further links within the text, so that researchers can have access to annotations, bibliography and other relevant information. Anyone can now publish his/her material/text on the Web and can attract the attention of international readers within a short time. The published material can be corrected and updated on the web page itself.

As a result of such highly useful techniques computing humanities has changed its earlier status as an archive of electronic resources to a field of new creations that can reshape the humanities. Multimedia has transformed texts into different forms like images, audio and video. Such expressions in different electronic forms have created tremendous scope for further research in computing humanities. We can witness various adventurous enquiries carried out by the researchers into computing humanities. Many researchers have interpreted hypertext in the light of the perspectives provided by postmodern and poststructural theories.

The nomenclature 'digital humanities' is of comparatively recent origin. It has been referred to by many terms like humanities computing, humanist informatics, literary and linguistic computing, digital resources in the humanities, and sometimes e-humanities. The term 'digital humanities' began to be widely used after the publication of the seminal book, *Companion to Digital Humanities* (ed. Susan Schreibman, Ray Siemens and John Unsworth, Blackwell, 2005). The merging of the Association for Computers in the Humanities and the Association for Literary and Linguistic Computing and the launching of the Digital Humanities Initiative, a funding programme by the National Endowment for the Humanities (NEH) in 2006 also made the term popular and gave impetus to research in this field.

Researchers working in the field of digital humanities present its history in the form of waves. The first wave (the late 1990s and the early 2000s) is considered to be quantitative in nature because during this phase digitisation projects were undertaken and technological infrastructure was established. The second wave (2000s onwards to the present) is qualitative in nature in that it has undertaken the interpretation of the interaction between digitisation and humanities and has generated a huge amount of research in visual representations and network analysis.

In a nutshell we can say that digital humanities promotes understanding of culture through digital technology. The perspective that stands out most prominently in digital humanities is the interest of the theorists in hypertext. Researchers have shown the convergence of hypertext and poststurctural theories. (For example George P. Landow in his book *Hypertext: the Convergence of Contemporary Critical Theory and Technology* [1992] makes a very insightful and exhaustive study of this kind). It is therefore worth knowing the parallels between hypertext and postmodern/poststructuralist ideas.

Hypertext	Literary Theory
Hypertext is an electronic text that contains links to other texts. It is a form of textuality composed of blocks of words and links that opens several other reading links. It is not limited to text but includes graphics, images, videos and sound. It is open to change and accessible to all. It is not based on any absolute and it remakes and is re-made constantly.	Literary theorists do not consider text as a closed piece of writing that allows no change but as an open continuum. They use the word 'text' in a somewhat similar sense to digital hypertext. It is not closed, unified, definitive and original for them.
Hypertext is not linear and compact. It is multilinear in the sense that it draws from several discrete sources, and actively encourages users/researchers to explore other media and fields of thought by making several further links available within the body of the text.	Literary theorists do not consider a text to be linear and unilateral. It is multilinear, multivalent writing that holds together information drawn from diverse sources.
Users/readers can customise the hypertext to the form and appearance they find best suited to their utility, purpose and desire.	Literary theorists observe that during the process of reading the text is reshaped into a different text and with every new reader the text becomes newly configured.
Electronic links provided within the hypertext reconfigure text and create an ever-multiplying and ever-changing chain. This chain of reconfiguration moves texts, readers and writers into a new writing space.	The act of reading radically changes the positions of text, reader and writer. The hierarchies collapse and give way to new arrangements where readers can enjoy the privilege of a writer.

The multiple reading links shift the power balance between reader and writer. Reconfiguration of the author and the authorial property constantly takes place as the reader plays the role of the author and reconfigures his text.	The shifting power equation between the reader and the author is very much like Stanley Fish's idea of the reader as the co-author of the text. It is also reminiscent of Roland Barthes idea of readerly text. In both instances the individual reader is not emphasised and his reading or re-writing is not taken to be full and final. The shift in emphasis and the multiplication of text are suggested through such ideas.
Hypertext is a network of connections to other texts. This can as well be understood as connections to knowledge which is distributed throughout the network. It is neither localised nor restricted to a particular electronic space/memory.	'Network' is a key term in the discussion of literary theorists. Major theorists like Barthes, Derrida, Foucault and Pierre Macherey have all interpreted text as a network that leads to some other text, thus forming a non-linear chain.
Networking leads to democratisation of the entire process of knowledge creation and distribution. Separations like main texts or original texts and annotations (which are texts in themselves) create hierarchical distinctions. But hypertext removes such distinctions.	The purpose of the conception of text as a network is to democratise the process of reading. Theorists reject the hierarchical distinctions of an original text and annotations. They see them as interconnected and interdependent. So every text works as a network for a host of other texts and vice-versa. The result is the collapse of hierarchies.

Salient Features of Digital Humanities

1) Digital humanities is the outcome of the efforts of researchers working towards the application of computation to humanities for more than half a century.

2) Digital humanities has immensely multiplied the potential of humanities disciplines and widened its reach both within and outside the academic world.

3) Its major concerns are—creation, preservation and interpretation of cultural data.

4) It has transformed from its initial role as a resource for texts and references to a serious intellectual enterprise with its own principles, rigorous norms and theoretical explorations.

5) Digital humanities does not have a history, like traditional humanist scholarship. This apparent weakness has proved to be an opportunity to digital humanities. Researchers in this field have had to invent new forms, tools and devices to study humanities. These inventions are the result of the shared premises of humanists, technologists and designers, and keep abreast with the contemporary world.

6) Due to digitisation communication has become varied, extensible and multiplicative. This has decisively influenced the communication process in humanities. Communication in humanities has also increasingly become varied, multifarious and extensive. This has resulted in multilinearity and multivalency of both electronic devices and texts.

7) Digital humanities is a generative field. It means that students and teachers in this field make things as they study and conduct research. They generate not only texts in the form of commentary, analysis or narration but images, interaction and software.

8) Digital humanities is based on visual elements like motion graphics, animation, screen capture, video and the appropriation and remixing of code. As a result textual elements have become secondary and visual elements are of primary importance.
9) Digital humanities has entirely changed the concepts and positions of the author, text and reader in humanities. Everyone who uses an electronic medium has the opportunity to write and publish or rewrite on the screen. So the centrality of the author is challenged. The unity, compact design and linearity of text have given way to extensibility, multiplicity and multilinearity of text. It has become hypertext. Readers have become active and dynamic due to electronic medium.
10) The very objectives, motivations and structure of disciplines in the humanities are radically changed due to digitisation.

Introduction to Stuart Moulthrop's 'You Say You Want a Revolution? Hypertext and the Laws of Media'

Stuart Moulthrop, in his essay, offers an insightful account of the history, nature and function of hypertext. He discusses the convergence of hypertext and contemporary critical theory in particular. We may understand the essay in three parts. The first part presents the history of hypertext, the second part offers a balanced view of the role and utility of hypertext and the last part discusses the relation of hypertext to contemporary critical theory. Unlike many supporters of hypertext and hypermedia, Mouthrop does not expect hypertext to bring any revolutionary change in human culture. However, unlike many critical theorists and cultural critics he does not underestimate the utility of hypertext either. Moulthrop is very balanced and impartial in his explanation and yet seriously committed to his topic of hypertext.

Moulthrop begins his discussion with a reference to the origin of hypertext. The concept of hypertext originated with Vannevar Bush (1890–1974) in 1945. He was a science advisor to President Roosevelt and an electrical engineer who designed an early computer.He wanted to build a machine called Memex to help researchers organise disparate sources of knowledge. His project did not succeed but the appearance of electronic computers on the academic scene proved that his projections were right and practically viable. The next development in this direction was the creation of an animation game called 'Adventure' by artificial intelligence researchers in the early 1960s. This was the first hypertextual narrative. Around this time Theodor Holm Nelson (b. 1937, an American philosopher, sociologist and expert in information technology) coined the term 'hypertext'. His dream project was to create a world-wide network of information. He called this project 'Xanadu' (like S. T. Coleridge's vision in a dream, a computer filing system for a great body of literature with all its details of authorship, ownership, interconnections and linkages) and projected it to be a centrally coordinated system through linking and retrieval. Nelson dreamt of putting every bit of information on screen and making it easily accessible to users. Computer scientists were impressed by Nelson's projections. One of the noted computer scientists, Douglas Englebart (one of the pioneers of user interface design) entered into a collaboration with Nelson. They prepared a hypertext system called FRESS (an abbreviation of a hypertext system called File Retrieval and Editing System) at Brown University in the early 1970s. Nelson saw hypertext as a dynamic computing system in which readers could both use and change the textual corpus. He argued that hypertext systems have immense political ramifications. But his concept of hypertext and its stated revolutionary potential did not excite the interest of scholar technologists until the mid 1980s. Around 1987 some important things happened. Nelson's books *Computer Lib* and *Dream Machines* were published by Microsoft Press, and Nelson joined Autodesk, a leading company in software development. This company resolved to support Xanadu as a commercial enterprise. It was also around this time that the Association for Computing Machinery sponsored the first of its international conferences on hypertext. Apple Computer began giving away HyperCard (a programming tool) to anyone who owned a Macintosh personal computer. HyperCard was a very useful model for operation—it was cheap, simple to operate and powerful. It was hoped that HyperCard and other computer applications would bring in a new era of textual communication. But the expected revolution did not take place in textual communication.

With this brief sketch of the origin and development of computational devices Moulthrop moves on to the relation of hypertext to humanities. He mentions some critics and their works that finally took note of hypertext and its utility in the study of humanities. Jay David Bolter's *Writing Space* (1991) offers a historical view of hypertext; Ted Nelson's *Literary Machines* presents for the first time the study of hypertext in hypertextual form; George Landow's *Hypertext* (1992) discusses the hypertext within the context of poststructuralist and postmodern theory. Moulthrop refers to the datedness of the technology that we use and the human tendency to look for the new. He agrees with the objection that hypertext has not fully lived up to its promises in the sense that it has not caused the expected revolution to materialise by replacing the old information order with a new one. But he argues that such expectations in the postmodern context do not make much sense. He mentions postmodern theorists like Baudrillard, Lyotard, Donna Haraway and Hakim Bey and their contribution to the digitisation of humanities. Jean Baudrillard (1929–2007), the French philosopher proposed his theory of simulation. He argued that in the postmodern condition representation is replaced by simulation and therefore there is no reality but hyperreality. Jean-Francois Lyotard (1924–98) another French philosopher and literary theorist rejected all traditional literary and cultural narratives as grand narratives and their consequent failure in explaining the complexity of the postmodern condition. Donna Haraway (b.1944) an American feminist critic has carried out interdisciplinary studies of technology and gender. Her approach to science, gender, nature and humanity has challenged the commonsense assumptions of and about these fields. Hakim Bey (b. 1945, pseudonym of Peter Lamborn Wilson) is an American philosopher and radical thinker. He is famous for his work called TAZ (Temporary Autonomous Zones) which was first published in 1985. He offered an anarchist view of the world and tried to relate the developments in science to poetry. By referring to these theorists with very different pursuits, Moulthrop brings out the parallels between hypertext and electronic medium.

Moulthrop then proceeds to discuss the necessity and distinctiveness of hypertext. He argues that it should not be dismissed as a local movement and as the preserve of a few in the technological elite. In order to prove this he relates and compares hypertext to the postmodern notion of simulation. Simulation is a postmodern theory proposed by Baudrillard which states that there is nothing real and primary in the original and pure sense in the world. The other connection of hypertext is to the vision in a dream seen by S. T. Coleridge (as described in his famous poem 'Kubla Khan'). Moulthrop sees no problem with revising Coleridge's dream in a new postmodern context when the line of distinction between reality and dream is blurred and the concept of originality complicated. Through computation this dream becomes a reconstruction of text not as a fixed series of symbols but a variable access database in which the reader/writer can forge new links. Ted Nelson's project of Xanadu is one such reconstruction of this dream. Before further elaborating his views on hypertext Moulthrop makes readers aware of the many criticisms of the postmodern notion of simulation. These criticisms are in fact a series of complicated issues (or 'technological abjection' as he calls it). According to Nelson, the entire world is a simulation. It means that there is only circulation and proliferation of discourses and methods. Simulation or hyperreality presents no clear agenda for social study and privileges no discourse as absolute and definitive. As a result the social critique becomes only a game and the multiplying view that it offers becomes a techno-social construction of reality. It is not truly radical and truly oppositional (as it has been claimed by the theorists like Lyotard to be against the grand narratives of modernism). This gets more complicated when the concept of hyperreality is brought in the company of media and technology. We all turn into mere 'simulacral subjects incapable of any radical or oppositional action'.

With his brief discussion of the objections to simulation theory, Moulthrop refers to the counterviews of critics in defence of the association between simulation theory and the electronic medium. He names critics like Bolter (b. 1951, J. David Bolter is a professor in the School of Literature, Media and Communication at the Georgia University of Technology, and wrote the textbook *Writing Space* in 2001 which offered an explanation of the use of computers for writing and research), Drexler (b. 1955, K. Eric Drexler is an American engineer who is known for his seminal work in nanotechnology, *Engines of Creation: The Coming of Nanotechnol*ogy in 1987), McCorduck (b. 1941, Pamela McCorduck is an American author of books on the history and philosophical significance of artificial intelligence; her famous book is *The Universal Machine: Confessions of a Technological Optimist*, 1985), and Zuboff (b.1951 Shoshanna Zuboff is a professor of Business Administration at Harvard Business School who has written on computer-mediated task environment in her famous *In the Age of the Smart Machine: The Future of Work and Power,* 1988) who strongly contend that technology can liberate humanity. These critics argue that postmodern modes of communication can destabilise social hierarchies and promote decentralising of authority, and thus can be of great use to humanity.

Moulthrop argues that the solution to these problems (whether electronic medium/hypertext can be of use to humanity, what are the ways in which its bad effects can be nullified and how it will bring about social revolution) lies not in theory but in practice.

Nelson's hypertext has the potential to offer the practical solutions required. It advances technological renaissance. It is different from Coleridge's Xanadu because that was an opium-induced vision and this is a well-envisioned business plan. It is not a fixed entity but a fluid database which is continuously remade by the users. Moulthrop defines hypertext as a complex network of textual elements. It consists of *lexias* (a term used by Roland Barthes to imply units of meaning) which may be pages, paragraphs, sections or volumes. Lexias are connected by links which work like dynamic footnotes. Hypertext is not book-bound so it can be modified by the reader/writer. It becomes a collective text that can expand limitlessly. Therefore Nelson calls hypertext 'docuverse.' Moulthrop further points out the utility to which hypertext can be put in the near future. Hypertext can bring about a complete 'renovation' of culture by unifying discourses, readers and writers. This is the world in which 'work' becomes 'text', not substance but reference, not containment but connection. Moulthrop briefly explains the political change or social order that this intertextual world can bring to human beings. Hypertext will bring a new *populitism*—a combination of populism with elite (a new coinage by Nelson). Populitism creates a society of text where no one is the author in a traditional hierarchical sense. In this populite culture everyone has access to information. This will be a kind of technological democracy.

In his discussion of the usefulness of hypertext Moulthrop does not disregard the troubles that the concept of populitism may cause. He mentions two problems. The first is that such a social/textual order will give benefits to only a few and that those benefitted will not understand the responsibility of distributing access among many. To substantiate the point Moulthrop considers the case of Clifford Stoll. Stoll in his book *The Cuckoo's Egg* exemplifies this problem. The paradox in his position is that he supports informational freedom on one hand but also regards digital information as strictly private and as property owned by elite experts employed by governments and corporations on the other hand. He believes that scientists alone must have access to databases. Stoll is partial and hierarchical in his approach. Further he supports the appropriation and utilisation of computer technology by the military and fails to understand the complicity between technology industry and the military. Moulthrop criticises such hierarchical positions and argues that they can foreclose the possibility of new change that hypertext promises.

The second problem is that information has virtually become equivalent to capital. Textuality shapes information, but this could be appropriated by capitalist systems to their benefit. So the promise of Xanadu to make information available to everyone becomes a complicated project. The trouble then is how the promised change will come about and how it will destabilise established hierarchies.

Moulthrop proceeds to explain the projected function or role of hypertext in creating a social/cultural order based on 'populitism'. He offers his explanation in the framework of the four questions provided by Marshall McLuhan (1911–1980, a Canadian cultural historian and media theorist. His notes on media and technology were posthumously published as *The Laws of Media: The New Science*, 1988). McLuhan formulates four basic questions that can be asked about any invention. Moulthrop applies these four questions and interprets hypertext accordingly. The first question is: 'What does hypertext enhance or intensify?' According to McLuhan communications media adjust the balance of human senses by privileging one sense over the other. For example, in print media sight is privileged over hearing. Applied to hypertext this principle reveals that hypertext is different from earlier media. Moulthrop argues that hypertext is not a new invention at all but an extension of an earlier form of symbolic discourse called print. It is significant to note that the effect of hypertext is not limited to senses but it extends to the mind, that is, it enhances our sensitivity. It encourages users to explore and construct links. It works on the ideas of affiliation, correspondence and resonance. Like literature it is an extended network of relations which readers and writers perpetually make and unmake. Moulthrop notes that hypertext may turn users into 'paranoids' as they may assume that all structures or arrangements they perceive are working against them. However he does not see it as a negative effect. It is a positive effect because it is a 'creative paranoia' in which the user can scrutinise the existing structures with the help of his ability to build and pursue links. The other concern that Moulthrop registers is that hypertext in the name of openness and interactivity predetermines choices for readers. Hypertext seems to open up new ways of access to readers but forecloses others at the same time. An article on a news site, for example, contains links to a few other articles the creators of the article deem relevant, and not to certain other articles.

The second question is: 'What does hypertext displace or render obsolete?' In addressing this question Moulthrop considers both print and electronic media. He records the justifications and objections to the arrival of electronic media. His answer to the above question is that hypertext does not render literacy obsolete. Hypertext implies a revival (Moulthrop uses the word *recursion* with a special computational sense) of typographic culture, a continuation and extension of print media. Moulthrop argues that print is not the only medium of information communication. Hypertext enhances the potential of information communication through several electronic devices. It can create interactive multimedia texts that incorporate voice, music, animated graphics and video along with alphabetic script.

The third question is: 'What does hypertext retrieve that was previously obsolete?' Moulthrop continues the discussion of print media and electronic media in the answer of this question. He argues that hypertext may be seen as the recursion to a new stage of typography of literacy. In order to explain the difference between these two media, Moulthrop distinguishes the word 'recursion' from mere repetition or return. 'Recursion' is self-reference with the possibility of progressive self-modification

(Moulthrop uses 'recursion' in at least two senses: a) a computer programming technique which involves the use of a procedure that calls itself one or more times until a specified condition is set, b) a self-referential medium that allows for further modification in its configuration). It consistently refers to itself and still maintains the possibility of change in its configurations. Repetition or return, on the other hand, is mere revival of the earlier self with no space for change. So the answer to the third question is that hypertext retrieves literacy, which was previously obsolete. Moulthrop carries forward the point of continuity between literacy and hypertext. Literacy in hypertext covers two fields—the ordinary, grammatical, rhetorical and tropological space generally called 'literature' and interactive discourse. The second field of interactive discourse is located in cyberspace. Moulthrop argues that beneath any hypertext system there is a lower layer called hypotext. On this level Xanadu becomes a creature of print. This happens because the command structures that control linkage, display, editing and accounting of the hypertext in the form of digital impulses can be translated into typographic text. Xanadu at its most intimate level is regulated by all the features of typographic medium. Therefore hypertext or hypermedia seems to lead to a secondary literacy. For Moulthrop this secondary literacy is recursion of hypertext to print. It can be seen happening in two important ways—a self-consciousness about technological mediation and a sensitivity to the way hypotext creates another order invisible on the screen.

The fourth question is: 'What does hypertext become when taken to its limit?' Moulthrop consults McLuhan's view on this point. McLuhan's view is that every form pushed to the limit of its potential reverses its characteristics. Moulthrop does not agree with McLuhan's self-negating reversal idea. Hypertext is a participatory media and will not reverse in the same way as other media. It is a complex, syncretic and interactive medium that does not take readers back to the earlier status quo. It is, in fact, a recursion to a new cultural space. When taken to its limit hypertext becomes a new cultural space. Moulthrop argues that because of its complex, syncretic and interactive nature hypertext does not play into the hands of capitalist imagination and informational industry. It stands against absolute property and hierarchy.

Moulthrop continues the same line of argument in succeeding paragraphs and dismisses William Gibson's (b. 1948, Gibson is an American-Canadian science fiction writer who coined the term 'cyberspace'. His early novels present dystopian narratives about the effects of cybernetics and computer networks on human beings) dark dream about cyberspace. He distinguishes Gibson's cyberspace from Nelson's hypertext. Gibson's cyberspace is a centralised hierarchical domain controlled and defined by scientists. Nelson's hypertext or Xanadu model is a de-centred space where ordinary readers can design their texts in whatever way possible or desirable. It opens the door to a true social revolution that goes beyond literature or mass entertainment. It transfers control of cultural work to the people working in culture like writers, artists, scholars, fans, punks, etc.

Moulthrop explains the utility and significance of Nelson's hypertext. But in his high praise for the dream project of Xanadu he does not ignore the risks it carries with itself. Thus he offers a balanced, impartial and insightful assessment of hypertext and convincingly claims that electronic media has the potential to create a new socio-cultural order.

Key Points

- The concept of hypertext originated with Vannevar Bush in 1945, though the term was coined by Theodor Nelson.
- The next stage in the development of hypertext was the creation of animation game called 'Adventure' in the early 1960s.
- Moulthrop's draws upon the ideas of postmodernist theorists like Baudrillard, Lyotard, Haraway and Bey in his essay.

- Moulthrop defines hypertext as a complex network of textual elements.
- The necessity and distinctiveness of hypertext is proved in connection with simulation and Coleridge's dream of Xanadu.
- Nelson's dream project of Xanadu is essentially a revision of Coleridge's dream for the postmodern period.
- Nelson believes that hypertext will usher in new populitism (combination of populism and elite). He warns that this may cause two problems: a) hypertext will give benefits to a few privileged people and deprive many ordinary people, b) information has become equivalent to capital.
- Moulthrop discusses the different views and counterviews about the usefulness of hypertext to humanity.
- Moulthrop refers to Marshall McLuhan's framework of four questions to determine hypertext's usefulness.
- McLuhan's *first question* is 'What does hypertext enhance or intensify?

The answer: Hypertext enhances our sensitivity.

- The *second question* is 'What does hypertext displace or render obsolete?'

The answer: Hypertext displaces 'post-literacy' in the age of television and revives typographical culture.

- The *third question* is 'What does hypertext retrieve that was previously obsolete?'

The answer: Hypertext retrieves literacy.

- The *fourth question* is 'What does hypertext become when taken to its limit?'

The answer: When taken to its limit hypertext becomes a new cultural space.

Exercises

Answer the following questions in 100–150 words.

1) Describe the project called Xanadu.
2) Define hypertext briefly.
3) What is populitism?
4) What does the example of Stoll suggest about hypertext?
5) What are the four questions that Moulthrop asks about hypetext?

Answer the following questions in 250–300 words.

1) How do you account for the combination of digitisation and humanities in the form of digital humanities?
2) What are the salient features of digital humanities?
3) What is Moulthrop's concept of hypertext?
4) How does Moulthrop correlate hypertext with critical theories?
5) What are the four laws that Moulthrop applies to hypertext? What are the results of this application?

GLOSSARY

Allegory

Allegory is a type of story with two meanings—a literal surface meaning and a deeper metaphorical meaning. It is very ancient in origin and is closely related to another didactic narrative, the fable. The earliest known example is Prudentius' *Psychomachia* (fifth century AD), which features the struggle between vices and virtues. Allegory in the medieval period can be found in the exegesis of Biblical texts in the form of morality plays. Some notable allegorical works of the modern period include Virginia Woolf's *Between the Acts* (1941) and George Orwell's *Animal Farm* (1945).

Allusion

An allusion is an indirect reference to another work, place, person or event. It enriches the reader's understanding by comparing the author's view/emotion about an external event to a reference in the text and thus gives depth to the work. It also often highlights the scholarship of the author, and the skill necessary for using them appropriately. Allusions can be from different sources—historical, mythical, Biblical, literary, topical and personal. Christopher Marlowe's *Doctor Faustus*, Milton's *Paradise Lost* and John Keats Odes, to quote a few examples, are full of mythical and Biblical allusions. The following stanza from John Keats's 'Ode on a Grecian Urn' alludes to Greek mythology:

> Sylvan historian, who canst thus express
> A flowery tale more sweetly than our rhyme:
> What leaf-fringed legend haunts about thy shape

Of deities or mortals, or of both,
In Tempe or the dales of Arcady?

'Sylvan' is a reference to the deity or spirit of woods in Greek mythology; 'Tempe' refers to the 'vale of Tempe', the place visited by Apollo and other gods (frequently referred to in Greek mythology); 'the dales of Arcady' refers to the home of Pan, the god of rustic music.

Ambiguity

In ordinary use the term refers to an unclear or confusing situation or expression. Ambiguity in language, written or spoken, has been traditionally considered as an error or flaw. But it was with the publication of William Empson's seminal book *Seven Types of Ambiguity* in 1930 that the term acquired new significance. Since Empson's reinterpretation, ambiguity has come to be regarded as a defining linguistic characteristic of poetry. He used the term to describe a literary technique in which a word or phrase conveys two or more different meanings.

Author

The word derives from the Latin 'auctor' which meant creator or originator. The common sense meaning of the term is a person who writes books. The ancient Greek idea of the author was that the author was a quasi-divine figure, because he had the ability to create. In the medieval period the idea of the author was differently understood. The author was an auctor which meant that he was one of the four persons responsible for the making of the book. The other three persons were the scriptor/ scribe (who simply wrote it down, added nothing to the book and changed nothing), compilator/compiler (who put together passages from other texts) and commentator (who added his own words to those of others). The auctor was expected to state his own opinions, as well as refer to that of other writers.

The Classical idea of the author as a creator and originator prevailed to a certain extent, but this status was restricted to the authoritative Latin writers. Vernacular writers were excluded and remained largely unknown to readers. In the eighteenth and nineteenth century, the author was viewed as a solitary genius and the source of the literary text and its meaning. Print culture and the establishing of copyright consolidated the status of the author as an originator and owner of a special kind of work. By the beginning of the twentieth century, critics and theorists began challenging the privileged status of the author. New Critics like Wimsatt and Beardsley argued that a literary work contained all the information necessary to understand its meaning and that it would be misleading to discover its meaning in the author's intention. The most radical opposition to the notion of the author as the creator of a text and owner of its meaning came from Roland Barthes, the French theorist. In his celebrated essay 'The Death of the Author', Barthes argued that the author is neither the source of the text nor of its meaning. The text is a construct that contains many voices or codes, and it cannot be reduced to the voice of a single person called 'author'. Barthes's negation of the author resulted in the increased significance of the reader. His argument was modified in turn by another French theorist, Michel Foucault. Foucault in his influential essay, 'Who Is an Author?' argued that the author is not the source of the text. Authorial intent is simply one of the signifiers of the text. Thus the idea of the author has been differently defined in different ages. The significance of the author varies with the changing ideas of literature, language, reading public and technology.

Byronic Hero

It is a term used for both the character of Lord Byron (George Gordon Byron, 1788–1824) and the heroes of many of his poems and plays. The Byronic hero rebels against conventional morality and defies fate. It became a major feature of Romanticism as it represented a proud, moody, cynical, conflicted, alienated and yet attractive hero.

Canon

The word derives from the Greek 'kanon' which meant a measuring rod or a rule. It was used to refer to the books of the Bible which were approved by church authorities as authentic. In literature the term applies to a body of works recognised as classics. It also applies to recognised works of a particular writer. In its wider application the term refers to those writers who have been considered great by tradition or by consensus. The term was used as critical shorthand to measure literary worth by the British literary critic F. R. Leavis. In his book *The Great Tradition* (1948) Leavis restricted the canon of the novel to the works of Jane Austen, George Eliot, Henry James and Joseph Conrad. But subsequently the concept and practice of 'canon' came to be variously challenged. The traditional canon itself was widened so that new authors could be incorporated into it. University courses began to incorporate texts from both 'high' and 'low' culture (many among the latter would not be classified as 'canon') into the curriculum. Finally, non-canonical writers started constructing alternative canons by publishing literatures of and by women or black writers.

Classic

The term has several meanings. The most significant among these are—a) something or someone that belongs to the first rank or authority, b) that which belongs to Greek and Roman art and literature. In Greek culture there was a clear division between writers writing for the upper class and those writing for the lower class. A 'scriptor classicus' wrote for the upper class and a 'scriptor proletarius' wrote for the lower class. For the Romans the 'classic' represented an author/work of the first rank. During the Renaissance the major works of the Greek and Latin writers were regarded as the classics. Dryden, Boileau, Pope and Johnson defined the features of the classic in their characteristic ways. Matthew Arnold explained the classic as work of the very best class. Apart from other meanings the term 'classic' signifies a general agreement about the excellence and merit of a literary work.

Decorum

Decorum is observation of the principles of propriety and appropriateness both in art and life. In simple words, this means that people should speak and behave as per their social status and abilities. It had its origins in the Classical Greek period as Aristotle and Horace dealt with it in their works. It entailed formal conventions, which good literary works were expected to conform to. It became an important critical term during the Neoclassical period. It governed the distinctions between literary genres and dictated the terms of language and subject matter suitable to particular literary genres. For example, it prescribed an elevated style for the epic to suit the heroic action and characters depicted, and a mean style for comedy to suit the vices and follies depicted. Neoclassicists like Dryden, Pope and Johnson respected the Classical rules and insisted on the use of appropriate language. In modern times writers do not observe decorum in the strictest sense of the term though they adjust their style to suit the subject matter.

Denotation and Connotation

Denotation is the literal dictionary definition of a word whereas connotation is the associations of meanings acquired by that word in its use. In simple words denotation is literal meaning; words mean what they say. Connotation is implicit meaning; it suggests rather than says. For example the denotation of the word 'hawk' is a large bird of prey symbol of destructiveness, suppression with sharp claws and very good eyesight. But its connotations are the different meanings that it acquires in a literary work. ,For example, in Ted Hughes' celebrated poem 'Hawk Roosting', it becomes a symbol of destructiveness, suppression of change, obsession with power and tyranny.

Diction

The term in general represents a specific set of words used and arranged by a writer. Aristotle in his *Poetics* gave diction a secondary role to the plot, in the six elements of tragedy he specified. According to him and some later critics, diction is a selection of words that clothe the structure of action; a dress of thought. Diction is selected and adapted in accordance with the requirement of a work. Therefore it is very common to speak of the archaic diction in Spencer's *The Faerie Queen* or the Latinate diction in Milton's *Paradise Lost.* In the case of poetry, diction differs with the poetic type or form. For example, satire requires urbane, cultivated and formal diction, while an ode requires an elaborate, formal and lofty style. The British poet Thomas Gray (1716–71) was an enthusiastic practitioner of poetic diction. He argued that the language of poetry was special because of how it differed from ordinary language. However this 'poetic diction' was challenged by William Wordsworth in the nineteenth century. He attacked the use of artificial language, its use of archaisms (use of old words), its Latinate nature (use of Latin words) and circumlocution (use of excessive words which cause vagueness). Wordsworth rejected the apparent differences between the language of prose and poetry. In spite of such opposition, the idea of 'poetic diction' continued to be effective even in the twentieth century. I. A. Richards tried to separate poetry from other kinds of writing on the basis of the emotive and scientific use of language. William Empson also emphasised the central role of diction in the composition of poems.

Discourse

The term is used in a number of different ways. In more general and traditional usage it represents written or spoken communication or debate. It is also a formal discussion of a topic. It is a specific context-specific form of language, and a few examples of this are academic discourse, legal discourse or medical discourse, which refer to the kind of language used in that specific field. Discourse acquired a new significance in the writings of the French theorist and historian Michel Foucault. Foucault argued that discourse is concerned with concrete examples of language used in specific fields of knowledge. He discussed fields like madness, sexuality and criminality as examples that illustrate the mode in which language and knowledge influence human behaviour in different historical periods. He further argued that particular discourses like law, medicine and psychiatry serve particular interests. For example, the history of madness illustrates that knowledge is used as a power to control and define the people who are termed as mad. Discourse/ language works in favour of dominant institutions by constructing people in certain ways. Further, Foucault argued that discourse not only consists of power but resistance to that power as well.

Fancy and Imagination

These two terms were synonymously used from the Renaissance period through the eighteenth century to refer to the faculty of creativity and madness. But the Romantic poet and critic S. T. Coleridge introduced the crucial distinction between the two terms in his literary autobiography, *Biographia Literaria* (1817). Coleridge defined fancy and imagination to be two distinct mental processes that create two distinct types of poetry. He argued that light verse comes from fancy and serious poetry from imagination. He gave more importance to imagination because it can unite separate or opposite elements. It can establish balance in disparate experiences and can create order and unity.

Gender

In a general sense it has been used as a term synonymous with a person's sex. But feminist critics and theorists have emphatically distinguished gender from sex. Sexual differences are biological and thus natural, while differences of gender are products of culture and society. Therefore they are ideological and cultural. Feminist critics explain that the patriarchal system (society in which the men hold all the power) assumed that genders arise out of sexual differences. The patriarchal system used this assumption to exploit women in the name of conventionally feminine roles and duties. The French feminist theorist, Simone de Beauvoir in her pathbreaking work *The Second Sex* (1953) elaborately dealt with the idea of gender as a cultural construction and as the source of women's oppression.

Genre

The term is used to denote a type or kind of literature. It is generally marked by a distinctive style, form or content. Aristotle's was the first to attempt classifying literary works into different genres based on their shared characteristics, in his *Poetics*. He classified literary works into lyric, epic and tragedy. In the succeeding periods of Renaissance and Neoclassicism genres were considered as fixed categories and governed by certain rules. The significant status of genres was somewhat challenged by the Romantic writers. In their emphasis on individual creativity they challenged the traditional rigidity of genres and made them more flexible. The discussion of genre and its criticism was revived in the twentieth century. The Canadian critic Northrop Frye made the most significant contribution to genre criticism. He presented a comprehensive typology of myth and archetype in his book, *Anatomy of Criticism* (1957). He explained the role of archetypal symbols, myths and generic conventions in creating literary meaning. René Wellek and Austin Warren in their *Theory of Literature* (1956) defined genres in terms of extrinsic or outer form and intrinsic or inner form. Extrinsic or outer form is the attitude, tone and purpose of a work, and intrinsic or inner form refers to specific metre and structures.

Hero

Originally a Greek word, it was applied to men of superhuman qualities. Heroes (like Achilles and Theseus) were supposed to be demigods, especially in the period before Homer's epics. Their superhuman status changed as they appeared in Homer's epics. The change was that heroes did not retain their individual status as the source of action in a text but became a part of the action of a literary work. As an established literary term it refers to the major figure in drama or narrative. In traditional usage it refers to qualities of courage and valour. But in modern literary works it has been replaced with the term 'character'. It is characteristic of modern life, which is complex and no character can be entirely 'heroic'. A corollary of every character having shades of grey is the rise of the 'anti-hero', who has no traditionally valued 'heroic' qualities.

Imitation

The first recorded use of the term was by the Greek philosopher Plato in his *Republic.* He used it to refer to the poet's creation as a false imitation of the appearances of the world. Aristotle in his *Poetics* defined the term in a radically different way and gave it a new aesthetic significance. According to him the poet does not imitate in a crude and mechanical form but does so by refashioning what he sees. He does not produce the exact copy of an object but its ideal version. It is important to note that Aristotle used the term to mean that a literary work reflects pre-existing reality on one hand but also presents it a new light. It is thus a new reality. Aristotle thus used the term to imply that a literary work possesses its own natural form and objective status.

Aristotle's theory of imitation has dominated Western aesthetics since the Classical period to the present day. However it has also been challenged by the Romantic authors and critics who argued that literary works are imaginative expressions of the authors and not just imitative representations of the real world.

Interpretation

It refers to a process by which the meaning of a text is constructed. Traditionally, the meaning of a text was thought to originate in the intention of the author. New Critics in the first half of the twentieth century believed the meaning was not in the author's intention but within the text itself. The aim of interpretation for both the traditional and the New Critical approaches is to extract meaning even though they differ in their methods. The opposite views have been posited by deconstruction and reader-response criticism. Deconstruction rejects the idea that meaning is determinable and reader-response criticism proposes that meaning is derived not from the text, but from the reader's perspective. Interpretation has been widely theorised as an art and/or science and applied to texts of various kinds as 'hermeneutics'. Hermeneutics was originally used to refer to the interpretation of the Bible, but in succeeding periods critics began to interpret secular texts as well. The main theorists of hermeneutics are Schleiermacher, Dilthey, Heidegger, Gadamer and Ricoeur. Schleiermacher (Friedrich Schleiermacher, 1768–1834, German philosopher known for his Romantic theory of hermeneutics) classified interpretation into 'grammatical' interpretation and 'technical' interpretation. Grammatical interpretation is based on the general discourse of a culture whereas technical interpretation is based on the individual subjectivity of the author. Schleiermacher argued that it is not enough for an interpreter to understand a text; he should also reconstruct the lived experience of its author. He emphasised psychological and subjective elements in the act of interpretation. Dilthey (Wilhelm Dilthey, 1833–1911, German hermeneutic philosopher) closely followed Schleiermacher in his conception of interpretation. However the German philosopher Martin Heidegger (1889–1976) brought about the most decisive turn in the theory of interpretation. He changed the focus of interpretation from knowledge (epistemology) to being (ontology). Interpretation for him is not only a process of *knowing* something but an inquiry into the human way of *being* in the world. According to him we understand the world because we exist. We exist only when we are out of our self and in the world. In other words our interpretation is the product of our being, our consciousness of time and our historicity. Gadamer (Hans Georg Gadamer, 1900–2002, German philosopher of hermeneutics) extended Heidegger's radical theory of interpretation and argued that knowledge of any kind has its roots in earlier lived experience.

Intertextuality

Intertextuality denotes the way in which a text becomes meaningful through its reference to other texts. The French theorist Julia Kristeva coined the term to refer to the interdependence of literary texts. For Kristeva, the term does not mean a simple act of identifying references in a particular text but a radical understanding that any text derives its identity from other texts. Thus for Kristeva (like her contemporary theorist, Roland Barthes) the text is not a singular, autonomous entity created by an author. It is an assemblage of previous texts. In her radical conception of intertextuality Kristeva dismissed Saussure's (Ferdinand de Saussure, the Swiss linguist) semiotic theory that signs get their meaning through structure in a specific text. She argued that readers in their interaction with a particular text are always influenced by other texts. So it is not the closed structure of the text but its open sharing with other texts and with readers that gives it its identity. A famous literary example of intertextuality is James Joyce's novel *Ulysses* (1922) which retells Homer's *Odyssey* but is set in the Dublin of his time.

Irony

Irony is a mode of writing in which words have a different meaning from what they appear to say. In this mode of writing the writer remains detached and demonstrates the gap between the ideal state of things and the real state of things. The earliest example of irony can be found in Plato's *Republic* (fourth century BC). In this dialogic work Socrates assumes the role of an ignorant questioner who asks the interlocutor naïve questions, undermines him and ultimately makes him see the truth of the matter.

Irony provides scope to writers to comment indirectly on social deformities and faults. That is why most satirical writing is ironical in nature. Writers like Dryden, Swift, Pope and Johnson consistently wrote in an ironical style. In the early twentieth century, the New Critics considered irony to be the essence of poetic language as it could help the poet achieve his meaning through contradiction. There are two broad categories of irony—situational irony and verbal irony. Situational irony works on the discrepancy between characters' understanding of a situation and the true nature of the situation. Verbal irony works when words mean something different from what they appear to say.

Metaphor

It is a figure of speech based upon the principle of similarity. It identifies one thing/idea with another and thus makes an abstract and difficult idea easy to understand. Metaphors are frequently used in poetry.

Poets from John Donne to Seamus Heaney have liberally used metaphors in their poems. In his celebrated poem 'The Sun Rising' Donne writes—'She's all states, and all princes I'. The line expresses the lover's strong conviction that he and his beloved are richer, in a sense, than all states, kingdoms and rulers in the world, due to their passionate love.

Point of view

It is a term used more often in fiction to signify the mode used to tell a story. There are three kinds of modes or points of view commonly employed by authors. The first is the *first person* point of view in which the main character tells the story. This point of view enables the author to enter into his protagonist's mind and relate his/her secret thoughts and feelings to readers. Charles Dickens used the *first person* mode in his novel *David Copperfield* (1850). The second is the *second person* point of view in which the second person 'you' is used. It is a rarely used mode of narration. However it is very effective because it brings readers close to the story. Jay McInerney's novel *Bright Lights, Big City* (1984) makes use of the second person point of view. The third is the *third person* point of view which has been widely practiced by the authors. In this mode of narration, the narrator comments on events and characters. The novelist Jane Austen adopted the third person point of view in her novels (for example, in *Pride and Prejudice*, 1813). The extended form of this point of view is omniscient narration. In this mode of narration the narrator is supposed to know everything about the characters and action and he/she relates the story. It is impersonal in nature and is commonly practised by modern novelists. Leo Tolstoy's *War and Peace* (1869) makes use of omniscient narration.

Polyphony

Polyphony, a term borrowed from music, originally meant 'multi-voicedness'. In literary studies it was introduced as a special feature of narrative by the Russian critic Mikhail Bakhtin (1895–1975). According to Bakhtin it is not an author, the individual, that speaks in a narrative but a polyphony of languages derived from different social contexts. Narrative for him is an interplay of many languages and not an expression of a single authoritative voice; not 'I' but 'We'. He referred to Fyodor Dostoevsky's (1821–81, Russian novelist) prose as an illustration of polyphony.

Round and flat characters

This distinction between types of characters was made by E. M. Forster in his work *Aspects of the Novel* (1917). Flat characters are characters that do not change with the changing course of action or narrative. Round characters are characters that change in the course of action or narrative. They are highly individualised characters that can decisively influence the course of action of a literary work. An example of a flat character is Mrs Micawber from Charles Dickens' *David Copperfield* (1850), while Rebecca (Becky) Sharp from William Thackeray's *Vanity Fair* (1848) would be an example of a round character.

Satire

Satire is a kind of writing in which the hypocrisy, follies and vices of society are criticised with a view to correct the conduct of people. It is divided into three broad categories— a) Horatian satire (based on the model developed by the Roman satirist Horace), b) Juvenalian satire (based on the model developed by the Roman satirist Juvenal) and c) Menippean satire (based on the model developed by the Greek philosopher, Menippus). The history of satire begins with the early Greek poets like Archilocus (680–645 BC) and Hipponax (541–487 BC). But satire as a form of writing flourished in the seventeenth century. John Dryden was an early and major practitioner in England who wrote satires like *Absalom and Achitophel* (1681) and *Mac Flecknoe* (1682). The two greatest satirists of the eighteenth century were Jonathan Swift and Alexander Pope. Swift favoured the prose form, and ridiculed hypocrisy, pride and cruelty. Pope was a brilliant satirist in verse and censured materialism and bad writing. Satire became increasingly rare in the modern period, especially from the nineteenth century onwards. A few satirical pieces continued to emerge, however. Poets like Tennyson and Browning wrote satire on occasions/incidents in the nineteenth century and novelists like Aldous Huxley and George Orwell wrote notable fictional satires in the twentieth century.

Setting

It is the time and place of a narrative and drama. It provides the necessary background to a play or a novel as per the need of the subject matter. It offers social and political contexts to the action in literary works. In some novels the personality and behaviour of characters is defined by the setting/environment from which they come from. For example, the French naturalist writer Emile Zola believed that environment determined the nature and action of characters and his novels illustrate his conviction. In some other novels locale/place becomes an informing and defining element, like Wessex in Thomas Hardy's novels.

Style

It is a unique mode of expression in prose or verse. Style is a comprehensive term as it consists of many different things about the mode of expression of a writer. It consists of a writer's choice of words, his/her use of linguistic devices, and his/her organisation of words into sentences and paragraphs. In view of its varying role, style has been classified into four broad categories. The first category is of style related to or representative of a particular literary period such as Augustan or Victorian. The second category refers to the style of an individual writer that has become his artistic signature, such as Miltonic (related to John Milton's peculiar mode of writing) and Shavian (related to G. B. Shaw's peculiar mode of writing). The third refers to the style that defines the genre of literary works such as a grand style for tragedy, a mean style for comedy, etc. The fourth category refers to the style that suggests a professional field such as legal, medical, journalistic, etc.

Subaltern

It is originally a military term used to refer to an officer of lower rank or subordinate. The Italian communist thinker Antonio Gramsci used it to mean non-elite classes. Gramsci's interpretation of the term influenced many intellectuals of the decolonised countries. For example, a group of Marxist historians in India in the late 1970s recognised the significance of Gramsci's mode of analysis. They established a group called Subaltern Studies Collective and used Gramsci's term to analyse the peasants as the biggest non-elite section of Indian society. The major argument of this group was that subaltern people (for example the peasants) as a non-elite class were completely ignored in the colonial historiography of India. The group aimed at constructing a subaltern history which could record the contribution of the non-elite classes and contest the dominance of the elite classes. But this endeavour raised the question of representation. Gayatri Spivak raised this question in her famous essay, 'Can the Subaltern Speak?' Her argument is that any subaltern consciousness escapes representation in a large section of society. This is so because it cannot entirely get rid of elite discourse to fully and independently articulate its viewpoint.

Subjective and Objective

The terms are usually used to distinguish each other. A subjective literary work consists of personal experiences of the author. It expresses the author's personal likes/dislikes, judgments and views. Therefore in a subjective work readers are compelled to identify the narrator or speaker with its author. William Wordsworth's 'Daffodils', P. B. Shelley's 'Ode to the West Wind' and Kamala Das' 'An Introduction' are examples of subjective literary work. An objective literary work, on the other hand, does not express the author's personal experiences. It presents the situation or characters, and their thoughts and actions in an impersonal and detached manner. Therefore in an objective work the readers need not identify the narrator or speaker with its author but with the invented character. T. S. Eliot's 'Love Song of J. Alfred Prufrock' and Wallace Stevens' 'The Emperor of Ice-cream' are examples of objective literary work.

Text

Traditionally the term refers to a literary work which is composed by its author and which derives its meaning from the author's intentional use of words. However structuralist and poststructuralist critics have given the term a broad significance. They have distinguished 'text' as an impersonal linguistic construction from 'work', which is a construction by its author. Poststructuralist critics argue that language is all-pervasive and that text being a linguistic construction encompasses everything in the world. The author as an intermediary only serves to organise the text by deriving from pre-existing verbal resources. This has led to the notion that text is not an autonomous, self-sustained entity but an intertext, a collection of diverse social and cultural contexts.

Three unities

It is a term used to designate the three categories of time, place and action necessary for the construction of a plot. Aristotle in his *Poetics* stated that the action in a play must take place in a single day (unity of time), in a single setting (unity of place) and have unified action (unity of action). Neoclassical critics considered these categories as inalienable rules for the composition of a play. The Greek tragedian Sophocles' *Oedipus Rex* is an example of a play that observes all the three unities.

FURTHER READING

General Surveys/Introductions

Eagleton, Terry. *Literary Theory: An Introduction*. 2nd ed. Oxford: Blackwell, 2005. Print.

McGowan, Kate. *Key Issues in Critical and Cultural Theory.* NY: Open Univ. Press, McGraw-Hill Education, 2007. Print.

Seldon, Raman, et al. *A Reader's Guide to Contemporary Literary Theory*. Delhi: Pearson/DK, 2006. Print.

Wexler, Philip. Ed. *Critical Theory Now*. London: Falmer Press, 1991. Print.

Classicism

Atherton, Carol. *Defining Literary Criticism: Scholarship, Authority and the Possession of Literary Knowledge, 1880-2002.* London: Palgrave Macmillan, 2006. Print.

Dorsch T. S. and Penelope Murray. *Classical Literary Criticism.* London: Penguin, 1981. Print.

Kennedy, George A. *A New History of Classical Rhetoric.* Princeton: Princeton University Press, 1994. Print.

Ford, Andrew. *The Origins of Criticism: Literary Theory and Poetic Culture in Classical Greece.* Princeton: Princeton Univ. Press, 2002. Print.

Neoclassicism

Habib, M. A. R. *Literary Criticism from Plato to the Present: An Introduction*. Oxford: Blackwell, 2005. Print.

Hardison Jr., O. B. Ed. *Medieval Literary Criticism: Translations and Interpretations*. New York: Frederick Ungar, 1974.

Romanticism and Victorian Criticism

Brown, Marshall Ed. *Cambridge History of Romanticism*. Vol. 5. Cambridge: Cambridge Univ. Press, 2000. Print.

Modernism and New Criticism

Hickman, Miranda B. and John D. McIntyre. *Rereading the New Criticism.* Ohio: Ohio State University Press, 2012. Print.

Levenson, Michael. *The Cambridge Companion to Modernism.* Cambridge: Cambridge University Press, 1997. Print.

Litz, A. Waltom and others. *The Cambridge History of Literary Criticism (Modernism and the New Criticism), Vol. 7*. Cambridge: Cambridge Univ. Press, 2000. Print.

Ross, Stephen. Ed. *Modernism and Theory: A Critical Debate.* NY: Routledge, 2009. Print.

Whitworth, Michael. Ed. *Modernism*. Oxford: Blackwell, 2007.Print.

Marxist Criticism

Eagleton, Terry. *Marxism and Literary Criticism*. London: New Left Books, 1976. Print.

Frow, John. *Marxism and Literary History*. Cambridge: Harvard Univ. Press, 1986. Print.

Jameson, Fredric. *Marxism and Form*. Princeton: Princeton Univ. Press, 1971. Print.

Macherey, Pierre. *The Object of Literature*. Cambridge: Cambridge Univ. Press, 1995. Print.

Structuralism

Berman, Art. *From the New Criticism to Deconstruction: The Reception of Structuralism and Post-Structuralism*. Urbana: University of Illinois Press, 1988. Print.

Fludernik, Monika. *An Introduction to Narratology*. NY: Routledge, 2009. Print.

Matthews, Peter. *A Short History of Structural Linguistics*. Cambridge: Cambridge Univ. Press, 2001. Print.

Sturrock, John. *Structuralism*. Oxford: Blackwell, 2003. Print.

Poststructuralism

Allen, Graham. *Roland Barthes*. NY: Routledge, 2003. Print.

Culler, Jonathan. *On Deconstruction*. Cornell: Cornell Univ. Press, 1982. Print.

Davis, Colin. *After Postructuralism: Reading, Stories and Theory*. NY: Routledge, 2004. Print.

Mills, Sara. *Michel Foucault*. NY: Routledge, 2003. Print.

Royle, Nicholas: *Jacques Derrida*. NY: Routledge, 2003. Print.

Zima, Peter V. *Deconstruction and Critical Theory*. NY: Bloomsbury, 2002. Print.

Psychoanalytic Criticism

Easthope, Antony. *The Unconscious*. NY: Routledge, 1999. Print.

Ellman, Maud. *Psychoanalytic Literary Criticism*. London: Longman, 1994. Print.

Reader- Response Criticism

Davis, Todd F. and Kenneth Wormack. *Transitions: Formalist Criticism and Reader Response Theory*. London: Palgrave Macmillan, 2002. Print.

Tompkins, Jane P. Ed. *Reader-Response Criticism: From Formalism to Post-Structuralism.* Baltimore: Johns Hopkins University Press, 1980. Print.

Feminist Literary Criticism

Benstock, Shari, et al. *A Handbook of Literary Feminisms.* Oxford: OUP, 2002. Print.

Madsen, Deborah. *Feminist Theory and Literary Practice.* Sterling: Pluto Press, 2000. Print.

Plain, Gill and Susan Sellers Ed. *A History of Feminist Literary Criticism.* Cambridge: Cambridge Univ. Press, 2007. Print.

Postcolonialism

Loomba, Ania. *Colonialism/Postcolonialism.* NY: Routledge, 1998. Print.

Mcleod, John. *Beginning Postcolonialism.* Manchester: Manchester Univ. Press, 2000. Print.

Young, Robert C. *Postcolonialism: A Very Short Introduction.* Oxford: OUP, 2003. Print.

Cultural Studies

Hartley, John. *A Short History of Cultural Studies.* NY: Sage Publications, 2003. Print.

Miller, Toby Ed. *A Companion to Cultural Studies.* Oxford: Blackwell, 2001. Print.

Ryan, Michael. *Cultural Studies: A Practical Introduction.* Oxford: Wiley-Blackwell, 2010. Print.

Digital Humanities

Berry, D. M. Ed. *Understanding Digital Humanities.* Basingstoke: Palgrave Macmillan, 2012. Print.

Burdick, Anne, et al. *Digital Humanities*. Massachusetts: MIT Press, 2012. Print.

Landow, George. *Hypertext: The Convergence of Contemporary Critical Theory and Technology*. Baltimore: Johns Hopkins Univ. Press, 1997. Print.

Schreibman, Susan et al. *A Companion to Digital Humanities*. Oxford: Blackwell, 2005. Print.